CHEATING THE SPREAD

SPORT AND SOCIETY

Series Editors
Randy Roberts
Aram Goudsouzian

Founding Editors
Benjamin G. Rader
Randy Roberts

A list of books in the series appears at the end of this book.

CHEATING THE SPREAD

ALBERT J. FIGONE

Gamblers, Point Shavers, and Game Fixers in College Football and Basketball

UNIVERSITY OF ILLINOIS PRESS
URBANA, CHICAGO, AND SPRINGFIELD

Manufactured in the United States of America
1 2 3 4 5 C P 5 4 3 2 1
∞ This book is printed on acid-free paper.

LCCN 2012037767

Photo research assistance by Feldman & Associates
(www.feldmans.net) is gratefully acknowledged.

To our daughter, Sunah, who left us too early
after a courageous battle with cancer,
and to our granddaughter, Song Yee,
who reminds us of the blessings of her mother.

Contents

Acknowledgments

A book of this nature is an endeavor requiring the skills, assistance, and cooperation of many people. The people mentioned here are special because they helped me retain the humbleness and persistence I needed to complete this book.

My wife, Jenifer, was exemplary in her patience, support, and understanding, though all too often she must have wondered why my mind was away from her and our son, Jeffrey, and daughters, Sunah and Janet. Words are insufficient to express my thanks to them.

Friend and Hall of Fame sportswriter Leonard Koppett, who lived in New York and wrote about basketball scandals until he moved to Palo Alto, California, was generous in sharing his insights and firsthand knowledge of many of the issues presented in the book.

Archivist and skilled researcher Judy Kerren, MLS, owner of Fact-Finder Research, provided a substantial number of difficult-to-find sources. Her speed in supplying information to corroborate the numerous events that were not easily accessible because of their status beyond the law allowed me to maintain a regular writing schedule. Experienced, astute, and collegial editor Stephen Barnett made the manuscript significantly more readable. His insights about how the corruptive aspects of major college sports relate to the gambling scandals described in the book fleshed out tangential and condensed repetitive material. The University of Illinois reviewers were very encouraging and motivating in the rewriting of the book to remove unnecessary content. Editor Ellen Goldlust-Gingrich's expertise in all aspects of editing is reflected in the final revisions of the book. Director Bill Regier's patience and cooperation were significant and responsible for bringing this book to publication, as was former director Richard Wentworth, who continually encouraged me to complete the book.

Introduction

Noted higher education scholar John R. Thelin, in his book *Games Colleges Play: Scandal and Reform in Intercollegiate Athletics*, has labeled intercollegiate athletics American higher education's "peculiar institution."[1] For the fans who follow college football and basketball, these sports offer a window into the colleges and universities that support, publicize, and play in Division I, the highest level of play offered by the National Collegiate Athletic Association (NCAA). The players and coaches in the major football and basketball programs at this level are similar to those in professional sports. The players' size, skill level, and execution are close enough to the professional leagues to generate billions in revenue each year. The costs of operating these programs include the construction, remodeling, and maintenance of football stadiums seating seventy thousand and basketball arenas seating twenty thousand; the salaries of the head coaches and assistants that exceed those of deans and professors; and budgets that exceed those of schools of law, engineering, and science.

Since their beginnings, college football and basketball programs have accounted for most of the serious scandals in American higher education. The practices within an athletic department raise important questions about excesses that bring unfavorable publicity to an institution. These questions could be answered by invoking a dictum used by many coaches: "It's okay to cheat until you get caught."[2] The implication here is that an athletic program has a unique role in a college and that whatever practices it employs are acceptable because the institution benefits from the "cheating axiom." If one accepts this precept, then the questions of who benefits and who pays when a college accommodates a corrupt athletic program on its campus become relevant as a matter of public policy. In matters of government, we are quick to prosecute individuals who have lost the public's trust by violating specific laws. In fact, compared to politicians, college coaches receive many fewer penalties and much more leniency. Sentencing a head college basketball coach who was found guilty of twenty-one felonies, a New Mexico judge stated,

> I'm asked to incarcerate a man who was only a cog in the machine of college basketball. Everybody looked the other way as the rules and laws were broken. The real hypocrisy is with the colleges and universities across the country that maintain and establish professional ball clubs while purporting to operate under amateur rules. I'm being asked to sentence a man because he got caught, not because his conduct was unacceptable. The question is how fair is it to incarcerate a man for doing what almost everyone in the community wanted him to do—namely win basketball games at whatever cost. All the money was used by the defendant to keep athletes happy or recruit them in the first place.[3]

This work examines one aspect of corruption in college football and basketball—gambling scandals. Though scholars, newspaper writers, and other observers have produced voluminous literature on abuses in recruiting, subsidizing, and academics, these works have exhibited a striking indifference to incidents in which players have fixed games for gamblers. When this author asked two football historians where to find data on gambling scandals in college football, the respective responses were, "I don't research stuff like that" and "I don't know much about gambling in college football." Except for a few newspaper writers who have responded to the major gambling scandals in basketball before, during, and after their occurrence, few scholarly studies and books have been written about this pervasive problem. The exceptions include two books written on the 1951 college basketball scandal, Charley Rosen's *Scandals of '51* and Stanley Cohen's *The Game They Played*, and Murray Sperber's *Onward to Victory: The Crises That Shaped College Sports*, which devotes five chapters to the 1951 scandal. Rosen's *The Wizard of Odds:*

How Jack Molinas Almost Destroyed the Game of Basketball examines the 1961 scandal. David Porter's *Fixed: How Goodfellas Bought Boston College Basketball* and a book by former Boston College play-by-play announcer Ted Sarandis, *Boston Eagles Men's Basketball: Boston College Point Shaving Scandals of 1978–79*, are two accounts of that scandal.

This book is based on court records, newspaper articles, books, government documents, magazine articles, documents found in university archives, scholarly journals, and interviews. However, many of those involved in the scandals, including players, gamblers, and fixers, were hesitant to be interviewed or declined altogether. Moreover, participants' accounts of the events in a specific scandal have not always meshed, as is to be expected: Time erodes memory, and the ignominy of youthful lapses in good judgment are more easily forgotten if talked about in ways that suit one's psychological level of comfort.

The book examines these scandals, putting together an accurate chronology of events that allows the reader to see how athletic corruption and an athlete's susceptibility to playing for a gambler intersected and placing these incidents in political, economic, and social context. For example, from 1940 until 1948, New York City's police department, with the blessing of the city's administration, actively participated in and benefited financially from a symbiotic relationship with bookies who took bets on college football and basketball games. To what degree this relationship influenced the rigging of games will never be known, but the gamblers and their emissaries who rigged basketball games no doubt were influenced by the prevalence of open gambling in New York and other cities. And post–World War II U.S. economic prosperity accounted for increased attendance, the beginning of television coverage, and the proliferation of athletic abuses that diverted attention from the alarming increase in fixed basketball games.

As college football and basketball evolved in the second half of the twentieth century, the nature of the fixing problem in both sports changed. Initially, when basketball games were fixed, gamblers contacted the athletes through emissaries. In recent times, the widespread popularity of gambling on college campuses has led these athletes to wager at the same rate as other students, often with student bookies, leading to the unthinkable act of players betting against their own team, as occurred in the 1994–95 Northwestern basketball scandal. Betting by student-athletes had become pandemic by the end of the twentieth century, leading the NCAA to pass a 2000 rule barring for life, with no possibility of appeal, any athlete found to be gambling on sports.

The athletic establishment and college police nevertheless have found it virtually impossible to prevent game rigging by college athletes. Instances have come to the attention of district attorneys accidentally as well as through their own investigations and through information provided by newspaper writers, illegal and legal bookies, rumors, gamblers who lost money on botched fixes, and athletes who found themselves in over their heads and feared for their lives. In only one instance—that of North Carolina State's Everett Case—has a coach reported his suspicions that his players were fixing games. Colleges' past inattention to the gambling problem may have been driven by fears of exposing illegal payments to players. "How can you blame these kids," asked former sports psychologist Thomas Tutko, "when they see everyone cheating around them?"[4]

Congress passed the 1964 Sports Bribery Act and the 1992 Professional and Amateur Sports Protection Act, which banned sports betting in the United States except for Nevada, Oregon, Delaware, and Montana, where sports lotteries were exempt, and New Jersey. Other states that allow sports betting as of 2010 include New Jersey, Delaware, and South Dakota. These statutes, in combination with antibribery laws in many states, have now placed the burden of ensuring that the public is viewing a legitimate college football or basketball game on the federal government and states. For the public, the expenses of investigating, indicting, and prosecuting individuals involved in the fixing business are another cost of the misdeeds in major professionalized and commercialized college football and basketball programs. Furthermore, the institutionalized athletic hypocrisy existing on many college campuses and the billons illegally wagered on football and basketball invite another scandal.

In 2009, $2.57 billion was legally wagered in Nevada's sports books—about 2 percent of the total money wagered in this country on all sports.[5] According to sports handicapper and gambling strategy author Wayne Allen Root, "There's no coincidence that the No. 1 sport to watch and bet on is football."[6] Driving the heavy betting are the point spread and football's dominance on television: between $80 and $100 billion per year is bet on the National Football League, with college football a close second at $60–$70 billion. The significant increase in wagering on college football is attributed to people who learned to bet on sports at a young age and then attended institutions involved in great rivalries—Michigan, Ohio State, Florida, Texas, Notre Dame, the University of Southern California, and Oklahoma—and to wealthy boosters who bet on their favorite colleges. Betting on college basketball generates approximately $50 billion per year, about 25 percent of that amount during the three-week NCAA Division I Basketball Tournament—March Madness.[7] The tournament is a paradise for gamblers, who can watch nonstop basketball on television while following their bets.

Gambling is America's largest industry, and where horse racing used to be popular, the new generation of gamblers favors human sports. States have taxed gambling in parimutuel horse racing, riverboat casinos, card rooms, and Indian casinos. However, lawmakers have resisted the idea of including sports gambling as a source of income, fearing the disfavor of their constituents and in response to the NCAA's lobbying efforts.

We only need to consider National Basketball Association (NBA) referee Tim Donaghy when asking whether another gambling scandal can hit college football or basketball. Donaghy had refereed in the NBA for thirteen seasons and was earning $250,000 a year. Yet as part of a broader investigation into organized crime, the Federal Bureau of Investigation (FBI) stumbled onto Donaghy's gambling-related debts, as a consequence of which he was sharing information with gamblers. He was ultimately convicted of passing inside information involving two games (though there were undoubtedly many more) during the 2006–7 NBA season, required to pay $30,000 in restitution, fined $500,000, and sentenced to fifteen months in prison.[8] Unknown is how much money other individuals, including organized crime figures, made by tapping into Donaghy's insider knowledge. The question, then, is not *whether* another gambling scandal will hit college football or basketball but rather *when*.

ONE
CREATING A GAME FOR GAMBLERS

The Rise of College Basketball

After its invention by James Naismith in 1891 at the Springfield, Massachusetts, YMCA, basketball quickly became popular with young men and women, especially in urban areas that lacked space to play games such as baseball and football.[1] Sensing its appeal to young people, high schools and colleges quickly incorporated the sport into their physical education and competitive athletics programs. By the early 1900s, many colleges sponsored teams that competed against YMCA, club, and professional teams.[2] Because colleges during this period did not subsidize the sport at the same level as football, college basketball players often competed in professional leagues, where they consorted with gamblers, even walking among the spectators to place bets on upcoming games.[3]

As basketball's popularity increased, colleges began to view the sport as a source of income. Large gymnasiums and field houses appeared on campuses, and with more spectators and more money, more gambling appeared.[4] In an early instance of gambling on the college game, Harry

Scholler, Wabash College's athletic director, reported that a professional gambler from Crawfordsville, Indiana, had attempted to bribe Benny Devol, a Wabash College player, before a 31 January 1927 game with Franklin College of Indianapolis; Devol scored more points than the entire Franklin team in a 47–32 Wabash victory.[5] If gamblers were attempting to rig games in rural Indiana, they might have been doing so anywhere basketball was played.

Yet court documents, newspapers, sports history books, magazines, personal memoirs, and other sources show little evidence of fixing in college basketball games until the mid-1940s. Professional gamblers, bookmakers, and players rarely memorialize their illegal gambling activities. However, the individuals who comprised most of the illegal bookie population between the two world wars were not the stereotypical gangsters of the 1920s and 1930s. Since bookmaking success required good business sense, most bookies differed little from the owners of neighborhood barbershops, bars, or restaurants. Because of the Great Depression and the anti-Prohibition sentiment of the period, many bookies began as bootleggers and expanded their businesses into gambling and prostitution. Needing a reputation for honesty, the money to quickly pay off winning bettors, protection from reform-minded political administrations, and the ability to spot rigged games to avoid bankruptcy, bookies ironically became law enforcement's first line of defense in combating sports bribery.[6]

In 1936, as college football and professional baseball suffered an economic downturn, John L. Griffith, editor of the coaches' magazine *Athletic Journal*, noted basketball's "ascendancy to the ranks of the elite," with more players participating and more spectators attending games.[7] Several factors were responsible for the meteoric rise of the indoor game. Franklin D. Roosevelt's public works programs and various state agencies constructed new civic auditoriums, college field houses, and high school gymnasiums, and by 1937, the Works Progress Administration had budgeted about $500 million for new recreational facilities, including outdoor neighborhood basketball courts.[8]

Seeking to fill the increased number of seats, college basketball rule makers aimed at creating "point-a-minute teams" by introducing a number of changes. The ball had to be advanced to the midcourt line in ten seconds, and the number of timeouts, personal fouls, and substitutions were increased. The ball was made two and half inches smaller in circumference and two ounces lighter, and its laces were removed, making it easier to handle. The three-second rule was introduced to allow more play in the lane, and the center jump after each basket was discarded in 1937 to force both teams to play hard the entire game.[9] The size of the court was increased to ninety-four by fifty feet, encouraging the fast break popularized by Purdue coach Ward "Piggy" Lambert and executed by all-American John Wooden.[10] Teams soon were scoring more than a point a minute: Rhode Island State's racehorse offense averaged an unheard-of 81 points per game in 1945. Teams also discarded the two-handed set shot, which featured one player holding the ball with both hands and planting both feet firmly on the floor behind a screen of as many as three men. Players such as Jumping Johnny Adams at the University of Arkansas were using the jump shot, as was Jumpin' Joe Fulks from Murray State, who became the NBA's first outstanding one-handed shooter.[11] This faster style of offense created more scoring, more turnovers, more excitement—and more opportunities for players to rig games.

America's economic downturn also gave rise to the sports-promotion business popularized by Tex Rickard's boxing matches in the 1920s. At the request of New York mayor Jimmy Walker, *New York World-Telegram* sportswriter Ned Irish and other notable sportswriters staged a basketball tripleheader at Madison Square Garden in January 1931 to support the mayor's Unemployment Relief Fund, drawing a capacity crowd. Similar exhibitions in the two subsequent winters also drew full houses at the Garden. After three other successful relief fund ventures, Irish, the Boy Promoter, began to schedule games at the Garden aimed at attracting fashionable socialites and the moneyed elite.[12] Students who attended the games were assigned the worst seats, behind one of the baskets. In December 1934, Irish produced a basketball doubleheader witnessed by more than sixteen thousand people, as New York University defeated Notre Dame 25–18 and Westminster (Pennsylvania) outlasted St. John's 37–33. The next season, eight college doubleheaders booked by Irish attracted close to one hundred thousand customers.[13] Sensing college basketball's increasing popularity, Irish began to schedule teams from outside New York and rented arenas in Boston, Buffalo, and Philadelphia, meaning that midwestern teams' traveling expenses could be offset by playing as many as five games on an East Coast swing.

Adding to the sport's popularity, radio broadcasts from Madison Square Garden featuring the staccato voice of Marty Glickman were introduced during the 1930s. Closed-circuit telecasts of basketball games were first viewed at a theater on Fifty-Third Street, and in February 1940 the Pitt-Fordham and New York University (NYU)–Georgetown doubleheader at the Garden was telecast by NBC, allowing the few thousand New Yorkers who had televisions to watch the games from the comfort of their living rooms.[14] The game's popularity did not escape the attention of gamblers, who openly plied their trade in the Garden and other large city arenas, with police and promoters usually winking and turning away.

As early as March 1931, the *Brooklyn Eagle* reported that Max Posnack, a diminutive guard who was one of St. John's Wonder Five, had been offered three thousand dollars (more than twice the average annual income for a U.S. worker at the time) to rig a game against Manhattan at Madison Square Garden.[15] Less than one month after Irish staged the first doubleheader at the Garden, the *New York Herald Tribune* sounded the alarm: "Those unerring feelers of the public pulse, the betting commissioners, have adopted basketball. Fifty thousand, the peak of the betting to date, changed hands on the recent Temple-N.Y.U. game at the Garden."[16]

When coach George Barsi brought his Santa Clara, California, team to the Garden for a morning workout, he found a sizable crowd in attendance. When asked, Irish told Barsi that the viewers were "just here to look you over"; Irish would not or could not admit that they were gamblers. But while practicing at NYU's gym, Barsi asked NYU coach Howard Cann about the faces pushed against the windows and was told, "They are gamblers sizing you up, looking for a sign on how to bet."[17]

When games were played in campus gymnasiums, campus police could remove brazen bettors. In public arenas, however, colleges relied on promoters to prevent gamblers from operating, and promoters, aware that the wagering attracted spectators, ignored the activity unless the police were directed by a reform-minded administration to stop the gambling. Later gambling scandals would reveal that the college establishment had developed a naive understanding of the gambling problem, as even the closest supervision of players did not guarantee that they would not succumb to the sinecures offered by gamblers. Until the problem was exposed in January 1951, college authorities simply hoped that it would disappear.

To maximize their gains and facilitate betting in college basketball, bookies in the early 1940s introduced the point spread—a 3-point range involving the final score. A team might be quoted as a 6–8 favorite, meaning that a bettor on the favorite would collect if the team won by 8 or more points, while a bettor on the underdog would collect if the team lost by 6 or fewer points. If a team won by 7 points, all bets were lost, and the bookies won. Bettors soon discovered the hazards of this system, as an unusually large number of games seemed to hit the middle. An adjustment was made in which only one point line was given, with half a point tacked on to avert a tie (a push). Thus, if a team were a 7½-point favorite, it would have to win by 8 for its backers to collect. If it won by 7 or fewer, a bet on the underdog won. Theoretically, the point spread made every game even.[18]

The point spread appealed to gamblers and opened up new possibilities for players. If the spread was big enough—for example, 9 points—one or more players on the favored team could work to make sure his team won by less than the spread. A gambler wanting to insure a big bet could offer a piece of the profit to one or more players; by shaving points, or winning by less than the spread, players could guarantee that a gambler who picked the underdog would win his bet without costing their team the game. Another method, dumping, involved players losing the game outright or allowing the favored team to win by more than the spread.[19] Both shaving and dumping carried the risk of detection, requiring crooked players to perform so badly that they risked arousing suspicion. Also, players on the favored team who were not involved in rigging might be playing above their usual levels, meaning that the fixers would have to play even more ineptly. Fixed games at times could be easy to spot, and disgruntled bettors would walk to a team's bench and scream, "What's the spread, huh, you bums!"[20]

The invention of the point spread has not been precisely documented. According to Ted Vincent, evaluating two teams by point differentials was initiated by Dayton, Ohio, sportswriter Dick Dunkel in 1929. Dunkel's system first involved selling rating sheets to football coaches through a mail-order business. After adding basketball, his weekly sheets gained popularity, with the Converse Shoe Company, Sears Roebuck, and the Pabst Brewing Company distributing them. In the early 1940s, Dunkel asserted that his method predicted basketball winners with 79.2 percent accuracy.[21]

Dunkel's system was based on the study of comparative game scores: the importance of Team A's victory over Team B was determined by team B's record over teams C, D, and E. To ensure the system's accuracy, almost every team playing basketball had to be evaluated, including industrial teams that played college teams. A New York office consisting of two men and three women gathered scores from newspapers from all over the country to make the necessary calculations. This rating system was a boon to small colleges located far away from metropolitan areas. High ratings by the Dunkel system could earn a team a better schedule the following year or assist an outstanding small-college team in obtaining a postseason bid. When Ohio University and Western Kentucky reached the finals of the National Invitational Tournament in 1941 and 1942, respectively, Dunkel's system appeared to be a reliable predictor of a team's strength.[22]

Some bookies and gamblers have attributed the implementation of the point spread to Chicago mathematics teacher Charles K. McNeil, a graduate of the University of Chicago. After he retired from teaching, McNeil worked for a brief time as a security analyst, drawing a small salary. He soon turned to gambling full time, taking advantage of the city's numerous bookmakers. McNeil recounted that he was such a successful gambler that eventually "the biggest book in town put a firm betting limit" on him.[23] Upset by these terms, he opened his own bookmaking system in the fall of 1940, labeling his form of betting "wholesale odds." McNeil's system analyzed and rated teams and then estimated the number of points by which one team would defeat the other. After the 1940 football season, he applied his system to college basketball, and his bookmaking business became so successful that he drove the bookie who had previously limited his wagering out of business. McNeil's methods anticipated using computers to collect information on teams. Most sports gamblers today believe that it is necessary to have accurate information about many team and individual factors to ensure a winning bet, and any small edge in information supports the illusion that sports betting is profitable. As noted handicapper Lem Banker has stated, "You have a better chance of becoming a rock star than becoming a [successful] professional gambler."[24] McNeil quit bookmaking in 1950 because "the mob wanted to go in[to] business with his brain."[25] At the end of the 1950 football season, he asserted that he had been a winner in twenty-five of the twenty-seven years he'd gambled on sports, a record others could only envy.

In another accounting of the point spread's beginning, crime reporter Dan Moldea interviewed Lexington, Kentucky, bookmaker Ed Curd, a friend of McNeil and of legendary University of Kentucky basketball coach Adolph Rupp. Curd did not know "who can take credit for [inventing the point spread]. McNeil fell in line with everyone else. But, in my estimation, he was the best handicapper who ever lived."[26] Curd was credited with inventing the 10 percent commission bookies earn from a losing bettor, known as the vigorish or juice.[27] Operating out of the Mayfair Bar in downtown Lexington, just five blocks from Rupp and the University of Kentucky's Alumni Gym, Curd employed four secretaries and had two Teletype machines and three phones solely for long-distance betting and other gambling-related business. He set lines on college and professional football games on Monday and distributed them nationwide. He became the most prominent college football bookie, and in the early 1950s, Mob boss Frank Costello testified before the Kefauver Crime Commission that "little Eddie Curd" was his friend and bookie.[28]

Other accounts of the point spread's invention credit Darby Hicks and Karl Ersin, oddsmakers in Minneapolis in the 1930s. Hicks was employed as a handicapper by the *Minneapolis Journal*, while Ersin was an avid football fan with an affinity for "keeping book after book on college football and reading everything I could." In the midst of the depression, the *Minneapolis Star Tribune* hired Ersin, who wrote a weekly article with Hicks that used the point spread to handicap games. According to Ersin, "Darby and I used the point spread as our way of handicapping and we had a contest to see who could do better."[29]

Ersin's role in developing the point spread went further than his work on the sports page when he met Billy Hecht, a Minneapolis liquor store owner who had just started the Minneapolis-based *Gorham Press*. According to Ersin, "Hecht did not know about setting a line and hired me and a couple of other handicappers."[30] In 1937, *Gorham Press* became the first national oddsmaking institution. Gamblers considered the newsletter to be their Bible—the first national service to set and distribute lines and point spreads on sporting events.[31] Its few hundred subscribers were invited to call the *Press* during the week to receive the latest adjustments. In 1940, Leo Hirshfield bought a majority of the *Gorham Press*, changing the name first to *Weekly Gridiron Record* and later to the *Green Sheet*. By 1948, the *Green Sheet* offered bettors and bookies lines and point spreads on college and professional football and basketball games as well as player statistics, team statistics, rosters, and schedules.[32] At its height, the company grossed ten million dollars annually. Ersin reported that he and other handicappers suspected that some college football and basketball games may have been fixed in the 1930s and 1940s, but they did not know for sure.[33]

The point spread increased the possibility that gamblers would solicit players to rig college basketball games. One way gamblers contacted players was by socializing with them during the summer. In the early 1930s, resort owners in the Catskill Mountains north of New York City saw the possibility of an added attraction: Let the guests watch college basketball players during their vacations at the resorts. Within a few years, nearly all of the area's two hundred resorts were fielding basketball teams. Basketball players jumped at the opportunity to earn extra money, have a good time, play competitive ball, and sharpen their skills. Players applied by letter, appeared in May when the hiring was done, or were placed by their coaches.[34] The average player's salary was forty dollars per month, with tips ranging from five hundred to one thousand dollars for the summer. Easier athletic staff jobs such as teaching tennis, swimming, and organizing games for guests paid three hundred dollars for the summer. Some resorts sent their teams on weeklong road trips around Sullivan County, usually playing two or three games per week and practicing every day.[35]

Coaches such as Nat Holman from City College of New York (CCNY) and Clair Bee from Long Island University (LIU) would visit the resorts and watch exciting games involving such college stars as Bob Cousy, Alex Groza, Bill Spivey, and George Mikan. The ball games kept the guests (some of them gamblers) and their money on the hotel premises. Each summer, as many as five hundred varsity basketball players were employed in the Catskills.[36]

In addition to salaries and tips, the players had another source of income. A hat was passed around the stands and guests could guess the total number of points that would be scored, with each pick costing a dollar. Players were often in cahoots with the winner, ensuring that a particular number of points would be scored. Thus, the players were shaving points even in the summertime, and the coaches watching the games were not oblivious to such chicanery.[37]

Professional gamblers in the Catskills would became friendly with college players, often beginning to soften them up with a fifty- or a hundred-dollar-bill. Players, too, initiated contact: Eddie Gard, who had fixed games while playing at LIU, was seeking money to finance as many corrupt teams as possible in New York City. He found his bankroll in Salvatore T. Sollazzo, a New York jeweler and gambler he met in the Catskills.[38]

University of Oklahoma players Jim Terrell, Marcus Freiburger, and Doug Lynn recounted to the Sooner student newspaper how they had met Sollazzo at a Catskill resort. The night before they played CCNY at Madison Square Garden, Terrell, Freiburger, and Lynn were invited to a lavish party at Sollazzo's Central Park apartment, where they discussed the possibility of rigging the game. The Sooners defeated 2-point favorite CCNY the following evening, 48–43.[39] Sollazzo, an inveterate gambler, also corralled National Basketball Association referee Sol Levy, whom he met at the Catskills, to rig NBA games by calling nonexistent fouls on certain players.[40]

In October 1944, Dr. Forrest "Phog" Allen, the legendary University of Kansas coach, warned of a coming gambling scandal "that would stink to high heaven." Allen's statement was made seven months after Utah coach Vadal Peterson reported that a gambler had approached him on the eve of the 1944 NCAA championship game between his team and Dartmouth at Madison Square Garden. The gambler's question was simple: How much it would cost to have Utah lose? Peterson answered the gambler's question with a quick right. Allen also cited a 1944 incident where two Philadelphia college players agreed to rig a game for one thousand dollars each but became scared and tried to return the money. One player developed an urge to join the navy, and the other became sick and dropped out of basketball.[41]

While the NCAA and Philadelphia college bribery incidents aroused flurries of indignation, college authorities and sportswriters did not view fixing as an endemic problem in college basketball. However, specific circumstances argued otherwise. Bookies, the police, and newspaper writers had for years routinely been alerted that certain baseball, basketball, and football games and boxing matches had been fixed.[42] Their information usually came from wiretaps or from bookies whose livelihood depended on honest contests.

In April 1945, New York's *Dunkirk Evening News* ran "You Don't Say, by Mac," an article citing the observations about rigged college basketball games by Sergeant John O. Jones, who had served as publicity director of a basketball minor league, the New York State Professional League (NYSPL), before joining the military. Jones recounted, "I know a lot of the boys personally, and their attitude in regards to sports. You couldn't trust them in a pro game. Hire one for twenty-five dollars, and if he made fifteen points he'd ask you for a big raise just before the next game started. Unless he got it, he would refuse to go on the floor, leaving you in the hole."[43]

College players frequently performed under aliases alongside professionals, with their coaches generally turning a blind eye; in one case, however, Jones recalled a coach who told his best player not to compete professionally before a big game so that he would not be tired. The New York City colleges where this practice was common, according to Jones, included Fordham, CCNY, St. Francis College of Brooklyn, Brooklyn College, St. John's, NYU, and LIU. Jones also observed, "Look over the professional backgrounds of Nat Holman of City College and Joe Lapchick of St. John's, both members of the famous Original Celtics, and you will understand why they might have had no objection to their charges playing a little pro ball on the side."[44] Because gambling in the professional leagues was at least as rampant as in colleges, it is highly likely that players who did business with gamblers as temporary professionals also did so when they played as collegians.[45]

By the mid-1940s, the rigging of basketball games had become more than a minor problem in commercialized college programs in various parts of the country. Later accounts highlighted New York City's open gambling environment as contributing to the unchecked fixing of games, but games were also being manipulated in Southern California, Oregon, Kansas City, Detroit, Kentucky, Louisiana, Florida, and elsewhere. College officials, the NCAA, and law enforcement contributed to the growth of the problem by developing a purblind attitude that would only deepen in the coming years.

TWO
THE GOLDEN AGE OF GAMBLING

College Basketball in the Postwar Years

College basketball's spectator appeal increased during World War II. Men over 6'6" were not drafted—the military lacked clothing and bedding for them, and they could not fit easily into the confines of ships and airplanes. "Big men" such as Don Otten of Bowling Green, George Mikan of DePaul, and Bob Kurland of Oklahoma A & M came to dominate a game already revolutionized by changes in rules and equipment and a faster, higher-scoring style of play. Many gamblers who favored the horses before the war switched to college basketball and football in the early 1940s. But the switch was not always easy: According to one Chicago bookie, "This basketball, it gives them all heart trouble. Ya see, a horse race starts, then bing, it's over in a few seconds. But the basketball starts, and boom, one team makes a basket. Boom, the second team makes a basket. Boom, the first team makes a basket. And this goes on for an hour. I tell ya, they're all getting heart trouble."[1]

The future of college basketball looked bright after the war, despite frequent and disturbing reports that players had been offered bribes to fix games. During the 1944–45 season, CCNY star player Paul Schmones was offered a bribe by teammate Lenny Hassman, who was reputed to be a dumper. Schmones reported the offer to CCNY coach Nat Holman, who immediately dropped Hassman from the team and reported the incident to Frank S. Lloyd, chair of the university's Department of Hygiene. The two decided to keep the offer a secret.[2] The profits the game generated could not justify the risk of giving the game a bad name by exposing a disease that by now was growing virtually unchecked. Many basketball players and gamblers remained cozy bedfellows, and at institutions such as LIU and CCNY, fixing had become such a time-honored tradition that even students were aware that some players rigged games with gamblers.[3]

In January 1945, five players at Brooklyn College were apprehended for attempting to rig an upcoming game. Bernard Barnett, Jerome Green, Robert Leder, Larry Pearlstein, and Stanley Simon confessed to accepting money to dump the Brooklyn College–University of Akron game scheduled at the Boston Garden. Their involvement was discovered by accident. Two detectives who were watching the home of Henry "The Mustache" Rosen, suspected of being a fence for teenaged garment thieves, spotted Barnett and Pearlstein entering and leaving. They followed the players to the home of gambler Harvey Stemmer, picked them up, and took them to police headquarters. The players readily admitted receiving a thousand dollars (equivalent to about twelve thousand dollars in 2010) as part of three thousand dollars to split among the other three teammates as payment for fixing the upcoming game.[4] They had also planned to fix another game with Brooklyn's St. Francis College at Madison Square Garden for two thousand dollars.

Brooklyn College president Harry D. Gideonse and the faculty council acted quickly. After conferring with Dean Frederick W. Maroney and members of the Committee on Men's Athletics, Gideonse expelled the five men. After the news of the expulsion reached the newspapers, one of the involved players commented, "Every college in the city is [fixing games] and I don't know why [the expulsions are] happening in Brooklyn." The player's reaction brought an immediate response from Holman: "That boy should have his head examined. It's absurd. College basketball is 99.9 percent on the level. I don't believe a college man has a price when his college is at stake."[5] Whether self-serving or naive, Holman's observation was proved false in 1951, when seven of his players were arrested for rigging games.

Rosen, Stemmer, and another man identified only as "Danny" were indicted. In summoning the grand jury, Judge Samuel S. Leibowitz stated, "To corrupt a boy is to destroy him in his formative years, and when these vermin stretch their filthy paws into our college halls they pollute the flower of our country's youth and they have got to be destroyed. . . . [T]ake forthright action. Smash the barnacles and smash them hard."[6] The Brooklyn College bribers were convicted and sentenced to a year in jail and a five-hundred-dollar fine.[7] In December 1946, Stemmer would engineer from jail the attempted fix of the 1946 National Football League championship game between the New York Giants and Chicago Bears at the Polo Grounds.

Because of rumors that other players had been approached by gamblers, Judge Leibowitz ordered an investigation into the extent of gambling on college basketball in New York City. During the course of the inquiry, Edgar Bromberger, commissioner of investigations under New York mayor Fiorello H. La Guardia, reported two other instances where gamblers had attempted to bribe college players. CCNY's William Levine revealed that during the 1945 season, gamblers had approached him prior to a game against Syracuse at Madison Square Garden. He also testified that Red Holzman, CCNY's captain for the 1941–42 season, had received two offers to rig a game. Both offers had been rejected.[8] Although Bromberger's investigation revealed no further evidence of fixed games, big money was still being wagered on college football and basketball. And each day that passed without the reporting of a bribe suggested that players were being approached and basketball games were being rigged. College officials may have rested easy, but bookies and bettors knew that any team with a winning record was a prime candidate for game fixing.

In his regular Sunday radio broadcast on 11 March 1945, Mayor La Guardia stated that "one of the players involved in the [Brooklyn College] scandal had, in fact, never been enrolled in the college although he had worn the school colors for a year." The player, Pearlstein, a war veteran, readily admitted he had never registered or attended classes. La Guardia described the situation as reflecting "laxity, indifference, and negligence by the faculty" and "border[ing] on the unpardonable." Moreover, he told his listeners, "It just happened that Brooklyn College was the school that was caught, but Brooklyn College is not the only one."[9] Sport columnist Grantland Rice also hinted at widespread gambling on college sports when he wrote, "It wouldn't be so bad if those Brooklyn College players were the only offenders. I know of more than one college football game under heavy suspicion. My informants were members of the FBI."[10]

Writing in January 1945 in the *New York Times*, Arthur Daley observed, "Long before the court addicts became entrenched in Madison Square Garden, there were rumors of games being 'thrown.' This reporter heard them as far back as fifteen years ago. He can even recall specific contests, the results of which had been questioned at the time."[11] Two weeks later, *Time* magazine reported that as much as two million dollars per night was bet on college basketball in the United States, a quarter of that amount in New York City, with individual bets ranging from fifty to five hundred dollars. In Chicago, one bookie operation alone was booking one hundred thousand dollars on college basketball on a good night.[12]

After the Brooklyn College legal proceedings, Brooklyn Borough councilman Peter V. Cacchione expressed his deep apprehension to Ordway Tead, chair of the city's Board of Higher Education, that "New York City institutions were allowed to play in arenas for private profit of an individual or corporation."[13] After obtaining reports from the presidents of Brooklyn College and CCNY and from various faculty members at the two institutions, Tead defended the use of Madison Square Garden because "students at the city colleges are anxious to be part of the intercollegiate games scheduled [there]. There is prestige in being included. They become part of the national community of colleges and many educators feel there is sound educational value in intercollegiate contests. It is not possible to have these on any of our campuses because we have no gymnasiums large enough."[14]

Bromberger, whom La Guardia had directed to investigate the problems that "participation in public arenas created for public four-year institutions in New York City," raised the possibility of an exceptional player being planted in a college by gamblers. Assemblyman William J. A. Glancy of Manhattan also brought up the possibility of gamblers planting a "dummy student" on a team who did not meet a college's admission and scholastic requirements. This followed the disclosure that like Brooklyn College's Pearlstein, Jack Laub, a player on the CCNY team, had played basketball without being a qualified student.[15] The increased concerns regarding the gambling problem in collegiate sports moved the New York State Legislature to pass the 1945 Wilson-Moritt Bill, which made it a felony "to extend or accept a bribe to throw a game" in a wide number of amateur sports, including baseball, football, hockey, and basketball.[16]

College football quickly reclaimed its position as the No. 1 college spectator sport after the war. Competing to fill the large stadiums that had been built before the war, several institutions increased the amount of money and attention lavished on their football programs. Some remodeled or built new stadiums and spent more money to field winning teams. Lacking the financial resources necessary to conduct competitive programs, many smaller schools dropped football and focused on basketball as a revenue producer. One successful example of this transition occurred at St. Louis University. Like other Catholic colleges whose football programs had enjoyed their place in the sun, such as Santa Clara University (winners over Paul "Bear" Bryant's Kentucky team in the 1950 Sugar Bowl), St. Mary's (California), and the University of San Francisco, St. Louis University dropped its football program in 1950.[17]

When the Reverend Patrick J. Halloran, S.J., a former athlete, was appointed president of the institution in the mid-1940s, he stated that "St. Louis University has nothing to apologize for academically, and we're not going to have anything to apologize for athletically."[18] Relying on local basketball talent such at two-time all-American Ed McCauley, the Billikens were soon filling the city's Kiel Auditorium with capacity crowds, often turning away as many as three thousand people a night. By 1950, the St. Louis team had won its first Missouri Valley Conference championship, the Sugar Bowl basketball tournament, by defeating Kentucky, and the NIT tournament and been ranked No. 1 in the country in the AP poll. The architect of the basketball program was diminutive Eddie Hickey, a 5'5½" dynamo who had previously practiced law and coached football and basketball at Omaha's Creighton University. Holy Cross coach Lester Sheary, whose team had lost to St. Louis in the first round of the Sugar Bowl tournament, commented on the Billikens' win over Kentucky, "The difference between Kentucky and Holy Cross and St. Louis is Eddie Hickey."[19]

Defeating Notre Dame, Marquette, and other Catholic and nationally ranked schools had washed away St. Louis's athletic inferiority complex, and alumni, students, faculty, and the St. Louis community now actively supported the university, regularly attending basketball games and providing generous financial contributions. Halloran became the director of the university's alumni federation and summed up the effect of the basketball program on the institution: "You could not purchase what basketball has done for this school."[20]

The costs of operating a basketball program were modest compared with football, and the recruitment of one or two outstanding players might ensure a team a postseason playoff, a high rating in the national press polls, free publicity, and profits. Men who had coached basketball in the military and then returned to the college ranks recruited players from their wartime teams. LIU's Clair Bee, for example, recruited future fixer Eddie Gard when both were serving in the Merchant Marines and placed him in night school until his grades were high enough to qualify for regular admission to the institution.[21]

Since a successful basketball program offered lesser-known small colleges a relatively inexpensive way to attract national attention, basketball coaches were increasingly hired for both their coaching and recruiting abilities. And given the inherent pressures of producing a winning team, their abuses of institutional and NCAA rules became as flagrant as many of their football counterparts.

A December 1947 *Collier's* article written as a preview for the upcoming season by Oklahoma A & M coach Hank Iba labeled basketball the "number one spectator sport of the country."[22] As the costs of administering a successful basketball program rose, the need to play in large arenas spread. Colleges that lacked large home playing venues sought lucrative road and neutral-site matchups. Following Ned Irish's lead, promoters across the country booked intersectional games, often between nationally ranked teams.[23] Irish was reportedly earning $150,000 per year as capacity crowds of eighteen thousand filled Madison Square Garden and three other venues under his control in Boston, Buffalo, and Philadelphia.

The Big Ten had barred its teams from playing in public arenas since most of the conference institutions had built basketball facilities that could accommodate sizable crowds. Writers speculated that LIU and other high-profile teams received forty-five hundred dollars for an appearance at the Garden, while lesser-known teams earned as little as two hundred dollars. Prior to a game between Brooklyn College and the University of Akron to be played in the Boston Garden, Brooklyn authorities were asked why the institution with the world's largest undergraduate liberal arts population was traveling to Boston to face a team from Ohio in a commercial venture entirely devoid of any collegiate spirit; they responded that the college was beholden to Irish for the finances needed for its entire athletic program and had signed a five-year contract to play in one of the four arenas he controlled. In the 1945–46 season, the total college basketball attendance at Madison Square Garden (including the NIT and NCAA tournaments) topped five hundred thousand.[24]

College basketball's popularity was enhanced when newspapers assigned beat writers to cover games during the latter part of the 1940s. Sportswriters such as Bruce Jacobs, Stanley Frank, Arthur Daley, and Tim Cohane wrote feature stories about teams, coaches, and players that appeared in such widely read magazines as the *Saturday Evening Post*, *Collier's*, *Look*, *Life*, and *Sport* and in syndicated columns.[25] Most of the writers depended on their relationships with the coaches and athletic administrators for stories and thus, not surprisingly, were rarely critical of the rampant abuses that were occurring in basketball programs, including the alarming number of games that were being rigged. At times, a magazine or newspaper editorial would point to the rigging of games, hinting that teams such as LIU were routinely working with gamblers.

Bookies had taken LIU's Blackbirds off the boards (suspended betting on them) because "unusual money" had come in too often on Clair Bee's team. Basketball cognoscenti, including bookies, gamblers, and fixers, and the New York City police were aware that college basketball game scores were routinely manipulated. An editorial in the March 1951 *Saturday Evening Post* placed some of the blame on "sportswriters, who might have been expected to evaluate this phenomenon critically, [but] were so intoxicated by their own sense of importance—so vitiated by their allegiance to Irish—that far from questioning, they joined enthusiastically in the general hoorah."[26]

After the Brooklyn scandal, relative calm characterized college basketball until 1948, when CCNY's Nat Holman stated at a weekly sportswriters' meeting that he believed "another scandal similar to the previous one at Brooklyn College would break out during the during the current season." In fact, Leonard Cohen reported in the *New York Post* that an attempt had been made to fix the game between CCNY and Syracuse at the Garden on 14 January 1948, but gamblers betting that Syracuse would win lost fifty thousand dollars.[27] Sam Winograd, the athletic director at CCNY, admitted that his superiors had instructed him not to comment to the press on the reported receipt of a telegram warning of the fix.[28] Bribe attempts across the country were undoubtedly going unreported as basketball officials apparently were hoping the problem would vanish on its own.

In a prophetic 1948 letter to CCNY president Harry N. Wright, Maude Stewart, director of information services for the New York Board of Education, offered her suggestions regarding the nefarious influence of gambling at Madison Square Garden:

> Possibly because of the rumors this would be a strategic time to consider taking the game out of the Garden and going to the public with a strong demand for funds to offset the loss from Garden receipts. You have the strongest plea in the world—character versus money—don't you agree? If something should happen (and I join you

> in devoutly hoping it doesn't), and if then you decide to leave the Garden, you lose almost all the advantage you have now for then it would be said, he knew about it, for it was published. Why did he wait until something happened?[29]

College authorities later revealed that Wright had informed Stewart that her suggestion was not acceptable to the officials in charge of the games. Thus, CCNY, NYU, St. John's, Brooklyn, Manhattan, and LIU demonstrated that basketball revenues supported their entire athletic programs, a situation that justified exposing their players to the "pressures of playing in the Garden." These pressures included accusations of consorting with gamblers, shouts of "He's dumping" after a missed shot, suspicions that players performing exceptionally well had bet on their own teams, and blatant offers to fix games. On many occasions during the last few minutes of games, crowds would be on their feet cheering for an underdog to score and beat the spread.[30]

Amid the rumors, reports, and proven incidents of bribes and fixing of games, college authorities and the NCAA viewed the problem as one created by a few gamblers who frequented Madison Square Garden. They pointed to the conviction of the three gamblers involved in the Brooklyn scandal and the expulsion of the five Brooklyn College players as sufficient evidence that the problem had been appropriately handled and expressed confidence that the punishment would warn gamblers and players that college basketball was no longer a place to do business.[31]

The NCAA further reassured college officials in 1948, when its members adopted the Principles for the Conduct of Intercollegiate Athletics, popularly referred to as the Sanity Code. The principles delineated the conditions under which athletes would receive subsidies but made no reference to the problem of gambling in collegiate basketball. In fact, at the association's business meeting, the NCAA president, Dr. Karl Leib of the University of Iowa, recognized "some sentiment for the return of the NCAA basketball championships to campus courts," a change that might occur "in the future as acceptable campus facilities become available. The need for revenue was paramount at the present time, and we owe a big debt to the Garden for saving basketball during the war years when we had to take the game to the public because transportation difficulties kept the public from seeing the game."[32]

In February 1951, the *Brooklyn Eagle* reported that the New York City Police Department had suppressed forty recordings of telephone conversations made before, during, and after the 1949–50 college basketball season that detailed accounts of a substantial fix involving players from every big-time college in and around New York.[33] Timely public disclosure of the recordings would undoubtedly have undermined and possibly collapsed the entire structure of college basketball, at least in New York City. College administrators, athletic officials, coaches, and players' lives would have been compromised, if not ruined. Former police commissioner William P. O'Brien had allegedly failed to reveal the information on orders from higher authority (presumably Mayor William O'Dwyer) and offered a "general denial" of the charges.[34] Chief inspector August Flath was ordered to uncover the "incriminating evidence" despite O'Brien's insistence that to his knowledge "no recordings were ever made."[35] Police files subsequently failed to reveal any such recordings, and the matter was dropped.

But the *Brooklyn Eagle* story was accurate: Since 1949, a Brooklyn grand jury had been investigating a gigantic bookmaking operation run by thirty-four-year-old Harry Gross and his brother, Frank, from an elegant suite at the Towers Hotel. Gross had opened a bookie operation in 1940 and quickly prospered. One day, while Gross was taking bets from a customer on the street, a police officer grabbed his hand and said, "You're a sucker for working, cheating this way. You ought to get an O.K." Gross gave the officer fifty dollars and asked, "How [do] I get an OK?" Gross met the officer again a few days later and was informed that permission from the division was possible, "but you're a sucker if you don't go all the way. We won't bother you, but what about the men from the other commands?" Gross expressed his wish to "go all the way."[36]

Between 1940 and 1948, Gross, who was known as Mister G, expanded his bookmaking to include horse parlors and wire rooms spanning New York City and its suburbs. He made semiannual payments totaling one million dollars per year to policemen, both uniformed and plainclothes; inspectors; and politicians, with two men delivering the money to the Dugout, a restaurant close to Ebbets Field. Large packages of fifty- and hundred-dollar bills were taken to the kitchen, where "cashiers" would funnel the money into channels of distribution. Gross often made additional gifts at Christmas, slipped police officials a few extra dollars for small favors, gave away watches and television sets, and maintained two accounts at Manhattan clothiers, where he sent favored law enforcement officials for free clothing.[37] When Rocky Graziano fought Tony Zale in Chicago in July 1947, Gross sent six policemen on an all-expenses-paid trip to watch. When Commissioner O'Brien's acting lieutenant, George W. McGirr, wanted $135,000 changed into smaller denominations, Gross was more than happy to oblige. All bribes were doubled at Christmas as a gesture of goodwill, and Gross doubled the ice (payoffs) if one of his horse rooms brought in above-average money.[38]

At the height of Gross's Brooklyn business, he operated twenty-five bookmaking businesses with four hundred employees, booked twenty million dollars a year in bets, and often paid less than two thousand dollars a year in taxes.[39] In 1950, however, he was arrested, and after spending four months in jail, he pled guilty and spoke freely before a grand jury about his police connections. The grand jury then indicted twenty-one policemen, some of whom quickly retired from the force, for accepting bribes and denounced fifty-six others as coconspirators. Gross was released from jail by posting a twenty-five-thousand-dollar bond and received twenty-four-hour police protection as a material witness.[40]

The young, dapper, and glib Gross dominated the ensuing trials with his Runyonesque theatrics. In one court appearance, he recalled that when he went broke betting on college basketball and moved to California, the New York Police came after him, brought him back, and loaned him fifty thousand dollars to resume his bookie operation.[41] He testified that he sat in a police wiretap room as detectives listened to calls involving Brooklyn bookmakers and identified those who were paying; the detectives "made a pinch" on those who were not.[42] But at one trial where Gross was to connect former policemen to graft, he refused to answer any questions and ultimately left the witness stand.[43] While the judge sparred with Gross over whether he might be held in contempt of court, the district attorney, in tears, moved to dismiss the indictments against the policemen, stating later that he had heard that Gross was offered seventy-five thousand dollars to protect all individuals tied to the scandal.[44] Because of Gross's unwillingness to cooperate, many of the policemen who had been indicted escaped trial. Nevertheless, at a police departmental hearing about whether five policemen could be discharged from the force and denied pension rights, Gross testified that he had bribed chief inspector August W. Flath, seventh deputy police commissioner Frank C. Bals, chief of detectives William T. Whalen, and police commissioner William P. O'Brien. When asked why these "big shots" had not been named in the indictment, Gross responded, "Maybe some money changed hands" and said he had implicated the department before the grand jury. When he asked whether the police big shots had been left alone because of favoritism, he received the annoyed response, "Don't be a lawyer."[45]

In the end, Gross spent eight years in prison, then moved to Long Beach, California, where he was jailed for manslaughter and arrested several times for gambling and bookmaking. He committed suicide at the age of sixty-nine after being arrested for attempting to sell heroin to an undercover federal agent, leaving a note saying he did not want to spend any more time in jail.[46]

Recalling the height of illegal gambling in New York in the late 1940s, Kings County district attorney Miles McDonald said, "It was like the selling of liquor in Prohibition days—everybody condoned it, from the Mob and police to the unions," and "Gross was central to grafters' success." William J. Kelly, McDonald's administrative assistant, commented that Gross "had carte blanche with bookmaking activities at that time. You had to have an O.K. to operate, and it reached all the way to headquarters."[47] The scandal led to the resignation of Mayor O'Dwyer and Commissioner O'Brien and to a number of sweeping police reforms. Many bookies employed by Gross, however, were not indicted in the police corruption case and were able to continue their operations unabated, virtually on the same side of the law as corrupt police, until the largest gambling scandal in American sports history unfolded in early 1951.

THREE

STINKING IT UP

The 1951 College Basketball Gambling Scandal

Sports historians, higher-education scholars, and sportswriters have described the 1951 college basketball gambling scandal as if it were an aberration or isolated incident. Their rationalizations in explaining the rigging of basketball games are characterized by healthy doses of righteous indignation about youthful indiscretions, attributing the acts of the players to the sinister influences of New York gamblers. In reality, the largest gambling scandal in the history of sports up to 1951 was a product of a disease that had been growing unchecked since the early 1900s. According to Stanley Cohen, author of a seminal book on the 1951 scandal, "All through the postwar years of the forties, every kid in the streets of New York knew that scores of college basketball were being manipulated."[1] At the close of 1940s, even casual spectators could not avoid the foul odor of corruption.

On 4 January 1949, New York County district attorney Frank S. Hogan announced the arrest of four men for attempting to bribe David Shapiro, cocaptain of George Washington University's basketball team, to fix a game against Manhattan College at Madison Square Garden that night. Joseph Aronowitz, one of the four men arrested, had initially approached Shapiro during the summer of 1948. Six months of intrigue transpired before he agreed to accept a bribe to fix the game with Manhattan. When Shapiro insisted on an advance, the conspirators agreed to pay the money to his uncle on game night at a bar and grill on Forty-Ninth Street and Eighth Avenue, across the street from the Garden.[2]

Pretending to be Shapiro's uncle, Max Rumack of the district attorney's staff showed up at the bar and grill and received an envelope. Aronowitz and Phillip Klein were arrested on the spot. Jack Levy and William Rivlin, two accomplices, were picked up at the American Overseas Airline headquarters at East Forty-Second Street. Aronowitz's sister-in-law, Sylvia Brill, was questioned about her role in attempting to lure Shapiro to a New Year's party with the four conspirators. Early on 4 January, large amounts of "wise money"—bets by people aware of the impending fix—had been wagered on Manhattan to defeat George Washington by 7 points. By noon, enough small-time gamblers had heard about the fix to cause a betting stampede. By the time Rumack entered the bar and grill, the big New Jersey bookie shops were no longer accepting bets on the game. Their explanation was simple and to the point: "The game stinks."[3] As the professional gamblers watching in the Garden waited for George Washington to fold, they began to squirm in their seats as Shapiro played little, possibly because of nervousness, and his teammates won the game 71–63.

While law enforcement officials believed this case was not part of a wider conspiracy, other factors indicated otherwise. Shapiro, a twenty-five-year-old war hero, the winner of four battle awards, and a law student living on the GI Bill, was hardly a likely candidate to risk his future career for a thousand dollars. Yet he was the gamblers' selection. If this incident were not part of a wider conspiracy, either Shapiro appeared to be the most corruptible player, or many other players had been offered bribes but failed to report the incidents. Later, players would admit that they failed to report bribes because they feared for their own or family members' safety. And although three of the fixers lived in New York City, they found it necessary to travel 250 miles to fix a game involving a team from Washington, D.C.

On 28 December 1950, spectators at Madison Square Garden would be treated to a doubleheader—and a double fix. In the first game, CCNY, facing a clearly inferior University of Arizona team, needed to win the game by less than the 6-point spread so that their backer, Salvatore T. Sollazzo, the gambler who had met many of the players during summers in the Catskills, could win his bet. Sollazzo intended to share some of the profits with CCNY players Ed Warner, Ed Roman, and Al Roth and former LIU player Eddie Gard. Because the Wildcats played so poorly, Nat Holman's team, amid a chorus of boos, did everything but shoot the ball for Arizona and lost 41–38.[4] In the second game, LIU was favored by 11 points over Western Kentucky, and Sollazzo had put his wise money on Clair Bee's Blackbirds to exceed the spread. But in a memorable instance of double-crossing and point shaving, LIU allowed Western Kentucky to score 13 unanswered points in the last two minutes of the game, winning by only 7 and costing Sollazzo his bet. The sizable crowd left furious, knowing that college basketball had become a "slot machine on wheels."[5] The blatant fixing of these games would be exposed just a few weeks later.

Max Kase, sports editor of the *New York Journal-American*, was not a basketball fan and had never seen a game. But after hearing the widespread rumors of corruption in college basketball in the late 1940s, he assigned a crime reporter to obtain evidence about game fixing during the 1948–49 season. He added another reporter the following year and intensified the investigation further during the 1950–51 season. On 10 January 1951, Kase presented evidence that the *Journal-American*'s crime reporters had collected to Hogan, who asked Kase to wait before breaking his story. New York County detectives spent the next month wiretapping and surveilling certain individuals.[6]

In early January 1951, Hank Poppe, one of Manhattan College's cocaptains during the 1949–50 season, offered Junius Kellogg, the first black player on a Manhattan College varsity basketball team, a thousand dollars to win the 16 January game with DePaul by less than 10 points. Kellogg, who had just completed forty months in the infantry in World War II, immediately reported the offer to coach Ken Norton, who informed Hogan's office. On orders from detectives, Kellogg asked Poppe to explain the nuances of fixing to him. Poppe's strategy, as recorded by Kellogg, demonstrated that Poppe was an experienced fixer:

> It's easy! You can miss a rebound once in a while. After you get a rebound, don't look to pass it down court. Hang on to it and give the defense a chance to set up. Then you can try shooting your hook shot a little hard. And don't try to block the other guy's shot. Throw the ball away when you get the chance. Just remember that Manhattan doesn't actually have to lose the game. All you have to do is control the margin of victory. It's easy, Junie. Everybody's doing it everywhere all over the country. The pros, too. But whatever you do, Junie, don't stink up the joint. Make it look like you're trying.[7]

Kellogg was so unnerved by the bribe offer that he played sloppily during the game. Norton replaced him with three-year substitute Charley Jennerich, who scored 12 points in twelve minutes, giving Manhattan a 62–59 victory. Poppe was arrested at his home in Queens at three in the morning after the game, and John Byrnes, the other cocaptain on the 1949–50 team, was apprehended two hours later. Three other men were also arrested: Cornelius Kelleher and Benjamin and Irving Schwartzberg. Kelleher had paid Poppe and Byrnes forty dollars per week prior to the 1949–50 season; during the season, Poppe and Byrnes were paid three thousand dollars each to ensure that Manhattan lost games against Siena, Santa Clara, and Bradley and two thousand dollars each to help Manhattan exceed the point spread against St. Francis (Brooklyn) and NYU.[8] After Poppe and Byrnes were arrested, they asked plaintively, "Why pick on us when others are doing the same thing?"[9]

On 17 February 1951, Nat Holman and his CCNY team boarded a train for New York after defeating Temple 95–71 in Philadelphia. After a stop in Camden, New Jersey, two detectives approached Holman and indicated that they wanted to speak to Roman, Roth, and Warner. The three players had been instrumental in leading CCNY to victory in the NIT and NCAA championships, the Grand Slam of collegiate basketball, during the 1949–50 season.[10] Hogan's strategy for interrogating the suspected players was explicit. He told his detectives, "While we're still investigating, bring these kids in late at night after the New York press has gone home. I don't want to see the name of a single college player in the paper until he's indicted. Then he gets his name in the paper."[11]

The next day, Hogan announced the arrests of Warner, Roman, Roth, Connie Schaff of NYU, and Gard, the former LIU player who was accused of working with Sollazzo and his bookie, Robert Sabatini. The CCNY players later admitted to rigging games during the current season against a clearly inferior Missouri team and against Arizona and Boston College. The Missouri venture netted each player $1,500, as did the Arizona game. Roth was the only one paid $1,400 after the Boston College game, however, as Sollazzo had apparently run out of money. Each of the three received $250 bonuses for a game CCNY won against Washington State and the same amount for a game CCNY lost to St. John's. Indictments were sought against Roman, Roth, and Warner for accepting bribes, against Gard for giving a bribe, and against Schaff for offering a bribe to teammate Jim Brasco. Sollazzo, who was indicted at the same time as the players, had reportedly paid a total of $30,000 to the players who manipulated scores for him over two seasons.[12]

After the arrests of the CCNY players, Kase broke his story. Hogan stated, "Without the *Journal-American*'s information, [the district attorney's] office would not have been able to locate many of the persons involved in the scandal."[13] Kase's investigative stories about the scandal earned him a Pulitzer Prize.

On 19 February 1951, two days after the arrests of the CCNY players, the *Sporting News* named Sherman White of LIU Player of the Year in college basketball. The next day, White and two other LIU players, Adolf Bigos and Leroy Smith, admitted their complicity in the slowly emerging scandal and were arrested. The three players received $18,500 to shave points in eight games during the 1949–50 and 1950–51 seasons. During the 1949–50 season, they fixed games against North Carolina State and Cincinnati as well as their NIT opener against Syracuse. During the

College basketball's leading scorer and the 1951 *Sporting News* Player of the Year, Sherman White of LIU, leaves court accompanied by two detectives after his arrest for fixing games. White's heartbroken father commented to reporters, "It would have been different if Sherman was raised on the streets. But Sherman had to go to college to learn something he was never taught at home."

1950–51 season, the players rigged games against Kansas State, Western Kentucky, Denver, Idaho, and Bowling Green.[14]

White, who had led LIU to a 20–4 record and a ranking of sixteenth in the country during the 1950–51 season, was only 77 points away from setting the all-time collegiate scoring record. The country's most prolific scorer now became a marked man and stood to forfeit a salary of sixty-five thousand dollars over five years and at least thirty-five thousand dollars from endorsements he would have received as an NBA professional. The New York Knicks had the territorial rights to White and would have chosen him as their first-round draft pick.[15] White's size and superlative skills would have made him a real asset to the struggling NBA, which would have heavily promoted his matchups against Minneapolis Lakers big man George Mikan, and with White, the Knicks, who had finished second to the Lakers in 1952 and 1953, might have won the NBA title, as their team included Nat "Sweetwater" Clifton, Dick McGuire, Harry Gallatin, and Carl Braun, all of whom were outstanding professional players.

White's father was heartbroken: "It would have been different if Sherman was raised on the streets. But Sherman had to go to college to learn something he was never taught at home." White's father had watched his son play since junior high school and regularly attended his collegiate games on the East Coast. He had suspected something was wrong with his son's play and asked several times, "What's the matter, Sherman? You don't seem to be playing like you used to. Is something wrong?" White later admitted that lying to his father hurt him deeply.[16]

On 27 February 1951, Natie Miller, a senior player at LIU during the 1948–49 season, was arrested along with Floyd Layne, who had played on the 1949–50 CCNY team and was named cocaptain after Warner, Roth, and Roman were arrested. Layne readily admitted his guilt and confessed to accepting three thousand dollars for rigging games during the 1950–51 season. Miller was charged with rigging two games against Bowling Green and Western Kentucky for fifteen hundred dollars.[17] Three more CCNY players—Irwin Dambrot, Norm Mager, and Herb Cohen—were subsequently arrested and charged with fixing games during the 1949–50 season. The three players, along with Roth and Roman, admitted to attempting to fix a game against Southern Methodist (though they failed to cover the spread) and successfully manipulating a loss to UCLA. Mager, Roth, and Cohen also admitted to fixing a loss to Niagara during the same season, though Warner and Layne were not implicated in the 1949–50 fixes.[18]

Still more arrests followed. Lou Lipman, a high scorer on the 1947–48 and 1948–49 LIU teams, was charged with fixing one game, while LIU's Dick Fuertado admitted to fixing three games during the 1949–50 season and one game during the 1948–49 season. Jackie Goldsmith, who as a sophomore had set a LIU single-season scoring record with 395 points, was reputed to be the "master fixer" of the scandal. After not playing his senior year, he had become intimate with the underworld and was described as "responsible for the corruption of more college basketball than any other single person."[19] Goldsmith reportedly had developed a source of income by advising gamblers that certain games were fixed. And if the game's outcome did not turn out as he sold it, Goldsmith would plead double-cross. He and Rivlin were later convicted of bribing Gard, Lipman, Fuertado, and Miller to fix the LIU-Duquesne game played at the Garden three days before the planned fix of the George Washington–Manhattan game. Goldsmith's Mob connections apparently influenced his decision to reveal nothing regarding his involvement in the scandal and to tear up his black book listing players who fixed games and the gamblers he represented.[20]

On 6 July 1951, Roman, Roth, Layne, Mager, Dambrot, Warner, and Cohen from CCNY; Fuertado, Bigos, Miller, White, and Smith from LIU; and Schaff from NYU appeared before General Sessions Court judge Saul S. Streit to change their pleas to guilty. By pleading guilty to the lesser charge of conspiracy, which carried a maximum sentence of three years in prison, the players escaped prosecution on bribery charges that carried a maximum sentence of ten years. Most of the players agreed to testify against Sollazzo. Gard pled innocent to two indictments charging him with accepting bribes and conspiring with other players to fix games and was released pending trial.[21]

As newspapers throughout the country reported the scandal, mainstream middle America tended to blame the entire problem on the "evil environment" of New York City. There, according to some midwestern writers, players were seduced by smooth city gamblers insinuating themselves into inexperienced lives with smiling assurances of the good life and an easy conscience. Kentucky coach Adolph Rupp echoed the parochialism, announcing, "Gamblers could not touch our boys with a ten-foot pole."[22] Stanley Woodward wrote in *Sport* magazine in January 1951 that he believed "most of the finagling has been centered in New York City where gambling on college basketball games is far more common than anywhere else in the country." He echoed Rupp's assessment that Kentucky was unlikely to experience such sordid events, describing Lexington as "a small-town community, crazy about its basketball team, where there is little betting. The citizens of Lexington are probably as basketball-conscious as any men and women in the country. But they don't bet much, and there is absolutely no organized bookmaking such as you find in the larger metropolitan areas."[23] Woodward's observations were uncharacteristically naive. For years, sportswriters had relied on their associations with bookies to report bribe offers and fixed games. About five blocks from the University of Kentucky's new field house, Woodward could have witnessed firsthand the nation's biggest college football bookie operation, run by Ed Curd, a major football handicapper and bettor who had regularly traveled with the university's basketball team.[24]

This unrealistic prevailing attitude was quickly dispelled as law enforcement officials learned of attempted fixes away from large civic arenas, proving that no town was too small for a rigged basketball game. All-American Don Lofgran from the University of San Francisco, winner of the 1949 NIT, revealed he had received multiple phone calls from an anonymous source from Portland, Oregon, asking if he and teammate Frank Kuzara would be interested in "doing business"; Kuzara stated that he had not reported the phone calls to his coach, Pete Newell, for "fear something would happen to us."[25] University of Oregon coach John Warren reported that a gambler came into the team's dressing room in Kansas City during the NCAA tournament and offered his star, Dick Wilkins, five hundred dollars to lose the upcoming game. Georgetown's Barry Sullivan and the University of Colorado's Lee Robins also reported having turned down propositions from gamblers; Colorado coach Forrest "Frosty" Cox indicated that he had informed Ned Irish, basketball director of Madison Square Garden, of the attempted bribe, but Irish claimed to have no recollection of the conversation. In Los Angeles, Southern California's Ken Flowers reported to his coach that he had been offered a bribe to lose a game against crosstown rival UCLA.[26]

In July 1951, the New York County district attorney's office announced that basketball scandals had spread to Toledo, Ohio, and Peoria, Illinois. The University of Toledo Rockets had concluded the 1950–51 season with a 22–7 record and were ranked fourteenth in the nation. Head coach Jerry Bush, captain of the St. John's varsity in the 1930s, had recruited several players from New York City and built such a powerhouse program that after the Rockets beat Michigan and Illinois decisively during the 1950–51 season, both schools removed themselves from Toledo's schedule for the following year.[27]

Gamblers had frequented Toledo's home games, and local bookmakers had informed university officials that Toledo players had wagered on and fixed a December 1950 game against Niagara.[28] Local law enforcement, urged on by the university, raided numerous Toledo gambling establishments, to little permanent effect. Toledo's rigged game against Niagara came to Hogan's attention because of surveillance on Jacob "Jack" Rubinstein, a bookie from Brooklyn and friend of Joe Massa, a star on Toledo's 1950–51 freshman team. Massa had worked in the Catskills with Bill Walker, a star on the Toledo varsity, and had introduced Walker to gambler Eli Kaye, who offered Walker $250 to fix games plus $250 per game for every other player he could recruit. Teammates Carlo Muzi, Bob McDonald, and Jumping Jack Freeman soon joined Walker and began rigging games with Kaye and his partner, Rubinstein.[29] Walker, Muzi, and McDonald implicated Massa but shielded Freeman, whose complicity was later reported by an intercollegiate investigatory committee headed by Toledo president Asa Knowles. Walker, Muzi, and McDonald admitted to shaving points in the 1950 Niagara game. Freeman did not know about the Niagara fix but admitted his complicity along with the three other players in games against Bowling Green and Xavier during the 1950–51 season.[30]

Detectives from Hogan's office also traveled to Peoria, where they arrested all-American Gene Melchiorre, Bill Mann, and Mike Chianakas for fixing the 1949 Bradley–Bowling Green NIT consolation game at Madison Square Garden. Bradley players Charles Grover, Fred Schlictman, Aaron Preese, and Jim Kelly, along with the three players arrested by New York authorities, admitted to a Peoria grand jury that they had also fixed games against Texas Christian University, Washington State, St. Joseph's, and Oregon State during the 1949–50 season. Only Melchiorre, who had been the contact man for the players, was indicted by the Peoria grand jury; he later received probation. In the 1951 draft, he and Bill Mann were slated to be signed by the Baltimore Bullets.[31]

Because the 1949 Bradley–Bowling Green NIT consolation game had been played in New York, Hogan's office obtained indictments against Melchiorre, Mann, and Chianakas, along with gamblers Nick and Tony Englisis of Brooklyn, Marvin Mansberg, Jack Rubinstein, Joseph Benintende, and Jack "Zip" West.[32] West, a former partner of New York mobster Dutch Schultz, had been questioned in 1947 in connection with an alleged hundred-thousand-dollar bribe offered to boxer Rocky Graziano.[33] West had also been indicted for offering Melchiorre ten thousand dollars to help Bradley lose the 1950 NCAA final against CCNY. Benintende was described by Hogan as "an associate of known narcotics dealers and the worst of the Missouri underworld." The "Kansas City hoodlum" was also being investigated for the murders of Kansas City Democratic leader Charles Binaggio and his top muscleman, Charles Gargotta.[34] Organized crime clearly had become deeply involved in rigging college basketball games.

The Bradley investigation spotlighted gamblers' methods of ensuring that players did not back out of rigging games. A member of a New York gambling syndicate threatened a Bradley player and his wife with physical harm if the player refused to fix games.[35] In another incident, West used a gun to force Tony Englisis to telephone his brother, Nick, in Philadelphia and get the Bradley players to call off a planned double-cross against West. During the game, Bradley played so poorly that coach Fordy Anderson asked his players, "Is something wrong?"[36] The Bradley players ultimately won the game, saving Tony Englisis's life.[37]

But the street ran both ways: Players also contacted gamblers, offering to sell games. Bradley's Aaron Preese repeatedly called Kaye in New York to see whether he would pay players to fix games. Anderson observed players receiving money after games in the locker room from unknown individuals, presumably Nick Englisis and the Bradley boosters; Anderson also revealed that Nick Englisis had traveled with the team, sharing a train compartment with Melchiorre, and had open access to Bradley's practices.[38] Players also testified that on some occasions players on opposite teams were attempting to fix the game in opposite directions. In the 1950 game against Manhattan, Kaye had offered Melchiorre five hundred dollars if favored Bradley won by less than the five-point spread, while Manhattan's Poppe and Byrnes had accepted money to lose by more than the spread.[39]

District attorney Hogan, known as Mr. Integrity for his investigation and prosecution of the scandals, revealed the extensive corruption in the University of Kentucky basketball program with the October 1951 arrests of all-Americans Ralph Beard and Alex Groza in Chicago and Dale Barnstable in Louisville, where he was teaching high school. The Kentucky program was the most successful in the United States after World War II, winning 93 percent of its games over a four-year period. Despite this success, Beard, Groza, and Barnstable had thrown Kentucky's first-round NIT game against Loyola at Madison Square Garden in 1949.[40] After the game, Coach Rupp had commented to assistant coach Harry Lancaster and athletic director Bernie Shively over a bottle of whiskey that he believed "something was wrong with his team."[41] His suspicions were not unfounded.

Hogan's office alleged that eleven of Kentucky's games were fixed during the 1948–49 season, beginning with the St. John's game at Madison Square Garden, which Kentucky won 57–30. Hogan also believed that while in New York, the Englisis brothers and Saul Feinberg, a former Harvard law student, planned with the implicated players to fix more games that season. Hogan's strategy was to prosecute the players for all games fixed after the St. John's game, since neither Kentucky nor the other states where the fixes had taken place had statutes prohibiting sports bribery.[42] However, the court did not accept his argument that its jurisdiction covered the games, indicting the Kentucky players only for the St. John's and Loyola games at the Garden.

Beard, Groza, and Barnstable admitted to rigging three games during the 1948–49 season: Each man received one hundred dollars for exceeding the spread against the DePaul game in Chicago and five hundred dollars for covering the spread against Tennessee; Barnstable and Beard received five hundred dollars each and Groza received one thousand dollars for rigging the NIT first-round game against Loyola at the Garden. Former *Lex-*

ington Leader sports editor Russell Rice recounted in his book, *Adolph Rupp: Kentucky's Basketball Baron*, that the 63–61 win over Bowling Green in Cleveland during the 1948–49 season was rigged; he cited as his source unnamed Kentucky players.[43] In a 1952 *True* magazine article, Tony Englisis asserted that the Kentucky trio had also rigged games in December 1948 and January 1949 against Notre Dame, St. John's, Tulane, Vanderbilt, and DePaul.[44] Groza and Beard vehemently denied Englisis's version of the events, but the trio's confession to manipulating only three games during their senior season strains credulity. Why throw the first-round NIT game against Loyola for such a relatively small sum? Winning the Grand Slam would very likely been worth more than the two thousand dollars they received, especially considering that two of them were about to become professionals. It seems likely that they had rigged so many other games during the season that the gamblers made them an offer they could not refuse. And since Kentucky possessed no statutes criminalizing amateur sports bribery, the players could be prosecuted only for the two fixed games in New York; players were unlikely to confess to rigging games for which they could not be prosecuted.

Like LIU's White, the losses incurred by Beard and Groza were substantial. Two years earlier, they had signed a fifty-thousand-dollar package with the NBA's Indianapolis Olympians that included a share of team profits and ownership of 70 percent of the franchise, with an option to buy the franchise within three years. The team was immediately successful, winning a divisional title its first year and qualifying for the playoffs each of its first two seasons. The team also drew well at home and on the road. Like the other outstanding players in the scandal, Beard and Groza were barred from the NBA for life, and they were forced to sell their stock at 10 percent of its initial purchase value.[45]

The New York County district attorney's office uncovered further evidence that University of Kentucky players Walter Hirsch, Jim Line, and Bill Spivey had continued to fix games during the 1949–50 and 1950–51 seasons. Line and Hirsch admitted their complicity, but Spivey steadfastly maintained that he had never fixed a game while at Kentucky. Hirsch told assistant district attorney Vincent A. G. O'Connor that Spivey had rigged the December 1950 Sugar Bowl Tournament game against St. Louis, which Kentucky lost 43–42.[46] Spivey disputed this contention.

Line later contended that "Spivey talked with Hirsch and me before practically every game played in December 1950 and January 1951 about the possibilities and arrangements for deals."[47] No charges could be filed against Line and Hirsch since none of the states where they fixed games had antibribery laws for amateur sports.

Spivey was later indicted for perjury in the first degree by failing to testify truthfully to a New York grand jury that he had received one thousand dollars from gambler Jack West for the Sugar Bowl game and money for games against De Paul and Notre Dame in January 1951. The death of Kaye, who had initially approached Spivey in the summer of 1950 in the Catskills, and West's insistence on withdrawing his guilty plea in exchange for his testimony against Spivey weakened the prosecution's case, and the jury was unable to reach a verdict. O'Connor moved for dismissal of the perjury charge against Spivey on 15 April 1953.[48]

University of Kentucky officials were less lenient. The board of directors of the University of Kentucky Athletics Association proclaimed unanimously that "there is very substantial evidence tending to show that William Spivey was involved in a conspiracy to fix the Sugar Bowl basketball tournament in December, 1950."[49] Spivey was suspended permanently from all athletic teams at Kentucky and banned for life by the NBA.

Like Smith, Groza, and Beard, the seven-foot Spivey sacrificed a great basketball career. He had led Kentucky to the NCAA title and was a consensus all-American in 1951, and he undoubtedly would have been a No. 1 pick in the professional draft. After he had played several outstanding seasons in the minor leagues, Cincinnati drafted him in his late twenties in the hopes of signing him to play the post with Oscar Robertson for the 1959–60 season. NBA commissioner Maurice Podoloff blocked the move.[50]

In 1951, Kentucky state legislators passed a law prohibiting the bribing of amateur athletes. Questions were also raised about the failure of local sportswriters to investigate corruption in the University of Kentucky's basketball program.[51] Unlike certain New York writers, who had written columns laden with innuendo about CCNY and LIU, the writers who covered the Wildcats treated statements by Rupp and Lancaster as Scripture.

After the Kentucky revelations in October 1951, Hogan shut down his investigation of college basketball gambling. He believed that the main gamblers and players involved had been apprehended and that the legal system would mete out punishments to prevent future corruption. But gamblers and basketball insiders knew the reality: The fixing had not stopped, and more players and gamblers remained in business than had been arrested.

Further, questions remained unanswered about why the scandals had scarcely touched Catholic colleges and universities in Philadelphia and New York (except for Manhattan College). Speculation centered on Hogan's Catholicism and the intervention of Francis Joseph Cardinal Spellman. Attorney Henry Urgetta, representing the St. John's players, prohibited the questioning of any player outside of his presence, a privilege not available to athletes from other schools, who could not afford to hire lawyers. Charles Rosen, a leading authority on basketball and author of three books on the college fixing scandals, included St. John's in his novel on the 1951 scandal, *Barney Polan's Game*. Rosen interviewed many college and professional basketball players who knew about or were involved in fixing games, and his inclusion of players from St. John's in the novel may reflect information he obtained that does not appear in the official records. Substantial evidence also exists that grand juries and prosecutors in other communities were less than eager to prosecute local players implicated in the scandal. The Toledo district attorney expressed virtually no desire to investigate the rigging of games, perhaps because the state had no law against bribing amateur or professional athletes or perhaps to shield the community.[52]

Judge Streit began sentencing the first group of convicted players and gamblers on 19 November 1951. This group included players from CCNY, NYU, and LIU along with Sollazzo, Gard, and Goldsmith. Of all the players from the New York City schools who were indicted, only Warner, White, Gard, and Goldsmith received jail time; the others received suspended sentences or complete freedom. Roth was sentenced to six months in a workhouse, with the sentence suspended if he agreed to join the army. Dambrot received a suspended sentence because the judge believed he had "realized the enormity of his misstep."[53] Lipman's war record earned him a suspended sentence, and Roman and Cohen avoided jail terms by joining the army. Bigos, Fuertado, Miller, Smith, Lane, and Mager escaped jail as well, and Connie Schaff was given a six-month suspended sentence. Gard received up to three years in prison for two counts of conspiracy, and Goldsmith was sentenced to between two and a half and five years. Sollazzo was to be locked up for eight to sixteen years. Warner received a sentence of six months, and White got one year. Poppe and Byrnes were put on three years' probation and were barred from professional sports for life. Gamblers Kelleher, Irving Schwartzberg, and Benjamin Schwartzberg were sent to jail for one year. Nick Englisis and Feinberg received up to three years, and Tony Englisis and Brown received six months. Benintende was sentenced to four to seven years in a state prison, while West received two to three years.[54]

In sentencing the men, Streit presented a scathing indictment of the role of college officials and coaches in corrupting not only college basketball but the entire system of collegiate athletics. Although his remarks were primarily directed at basketball programs, he had also researched corruption in selected prominent football programs. He chronicled commercialization, subsidization, and recruiting violations along with a multitude of academic abuses. He recounted how college administrators doctored high school transcripts and enrolled athletes in perfunctory college courses. He described how coaches openly bid for athletes' services with gifts and money, ensured that wages were paid for nonexistent jobs, and committed forgery, bribery, and fraud. He illustrated how coaches' expenses for salaries, scholarships, travel, equipment, and publicity transformed basketball into a business venture worthy of investment by college officials. He cited Michigan, Bradley, Ohio State, Oklahoma, and Kentucky as institutions whose commercialization of athletics made LIU look like a small-time operation by comparison.[55]

During his 7 December 1951 sentencing of Bradley's Chianakas, Melchiorre, and Mann, Streit vigorously castigated the school's president, David B. Owen. Noting that Owen accompanied the team to all of its away games, Streit blamed the president and especially the booster club for openly giving money to players after games, paying for bogus jobs, and creating an atmosphere at the university "inimical to sound educational practices."[56]

The judge dispensed his most serious condemnation of "money-mad athletics" at the sentencing of Beard, Groza, and Barnstable on 29 April 1952. Streit issued a sixty-three-page report that included a fifteen-thousand-word litany of abuses in the University of Kentucky's football and basketball programs, including covert subsidization and ruthless exploitation of players; cribbing on examinations; illegal recruiting; a reckless disregard for players' physical welfare; matriculation of unqualified students; demoralization of athletes by the coach, alumni, and townspeople; and flagrant abuses of athletic scholarships. Streit labeled Kentucky's program "a highly systematized, professionalized, and commercialized enterprise" with a budget exceeding that of a professional franchise, "an acme of commercialization."[57] The Southeastern Conference and the NCAA agreed: On 11 August 1952, Kentucky was barred from conference and postseason tournaments for one year and placed on one year's probation.

In the 1951 college basketball scandal, a total of thirty-five active and ex-players were accused of accepting $50,000 to fix eighty-six games. Sixteen players reported that they had spurned bribe offers totaling $22,900. Twenty-one gamblers and go-betweens were also implicated.[58]

In 1954, CCNY's Holman told a gathering of New Jersey writers that "gambling in college basketball was as rampant as ever" and "soon the game would again be tainted by a scandal."[59] Holman seemed to have suddenly seen the light after seven of his players had been implicated in fixing games. He was right. Gambling, game fixing, and corruption would increase in the coming decade, with the jail sentences, the words of Judge Streit, the ruined lives, and the destroyed careers quickly forgotten. Certain institutions would become veritable schools for scandal where game-fixing was a time-honored tradition and college basketball would be seen as more corrupt than politics.

FOUR

DO NO EVIL, SEE NO EVIL, AND HEAR NO EVIL

Coaching and Presiding over College Basketball Scandals in the 1950s

The year 1951 was scandalous in college athletics: Widespread fixing had been revealed in college basketball, and academic fraud and illegal recruiting had been exposed in college football.[1] After the basketball scandal broke in January of that year, colleges, with the aid of many writers, were quick to label the players' misdeeds "criminal" and to attribute them to players' lack of moral values and flawed characters.[2] LIU basketball coach Clair Bee, who also served as LIU's acting president, said that "the present mess is one of individuals and not the result of policy."[3] Bee had been a particular target of New York General Sessions Court judge Saul S. Streit when he stated, "The naiveté, the equivocation and the denials of the coaches and their assistants concerning their knowledge of gambling, recruiting, and subsidizing would be comical were they not so despicable."[4]

In September 1951, *Life* published an editorial, "Football Is a Farce," that laid the blame for the pervasive corruption in college athletics squarely on the shoulders of college coaches, athletic administrators, boards of trustees, and presidents. The editors argued that behind a curtain of hypocrisy, college football and basketball players had become pawns in a commercialized system characterized by falsified admission records, fraud, academic forgery, recruiting violations, proselytizing, and subsidizing.[5] And Yale basketball coach Howard Hobson, writing in *Collier's* at the end of the year, cited a conversation between a reporter and a college official whose players were involved in a gambling scandal. The college official stated that he could not believe that "our boys could do such a thing." The reporter replied, "Why not? You paid them for campus jobs they didn't work at; you gave them passing grades for classes they did not attend. You bribed them to play for you; the gamblers bribed them not to play too well. What's the difference?"[6]

The players who rigged games in the 1951 scandals paid an inordinate price for crimes that would soon be dismissed and forgotten. Shattering the myth of amateurism in college sports would carry a sentence even greater than losing the opportunity to play professional sports: a lifetime label as a dumper and condemnation that would follow them until death.[7] But their coaches escaped the taint of scandal. Said Ed Roman, a member of the 1949–50 CCNY Grand Slam team, "All of [the head] coaches yelled their innocence from the rooftop, but we [players] took the rap." Teammate Floyd Layne, who later became the head basketball coach at his alma mater, saw through the coaches' pronouncements of innocence: "If you told the truth, as the players did in their confessions, you were crucified. But if you lied and maintained an air of respectability as the head coaches did, then you could ride through and everything would be okay."[8]

Basketball coaches' baseless proclamations of innocence reflected their mentality as victims of a conspiracy between their players and the gamblers. Given the choice of detecting or ignoring the fixing, every coach whose players rigged games chose the latter to preserve his career and the money associated with winning.[9] Understanding how basketball coaches at the University of Kentucky, CCNY, and LIU made that choice shows the essential role their passive complicity played in the size and shape of the scandals.

The sport that brought the University of Kentucky the regional and national attention it desired was basketball, and the coach was Adolph Rupp. Born on a farm in Kansas in 1901 to a German Mennonite family, Rupp played basketball at the University of Kansas under pioneering basketball coach Forrest "Phog" Allen, then coached at the high school and college levels before being hired at Kentucky. Rupp built a strong basketball program at Kentucky, unlike those at the other Southeastern Conference (SEC) schools, which focused more on football. Arriving in Kentucky in 1930, Rupp immediately began to field winning teams, produce conference champions, and garner high national rankings, including NCAA titles.[10]

Coinciding with Rupp's arrival and success, Kentucky state legislators began to demand that presidents of the university build a football program that "the university could be proud of."[11] They found their man in Herman Lee Donovan, who occupied the president's office from 1941 to 1956. In 1945, Donovan raised $113,000 to create, with the approval of the state's attorney general and the university's board of trustees, the University of Kentucky Athletic Association (UKAA), an athletic booster organization whose members included some of Lexington's most wealthy and prominent citizens. This organization could hire a coach for more than the state's constitutional limit of $5,000, prevent outside alumni from controlling athletics, and enable funds to be spent more freely than under rules established by the state legislature.[12] The UKAA allowed the university to hire Maryland football coach Paul "Bear" Bryant after the 1945 season; it also funded a number of non-revenue-producing sports, intramurals, the expansion of the football stadium, and the construction of a new basketball arena. Through the UKAA, the athletic program essentially become a separate part of the university, largely independent of its administration but still connected enough to be in concert with state laws governing the institution.

In 1947, the governor of Kentucky hired Griffenhagen and Associates of Chicago to study the university's role in the state. The study's data would in theory allow the university and its citizens to lobby the legislature for more funding so the university could join in the surge of prosperity after World War II. The Griffenhagen Report was related to college athletics in two significant ways. First, it illustrated that a successful football program would not ensure larger funding for the university, as Donovan believed. Second, the report recognized the value of athletics on a major campus but pointed out that the imbalance between athletics and academics was detrimental to the university and stated that intercollegiate athletics should be returned to "an amateur sports basis." The report acknowledged that equalizing the university's athletic program with educational values was not likely because of the "boosterism" in Lexington:

> Still it is really impossible to put football and basketball in its proper place in university education because some of the alumni, other fans, and sports writers demand winning teams with such force that their demands cannot be resisted. It can be assumed that the university faculty in general is not proud of the position of university athletics among the university's activities. But, in viewing the situation realistically, it must be concluded that the university administration, in establishing the University of Kentucky Athletics Association Incorporated, took a step toward making the most of a bad situation, from an educational point of view.[13]

The report criticized the fact that the UKAA was separate from the university and operated as a business yet derived part of its funding from student fees. It pointed out that the nominal total annual fee of one dollar the university paid the state was vastly insufficient, since the state had paid two million dollars to increase the football stadium's seating and build the new field house, which drew capacity crowds for basketball, and it noted that the UKAA derived income from these new facilities at the expense of the state's citizens. Finally, the report criticized athletic financial aid because part of the aid was derived from student fees, and athletics, as a form of entertainment, should have been self-supporting.[14]

Donovan and the board of trustees accepted only the Griffenhagen Report's recommendations regarding rental fees for Alumni Gym and the football stadium. They rejected without comment the proposal to return athletics to amateur standing and nixed the idea that student fees should not be used for athletics, arguing that students were paying to participate in the university's many extracurricular activities, including attending athletic contests. They simply ignored the report's criticism of the practice of giving student fees to the UKAA and dismissed the recommendation that the state be repaid for the upgraded stadium and new field house.[15]

The university now had in place the professionalized and commercialized athletic program it wanted. Classroom, dormitory, and laboratory construction had been subordinated to the construction of the basketball arena and expansion of the football stadium. Because of the coaching and recruiting talents of Rupp and his longtime assistant, Harry Lancaster, Kentucky's basketball program continued to dominate the SEC. And Bear Bryant brought Donovan, the board of trustees, and the UKAA the kind of football program they had envisioned. From 1946 until 1952, when he assumed the head coaching position at Texas A & M, Bryant's teams won an SEC championship and three out of four bowl games.[16]

Still, the university's athletic program was tarnished by Kentucky's involvement in the 1951 basketball scandal, which led the SEC to bar the school from playing any basketball games against NCAA institutions in 1951–52 and the NCAA to place Kentucky on probation for one year.[17]

Donovan admitted that the university might have overemphasized athletics in response to media stimulation of public interest in college sports but placed most of the blame on Madison Square Garden, an environment where "gamblers operated and racketeering prevailed," although Kentucky's basketball team had played in many other public arenas, including venues in St. Louis and Louisville that were two of the nation's most active illegal betting centers. He blamed the players for accepting easy money in the "big cities over which the university had no control."[18] And most tellingly, Donovan conveniently omitted that five blocks from Rupp's office in Alumni Gym was the Mayfair Bar, owned by Rupp's friend Ed Curd, bookie for Mob boss Frank Costello.[19]

Donovan also played dirty politics against his adversaries. On 16 May 1952, he wrote a confidential letter to U.S. senator Thomas R. Underwood of Kentucky requesting information about Judge Streit: "Would it be possible for you to obtain from the FBI and from [the House Un-American Activities Committee] information on the standing and status of Judge Saul S. Streit? If this information is available, the Board of Trustees, the

Athletics Board, and many of us here at the university would like to have these data." On the same day, he forwarded a "a personal and confidential" note to University of Maryland president Harry C. Byrd stating "our mutual friend, President [George Duke] Humphrey of the University of Wyoming, telephoned me a few days ago saying he believed you had a file of information regarding Judge Saul S. Streit of New York City. He suggested that I communicate with you and ask if you have such information as you may have collected. I can use it to good advantage if you have such a file." One month later, Byrd responded with well-reasoned letter advising Donovan to ignore Judge Streit and consider the matter closed. President Donovan wisely followed Byrd's advice.[20]

Rupp's role in the fixing of games has been overshadowed by his success in winning SEC championships and NCAA titles and by his racism, highlighted when his all-white 1966 team lost the NCAA title game to Texas Western, which started five African American players and was coached by Don Haskins.[21] Rupp consistently overrecruited top talent by paying players to attend the university and exceeding NCAA limits on athletic scholarships.[22] (Eight players from his 1947–48 roster were named to the fourteen-member U.S. team that easily won the gold medal at the 1948 London Olympics.)

Three Kentucky players on the Olympic team, Groza, Barnstable, and Beard, admitted to rigging games during the 1948–49 season, and the evidence that Rupp was aware of their fixing is convincing. For example, the three players engineered Kentucky's loss to lowly Loyola in the first round of the 1948 NIT. Watching that game, Yale coach Howard Hobson observed that Groza played Loyola center Jack Kerris "soft," picking up early unnecessary fouls and playing defense behind him instead of beside or in front of him.[23] Groza, who was much faster than Kerris, failed to put himself in position to receive a single pass from the normally sharp-passing Beard, scoring only twelve points and fouling out of the game. Asked by sportswriters after the game if he had instructed his team to not feed Groza, Rupp replied, "Good Lord, didn't you hear the whole bench yelling at them?"[24] Rupp, who demanded and usually obtained perfection on offense and defense, had chosen to ignore his players' obvious lapses.[25]

Groza informed Judge Streit that "Rupp used to show the players slips showing the number of points by which they were favored before

Adolph Rupp and the University of Kentucky basketball team admire the trophy they received for winning the 1949 NCAA basketball title over Oklahoma A & M. When the first arrests were reported in February 1951, Rupp stated, "Gamblers could not touch my boys with a ten-foot pole." When Kentucky all-Americans Ralph Beard and Alex Groza and teammate Dale Barnstable were sentenced in October 1953 by New York judge Saul S. Streit for their involvement in the scandal, the jurist labeled Rupp a coach "with an ear to the betting odds."

every game." Barnstable testified that in the Sugar Bowl game with St. Louis in January 1949, he missed a shot and after the game "Rupp came back and gave me the devil and said that shot I missed just cost his friend Burgess Carey [a former All-American, heavy gambler, and Rupp player] five hundred dollars."[26] Beard testified that while in Cincinnati, Rupp came into his hotel room and said, "I just called Ed Curd and got the points. We are favored by fifteen. Now these guys will be tough, so let's pour it on." The players also reported to Judge Streit that Rupp's coaching strategies and substitutions were dictated by the point spread.[27] Kansas's Allen had repeatedly warned Rupp about Curd, who handled more than five hundred thousand dollars per year in bets on college and professional football games.[28]

Rupp denied being aware of this rigging despite filming and analyzing all of his team's practices and games. NBA Hall of Fame coach Red Auerbach believed that Rupp was a master at evaluating players and relied on his opinions when drafting future Celtics.[29] Rupp and his staff must have spotted these playing lapses, but any hint of rigging would have destroyed the Kentucky basketball program and more than likely forced Rupp and Lancaster to resign. Rupp's public statements about the gambling scandal began with denial and changed to rationalization: "People told me I should have known what was going on. Hell, we won the NCAA and NIT and we sent the team to the Olympics with those same players. If I was supposed to know what was going on when a team like that is winning, then why doesn't a coach of a losing team think his players are fixing games?"[30]

The university's official response to the evidence presented by the players was that point spreads were common knowledge and that Rupp might have used the point spread as a motivational tool. Administrators saw the coach's association with Curd as "accidental and given an appearance of evil that is not warranted."[31]

Before the 1951 scandal, Rupp had contemplated retiring because of health reasons. His resignation would have spared the Wildcats' one-year death penalty and NCAA probation. In August 1952, President Donovan wrote to Rupp,

> In my conversation with you I stated you would be held strictly responsible for observing every rule of the Southeastern Conference and the NCAA. I also told you that your failure to be aware of violations that might occur would be regarded as negligence on your part, even if you were not aware of these violations. You cannot escape responsibility for your team. It is the coach's business to know what his team is doing and to know that his players are strictly observing the rules under which we operate.[32]

But the scandal in his program changed Rupp's mind. He won one final NCAA championship in 1958, was inducted into the Naismith Memorial Basketball Hall of Fame in 1969, and retired in 1972 as the winningest coach in basketball history.

Did Kentucky's successful athletic program fulfill the dreams of President Donovan and the university boosters? If it did, the price the university had to pay was the humiliation of a gambling scandal that marked the beginning of repeated allegations and investigations of corruption that have tainted the university's legacy.

CCNY had begun its athletic program in the early 1900s, and by the 1930s it had developed a respected basketball program composed mostly of Jewish players who had learned to play as children in settlement houses on New York's Lower East Side. Because the CCNY gymnasium was small, its primary venues for playing home games were Madison Square Garden (the third Garden, opened in 1925 and closed in 1967) or one of the armories built in the early 1900s to train soldiers and store military equipment.[33]

Nat Holman, born Nathan Helmanowich on the Lower East Side in 1896, had graduated from the city's Commerce High School in 1916, where he lettered in football, soccer, and baseball but truly excelled at basketball. Upon graduation, he declined a contract to play professional baseball with the Cincinnati Reds, instead entering the Savage School of Physical Education. He received his degree and accepted a position as CCNY's junior varsity basketball coach before leaving to serve in the U.S. Navy during World War I. He returned to CCNY as the country's youngest collegiate head basketball coach at twenty-three. He split his time between coaching and playing on professional teams until 1928, when he devoted himself to coaching full time. Regarded as one of basketball's all-time greats, Holman had a sonorous speaking style sprinkled with mixed metaphors, literary references, and classical allusions. When he spoke a phrase such as a "no-good expurgated bum," he would add, "if you don't mind the English." Opposing coaches would mock his speaking style as pretentious.[34]

Holman was a demanding coach who earned the enmity of many of his players. William "Red" Holzman, two-time CCNY all-American under Holman, National Basketball League star, and Hall of Fame NBA coach, described Holman's coaching style as emphasizing unselfishness, constant movement, court savvy, and relentless teamwork. Holzman also had a strained relationship with Holman. During practices Holman would caustically correct mistakes while the team stood and listened. "I have no patience with mediocrity," he said. "I'll string along with a sophomore, but after a boy has had a full year of my teaching, I want a passing grade, just like the teacher of mathematics or history. . . . As the French say, by dint of great hammering one becomes a blacksmith. You correct mistakes by pounding at them. Easygoing guys who don't demand the best from their players don't win many games." A former player observed, "There's no satisfying Holman. He undermines the confidence of his men by riding them for mistakes without giving credit for good work. You've got to have an awfully tough hide to take it." This enmity for Holman could have lessened the feeling of betrayal when CCNY players were solicited to rig games. When Holman lost his temper during a game, his able assistant, Bobby Sand, would take over. Sand, a mediocre CCNY player from 1936 to 1938, had a fine basketball mind. Coaching magazines sought his articles, but Holman prohibited Sand from publishing them because they might diminish Holman's stature as Mr. Basketball.[35]

At the beginning of the 1949–50 season, Holman's team, known as the Cinderella Team, was considered as talented as any team in the country and was expected to attain a high national ranking, but it underperformed. One player, Norm Mager, hated Holman with a passion and reportedly "would have dumped for nothing."[36] Mager would be the contact man between gambler Eli Kaye and another group of gamblers and the players who wanted to rig games. The "fixers group"—Mager, Irwin Dambrot, Herb Cohen, Ed Roman, and Al Roth—manipulated a game against SMU for which they were not paid because they did not cover the spread and as well as losses to UCLA and Niagara. They also lost to the University of Oklahoma, Canisius, and Syracuse, finishing the season with a 17–5 record and receiving the last berth in the NIT.[37] The team then came seemingly from nowhere to win three NIT games, including an 89–50 thrashing of Rupp's Kentucky Wildcats, and reached the NIT finals, where they defeated Bradley 68–61. They completed the Grand Slam by defeating Bradley again to capture the NCAA championship.

According to the *New York Journal-American*, when New York County district attorney Frank S. Hogan arrested the first CCNY players on 18 February 1951, Holman's response was "Tell Them Everything." The article portrayed Holman as a victim of the fixes when he stated, "This is the hardest thing I have ever had to swallow in all my years in sports." He continued, "I feel punchy. I can't make head or tail of it. I can't find words to tell just how I feel." And with seven players working against him, the odds were uneven and "he was strapped."[38] Because of his stature with the New York sportswriters, Holman was able to persuasively argue that he had been deceived. At their first practice after the arrests, Holman told his ten remaining players, "It started so far back. The Missouri game and [Warner, Roman, and Roth] showing straight faces when we talked and were together. It's a terrible thing. There's a lesson to be learned from this, boys, but it's a terrible price to pay for it. . . . Believe me, boys, I have no sympathy for them if they are guilty because they did as fine a double-crossing job on me and on you as ever has been done."[39]

In January 1951, University of Kansas coach Phog Allen condemned coaches for failing to investigate or dismiss players suspected of dishonesty: "The coach is responsible. Some of these coaches don't give a darn, figuring it's enough if their team wins. But the whole evil is rooted in the Eastern practice of letting college players play [minor league] pro ball on Sundays and odd nights."[40] Allen also suggested that coaches should investigate any player suspected of rigging and dismiss those found to be consorting with gamblers. If one or more players were controlling a game's outcome, a wiretap should be used verify or absolve players of any wrongdoing.[41] LIU coach Clair Bee retorted, "I've worked with boys a long time and could be wrong. I know the two Manhattan boys accused in New York and they always seemed to be nice boys. Anyway it's silly to try to bet on basketball. Smart operators don't touch basketball. It's too uncertain. Too many substitutions. Too many hot and cold nights."[42] Holman and other coaches used the same self-serving analysis to escape the consequences if any action against players they suspected of game fixing was taken.

Writers such as Joe Williams of the *New York World-Telegram and Sun*, Dan Parker of the *New York Mirror*, and Milton Gross of the *New York Post* began to place the blame for rigging games on coaches, athletic directors, and college administrators. One February 1951 Williams column was headlined "Coaches Couldn't Have Missed All the Dumps" and argued,

> What seems to puzzle the innocent most is why the coach, who is so familiar with the talents of his players and so insistent on perfection of play, is unable to recognize Felix J. Faker on the basketball court? . . . But when the coaches say, as they are saying now, that [they] at no time entertained suspicions they are not telling the whole truth. They were simply reluctant to believe their eyes. So they would take refuge in human considerations; their men were too decent to cheat; they were having an off night.[43]

Parker wrote the following November that he believed Holman was aware that he was "harboring mercenaries"—CCNY players who worked and shared gambling pools in the Catskills. Parker also stated that Holman at least knew about the crooked basketball program because Sand had testified that he was "aware of the corruptness but was powerless to stop it."[44]

During a December 1950 game against Missouri, Sand told Holman that the starters were "dumping" and advised him "to get them out of there." Sand was told to "quiet down and mind your own business."[45] After the game, Sand called a few bookies he knew and was informed that betting on the game had been halted, acknowledging the strong suspicion of rigging. Sand shared his suspicions with a member of CCNY's Intercollegiate Athletics Committee, who agreed to investigate. When questioned, however, Holman stated, "There was no chance in the world a City College player would ever do such a thing."[46] Holman's style of coaching, which included filming practices and games, criticizing the slightest mistakes, and requiring precision and teamwork, made it virtually impossible for him, Sand, and his other assistants to fail to spot intentional lapses. CCNY reserve Ron Nadell commented in 2000 that "the subs on CCNY knew something was not right. I know our coach Nat Holman has always claimed he was unaware of any wrongdoing. But a layman watching our game films could determine that some of the players were missing shots and fumbling passes that they normally would not do."[47]

In November 1952, seven months after the sentencing of participants in the scandal and in response to Judge Streit's admonitions, the New

York City Board of Education's Committee on Intercollegiate Basketball reported that

* between 1945 and 1951, fourteen records of athletes had been fraudulently changed in such a way as to raise the high school average and establish eligibility for admission to the college.
* make-up examinations were administered in the registrar's office for athletes and other students with little supervision or safeguards normally present during examinations.
* high school coaches were put on the payroll of the so-called Athletic Guidance Committee to recruit promising athletes. A member of the registrar's office was also on this payroll to "ease" athletes through college.
* The Athletic Guidance Committee was in reality a recruiting program for the promotion of athletics at City College and by its activities helped to create the atmosphere of cynicism and disregard for academic and ethical standards that led to the gambling scandal.
* the withholding of vital information from the committee until statements were being taken under oath, as outlined later in the report, was part of a deliberate pattern of concealment.[48]

The report concluded, "Our committee is convinced that either Professor Holman knew very well many of the big-time aspects dealt with in this report or else was so naïve about matters involving his own job as to throw doubt on his fitness as a teacher."[49] The committee had sound reasons for its conclusion. Holman had stated that he knew nothing about the details of recruiting and insisted that a coach had to believe in the honesty of his players. He said nothing to the committee about CCNY player Paul Schmones's bribe offer to Lenny Hassman in 1945 or about his and Frank S. Lloyd's decision to keep the incident secret. He failed to mention that Sand had brought suspicions of game fixing to his attention or that Sand had written to Warner about a planned trip to South America that would have violated NCAA rules involving paying a college athlete to play a sport. Holman replied that "it was no concern of mine" when asked whether he had checked or confirmed the final score with the point spread of the game, a response that the committee called "evidence of cynical disregard of elementary precautions that were his direct responsibility as a coach." Holman's testimony was seen as "an attempt to show that he remained aloof from the sordid details that actually were part and parcel of the system of big-time basketball."[50] The committee suspended Holman, accusing both him and Sand of

* failure to report the Hassman-Schmones 1945 bribe attempt to the college administration.
* fraud for the fourteen fraudulent transcripts uncovered in the registrar's office between 1945 and 1951.
* creating the Student-Athletic Athletic Council, which was in essence an illegal recruiting mechanism for basketball.
* participating in the plans for the South America tour that would have paid the players.[51]

On 24 February 1954, nearly two years after sentencing in the scandals, the majority report of a three-member trial committee created by the board of education exonerated Holman of all accusations except showing bad judgment. A forty-page minority report, however, pointed out a number of Holman's transgressions. The committee found Sand guilty of all accusations and recommended that he be suspended for one year without pay and then be assigned to duties outside the Hygiene Department.[52]

In March 1954, after conferring with several attorneys, ten of the fifteen board of education members present (five were absent) voted to dismiss Holman as of 2 November 1952, the date of his suspension. Because eleven votes were needed to dismiss him under CCNY's tenure rules, the dismissal did not pass. Twelve members of the board did, however, vote to extend Holman's suspension without pay until 2 April 1954, at which point he would be dismissed; if he filed an application for retirement before that date, he would be dismissed on the date of his application. The board voted Sand guilty of conduct unbecoming a teacher and suspended him for one year without pay.[53]

Holman appealed the board's decision to state commissioner of education Lewis Wilson, who ordered Holman reinstated to faculty status with full back pay.[54] However, Wilson also observed that CCNY's basketball program had become commercialized and that Holman and others should be "censured"; he also noted that Sand's letter and the 1945 bribe offer should have been reported to the university president. Writing in the *New York Times*, Arthur Daley praised the board's decision and commended the CCNY authorities for their relentless and unsparing pursuit of the investigation: "There was not an attempt to whitewash, such as the University of Kentucky produced."[55]

In response to the 1951 scandal, CCNY's governing body reduced the basketball program from the NCAA Division I level to Division III. Basketball officials felt that the scandal had compromised the university's reputation for academic excellence, and they were also aware that a big-time basketball program would repeatedly bring unwanted publicity to the institution. Unlike Bradley University, the University of Kentucky, the University of Toledo, and the other institutions involved in gambling scandals, CCNY placed athletics at a level where it could never again taint the school's academic reputation.

Long Island University opened its doors in 1926 during the Golden Age of Sports with the mission of providing young people with job skills in business. The Brooklyn campus consisted of a series of industrial buildings that had been converted into classrooms; some classes were held in rooms above a bowling alley. The university president believed that an athletic program would increase the institution's visibility, generate free publicity, and help recruit new students. To this end, the university hired Clair Bee in 1931 to coach football, basketball, and baseball. In just two years, the LIU basketball team would compile a 27–1 record, and by 1939, it had a record of 150–10. Its 1935–36 team, with a 26–0 record, decided to boycott the 1936 Olympic trials because of Hitler's policy toward Jews in Germany.[56]

Bee was born in 1896 in Grafton, West Virginia, and attended Pennsylvania's Waynesburg College, Ohio State, and Rutgers, earning four degrees, including one in accounting. Bee's accomplishments in basketball earned him enshrinement in four halls of fame and numerous awards for outstanding contributions. He wrote more than fifty technical books on basketball as well as the twenty-three-volume Chip Hilton series of sports novels popular among youngsters from the late 1940s until the early 1960s. He is credited with a number of basketball innovations, including the one-three-one zone, the three-second rule, and, in some accounts, the twenty-four-second shot clock. Many outstanding coaches, including Bobby Knight and Frank McGuire, have claimed that Bee had "greatest basketball mind of all time."[57] His winning percentage of 82.7 over a twenty-year college career makes him one of the most successful coaches in college basketball history.

In January 1951, Bee was serving as the university's comptroller and assistant to the president as well as the head basketball coach, earning a total of twenty thousand dollars per year. That same month, an article, "Basketball Betting: An Open Scandal," quoted Bee as saying,

> I've got good boys on my team. And I can't imagine that any of them would as much as speak to any of the shady characters who roam around the West Side. So let's disregard personal and associated aspects. But if, in another era, I were coaching another team that was less ethical, and if one or more of these theoretical players were to have been fixed by gamblers, I think I would know it. I would see a man do something that I knew he never did, and I would make one of two conclusions: a. I would think he was sick and off his game: b. I would think that some mental handicap—and in wild theory, it could be interference by an outside person say, a gambler—was accomplishing that same result.[58]

A month later, three of Bee's players—Sherman White, Adolf Bigos, and Leroy Smith—were under arrest for fixing games, and within a few more months, five others had also been caught, including Jackie Goldsmith, whom the district attorney's office called the "master fixer" and "the sum of all that has been wrong in the basketball picture in recent years."[59]

In March 1951, the *New York Times* published a series of articles by Charles Grutzner on "The Impact of Athletics on Education." Grutzner focused on corrupt football programs but described LIU's basketball program as just as shady. LIU awarded basketball players athletic scholarships, free tuition, alumni funds for books, free meals, private rooms in a special building, and expense-paid preseason training trips.[60] Grutzner did not mention that Bee and his assistants placed basketball players in soft jobs on campus and gave them money beyond their athletic scholarships. And Grutzner did not describe the institution's involvement in admitting academically deficient basketball players. LIU enrolled prospective athletes in prep schools paid for by alumni or in its night school until they could receive the grades needed for admission; the school then placed them in easy courses. Its tryout system consisted of allowing prospective players to play a full-court game with numbered jerseys, and Bee and his assistants would offer athletic scholarships to those they liked, a system that clearly violated NCAA rules.[61]

In response to the arrest of the LIU players, Bee vigorously defended his actions and his program. His actions compare unfavorably with the behavior of Coach Henry Bramwell, the fictional coach Bee created for the Chip Hilton novels. Unlike Bee, Bramwell could spot sinister activity involving his players and their friends. In *Championship Ball* (1948), for example, Coach Bramwell removed a player discovered to be playing on an outside (professional) team; later in the season, he removed two more players because they had been seen in a billiard parlor where gamblers were known to congregate. Coach Bramwell commented, "Peers of players can't be trusted to turn in teammates who violate team rules."[62] But Bee's actions were far different from those of his ideal.

Shortly before the basketball scandal broke in January 1951, Stan Isaacs, a reporter for the *New York Daily Compass*, wrote about an unnamed basketball team on which bookies regularly refused to take bets. Isaacs cited as his source an ex-player who "was one of the biggest names in collegiate basketball a few years ago." The ex-player's performance had fluctuated dramatically, raising suspicions of game fixing. Many bookies and bettors thought that LIU's Jackie Goldsmith was the source and LIU was the team. An unidentified coach—conceivably Bee—had shown Isaacs the column a week after it appeared and commented that "stuff like that should not be written as it was not good for the game." Isaacs responded that "unless someone starts writing 'stuff like that,' something's going to break that won't be the least bit good for the game." The coach answered, "When something happens, then talk to me."[63]

Bee must have seen many cases where one of his players did "something that I knew he never did." Even Sherman White's father had spotted his son's suspiciously sloppy play during some of the games fixed during the 1950–51 season.[64] That season's Bowling Green game was so poorly fixed that several fans wrote letters to LIU authorities alleging that the game was rigged. During the previous season, when Eddie Gard was fixing games, he had thrown several passes at White's feet that led to a confrontation and near fistfight. Nearly thirty years later, White recalled,

> Much as I respect Clair Bee, you tell me that he didn't know the difference between a guy controlling or not controlling a game. You tell me Nat Holman would not know these guys were playing up to par or not playing up to par. When you got five guys playing bad at one time, it wouldn't take a rocket scientist to understand that these guys were doing something that was wrong or not right. It's too late in the game to throw stones, but I never hear nobody talk about the coaches.[65]

A year after the scandal broke, Bee published an article in the *Saturday Evening Post* in which he described his role in creating an environment at LIU that made the fixing of games inevitable. Unlike Holman and Rupp, who accepted none of the responsibility for running corrupt programs, Bee wrote about the corruptive aspects of the LIU program as if he were confessing his guilt, saying, "they say the loudest psalm singer is a reformed sinner—and I'm singing," as if Coach Bramwell had finally been heard. Bee described having to wait from four in the afternoon until six in the morning for Smith, Bigos, and White to return after being picked by up detectives as a terrible ordeal. Perhaps he was afraid that the team for which he had such high aspirations would be dismantled and his program would be identified as one of the most corrupt in college sports.[66]

But Bee also attempted to contextualize and thus mitigate his misdeeds, noting that abuses were widespread in college sports—overemphasizing sports by offering scholarships, paying cash subsidies, guaranteeing passing grades in the classroom, scheduling extended road trips, playing too many games, conducting year-round practices, and regularly playing in off-campus arenas. Bee admitted guilt only to overemphasizing sports. Yet Dick Fuertado, an LIU player arrested for fixing games, stated that his part-time campus job was "shooting fifty foul shots a day which earned him eight to fifteen dollars a week" from the bursar's office; when he complained to Bee that other players were making more than him, Bee sent twenty dollars to his mother. And before the Blackbirds' first game against Stanford in 1936, Bee took his team to Grossinger's resort in the Catskills for three days, a lavish outing in the midst of the Great Depression. Ultimately, Bee argued that a major sports program lifted student morale, increased school pride, unified the student body, and provided other intangible benefits such as being part of "the American tradition that admires and strives for top ranking in any field."[67] But students were assigned the worst seats at the Garden, far removed from the court.

Despite its success, the LIU basketball program ran a deficit nearly continuously from 1933 to 1951. Bee attributed the shortfalls to scholarships, cash payments, hidden expenses, costly road trips, flashy equipment, a training table, publicity, scouting, and office "overload." During the 1950–51 school year alone, the basketball program lost $24,000; the university had to make up the difference, taking money away from such academic essentials as new buildings, laboratories, and raises for professors. Bee admitted to being a "lousy businessman."[68] Why did the board of trustees, the university president, faculty, and other personnel allow a money-losing program to continue and Bee to receive his substantial salary? The basketball program's success may well have been seen as compensation for draining the institution's budget.

Bee adjusted his defense in another article published in 1952, confessing that he had learned that "basketball can be made to be crooked, that the game could be rigged." At the time, Bee had looked at the rigged games and seen "the usual evidence of a player having a bad night, another having indescribable bad luck, and as in many other games, the contests merely appeared to be those in which one team was getting the breaks, while the others just couldn't do anything right." And as long as his players looked him in the eye and denied involvement, he could not possibly "doubt them and still coach them."[69]

When Chip Hilton reaches State U in *Freshman Quarterback* (1952), he refuses a scholarship, and through a series of implausible twists, his freshman nonscholarship dormitory football team defeats the freshman scholarship team as Chip kicks the winning field goal in a snowstorm. In a parallel plot, the booster club president resigns and excoriates the "hired hand system" in college sports: "We expected too much from our hired hands. We set those boys apart and expected them to maintain the same enthusiasm as the regular student body. We placed them under outside supervision just as we've placed the coaching staff under outside supervision. We disassociated them from normal student life just as we've disassociated our coaches from the regular administration of the university."[70]

LIU's role in the 1951 basketball scandal is the story of a brilliant coach who operated a corrupt basketball program by shielding his eyes from the truth with self-serving excuses and justifications, all the while fictionally portraying an idealized version of himself that had never and could never exist in college basketball. When the corruption was revealed, he defended himself with pious denials full of contradictions, omissions, and inaccuracies.

FIVE

"DO YOU HAVE ANYTHING FOR ME?"

Gambling Scandals in College Football from the Big Three to Bear Bryant

Gambling in college football has grown steadily from its beginnings in the latter part of the nineteenth century. Despite repeated abuses in recruiting, subsidizing, and academics, the sport escaped the game-fixing scandals that had plagued college basketball. Since the 1990s, however, college officials, the NCAA, and law enforcement at the federal, state, and local levels have investigated and indicted an increasing number of college football players who have bet on sports, in some cases against their own teams.

As early as 1893, college football's founder, Walter Camp, was keenly aware of the possibility that players could fix games. Observing the open bidding and money offered by colleges to obtain the best players, Camp stated, "A man who begins by selling his skill to a college may someday find himself selling an individual act in a particular contest—selling games."[1] The Ivy League institutions of Yale, Princeton, and Harvard—the Big Three—created college football and simultaneously promulgated many of its scandals. In 1880, when Princeton played Yale in the Big Three championship at the Polo Grounds in Manhattan, newspapers reported that an "unusual number of young collegians swung handsful of greenbacks in the air, loudly calling for bets." The 0–0 final score undoubtedly disappointed the young bettors. The number of spectators attending the Big Three championship grew from five thousand in 1880 to twenty-five thousand in 1890; the crowd for the 1893 game, in which Princeton upset Harvard, was estimated at forty thousand. For bookies, the game presented an opportunity to make big money. The week before the game, alumni of the two institutions and many nongraduates booked bets on the floor of the New York Stock Exchange and wherever else one could tender a bet. The press reported that in 1890, four thousand dollars was sent to Princeton accompanied with orders to bet the money on Yale at odds of 5–1 or better. In 1891, Henry Ward Beecher, a former Yale star and the grandson of the famous minister and social reformer by the same name, was observed offering the princely sum of two thousand dollars on the street that Princeton would not kick a field goal and one thousand dollars that his former team would win by more than 20 points.[2]

In 1880, noted physical educator Dudley Sargent deplored college football's trend toward professionalism, predicting, "Betting will be the bane of competitive contests."[3] The basis for Sargent's observation was that many college football teams played town or semiprofessional teams that were widely known to wager on games to earn extra money. College authorities were also keenly aware that gambling in professional baseball and boxing existed virtually unchecked, and the sorts of scandals that plagued baseball from 1877 up to and beyond the fixed 1919 World Series could easily become a menace in college football.

Until the early 1900s, most of college football's spectators were students and graduates along with social elites who could afford the high-priced tickets. The 1893 Yale-Princeton game attracted future president Theodore Roosevelt, New York City mayor Thomas Francis Gilroy, House Speaker Thomas B. Reed, and financial giants Richard Whitney and Cornelius Vanderbilt. While betting may have been brisk among the alumni and students, the games generally did not have serious gamblers attempting to bribe players to fix the outcome.[4]

Beginning in the late 1880s, the telegraph allowed people instantly to learn the results of college football and professional baseball games, horse races, prizefights, and other sporting events. The appearance of the sports page in newspapers coincided with the public's increased interest in sports. These new ways of communicating allowed bookies to become more prominent: Newspapers set up bulletin boards outside their premises where bettors and fans could learn the outcomes of games. In large cities such as Baltimore, writer H. L. Mencken recalled, "The high-toned saloons of the town catered to the fans by putting in telegraph operators who wrote the scores on the blackboards."[5]

By the turn of the century, athletic bums, saloon owners, gamblers, and other parasites of the sporting world had earned public suspicion and hostility, but at the same time they satisfied the urban populace's voracious betting appetite. Some supporters of college football cited gambling as a parasite that needed to be eradicated, as the sport was viewed as a training ground and preparation for life for the sons of the upper classes.[6]

In the early 1900s, eastern college and athletic administrators, observing that students, alumni, and the public were interested in football and that the sport could provide financial benefits, began to construct large stadiums. By 1914, Harvard (40,000-seat capacity), Syracuse (40,000), Princeton (45,275), and Yale (70,657) had built U- or bowl-shaped steel-reinforced stadiums in architectural styles that reflected features of ancient Greece and Rome.[7] With spectators needed to fill the stadiums and provide funds to repay the loans obtained to construct them, the commercialization and professionalization of college football became more widespread, and even some of the smallest colleges believed that football programs could bring big paydays. Admitting academically unqualified players to an institution, paying off talented high school players, subsidizing players while in college, and giving control of football programs to alumni and later to groups known as boosters became a common practice.

College football players also temporarily joined the professional ranks under assumed names. Beginning in the late 1800s, semiprofessional football teams had been formed in cities where the college game was not played. In the beginning, these town teams were composed of individuals who worked six days a week and played their games on Sundays, providing popular entertainment. When the games involved cities that were in close proximity, such as Canton and Massillon, Ohio, they assumed an importance analogous to a collegiate rivalry and gave bookies a healthy business. On some games, citizens and professional gamblers wagered as much as one hundred thousand dollars. To strengthen their teams and help ensure their bets, team officials often queried college players about their interest in making money by playing on Sunday afternoons.[8]

The American Professional Football Association, organized in 1919, soon became embroiled in recruiting collegiate players. The Green Bay Packers had their franchise revoked in 1921 because they recruited three Notre Dame players—Hunk Anderson, Ojay Larson, and Hec Garvey—for their final game of the season at Milwaukee. The story was broken by the *Chicago Tribune*, home of the Packers' archrival Staleys (later the Bears), coached by George Halas. The Green Bay franchise was reinstated in 1922 after Curly Lambeau paid a fee.[9]

In another widely publicized incident involving Notre Dame players, Carlinville, Illinois, hired ten members of the Irish squad, offering them two hundred dollars each to play for the town in its 21 November 1921 game against nearby Taylorsville. Carlinville businessmen and bankers bet the enormous sum of fifty thousand dollars on their team to win; later reports indicated that professional gamblers had put up more money, raising the pot to one hundred thousand dollars. Taylorsville responded by hiring nine players from the University of Illinois. Taylorsville prevailed 16–0, as the Notre Dame quarterback was not among Carlinville's ringers and an end was directing the offense.[10] All nineteen players were barred from future collegiate athletic competition, and controversy subsequently arose about how much the Notre Dame and Illinois coaches knew about their players' participation. Illinois coach Bob Zuppke indicated that he had not known about his players' participation until late January 1922.[11] However, local newspapers had widely reported the game's results, including the participation of the collegians. The manager of the Carlinville squad, Grover Hoover, said that Notre Dame's Knute Rockne became aware of his players' involvement shortly after they agreed to play, but Hoover retracted his statement when the legendary coach threatened to sue for libel.[12]

After World War I, during a time when the federal government shut down horse racing tracks, many gamblers shifted their business to college football. As more colleges constructed football stadiums, many football programs reported increased profits and attendance, along with widespread drinking, gambling, and ticket scalping. Big Ten athletic directors noted in 1922 for the first time the "alarming" amount of wagering that had occurred on games involving conference teams and officials' inability to stop the practice.[13] Yale's Walter Camp saw football revenues as financing "elaborate and expensive coaching staffs" and observed, "Commercialism will be the evil if the premium is all on winning."[14]

The introduction of radio broadcasts and intersectional games also increased gambling in college football. According to sports historian Ronald A. Smith, the first college to broadcast its football games was the University of Minnesota, in 1912.[15] Eight years later, the in-state rivalry between the University of Texas and Texas A & M was broadcast from College Station. In 1922, an intersectional game between Princeton and the University of Chicago was broadcast to New York City, where thousands listened as Princeton won in a nail-biter. NBC estimated an audience of twenty-five million for its radio broadcast of the 1928 Rose Bowl game.[16]

The advent of television would have an even greater influence on the country's betting clientele.[17] During World War II, RCA and CBS worked to develop the new medium, and when it became publicly available, it would allow bookies and gamblers to create sports betting as we know it today.[18] Radio and television enabled bookies and gamblers to follow the progress of their bets from the comfort of their homes, a Nevada casino, or a neighborhood bar.

Intersectional games were regularly scheduled during the 1920s at campus stadiums and at neutral sites such as the Polo Grounds in Manhattan, the Los Angeles Coliseum, and Chicago's Soldier Field (first named Grant Park Stadium), with promoters and competing colleges receiving handsome sums of money. Such matchups between teams with the best records in college football attracted bookies and gamblers as well as spectators, who commonly paid two to five dollars to join the crowd, with the 1928 game between Navy and Notre Dame drawing an estimated 120,000 (at fifteen dollars a ticket) to Soldier Field.[19]

A number of small colleges sought to grab some of the largesse from football mania, including the 270-student Centre College in Danville, Kentucky. Lacking the money or population base to construct a large stadium, school officials decided that a barnstorming football team would enrich the college. The squad, nicknamed the Praying Colonels because of the team's pregame locker room devotions, compiled an undefeated record in 1919 and claimed the mythical national championship. Playing from coast to coast, the football team may have recruited players by pointing out the money they could make by betting on their team to win. In 1920, the team lost only one game—to Harvard, which had not lost since 1916 and featured All-Americans Alvin "Bo" McMillin, James "Red" Weaver, and James M. "Red" Roberts. In an October 1921 rematch on a muddy field at Cambridge, Centre defeated the Crimson 6–0 in what the *New York Times* labeled the "upset of the century."[20]

Like Notre Dame's legendary George Gipp, McMillin was reputed to have supported himself through college by rolling dice and betting on Centre to win by large margins. When the team traveled to Boston in 1920 and 1921, McMillin and Roberts appeared at a pool hall and bet lavishly on Centre. The 1921 team was almost identical to the 1920 team except that Weaver, who set a record for ninety-nine consecutive extra points, had left the team for a high school coaching position. Also, receiver and punter Lefty Whitnell did not travel to the game because of "poor grades," a McMillin shortcoming overlooked by the faculty. While returning home the evening after the game, Earl Ruby of the *Louisville Courier-Journal* reported that McMillin "had more folding money on the night of October 29, 1921, in a lower berth on a Pullman heading back to Kentucky than could normally be found in a lot of small town Kentucky banks."[21]

Rockne traveled to Danville's Busy Bee Café to offer Centre's head coach, Charlie Moran (also a National League baseball umpire), the opportunity to play Notre Dame at Soldier Field. Rockne's bid was refused, just as Moran had also refused offers from the Polo Grounds, the University of Detroit, Princeton, Yale, and the Rose Bowl. The Rose Bowl offer was later rescinded when the University of California at Berkeley refused to play a "third rate school" in the New Year's day classic. In addition to upsetting Harvard, Centre defeated Tulane 21–0 on Thanksgiving Day in New Orleans and Arizona State 38–0 on 26 December in San Diego, but the team lost its final game to Texas A & M 22–14 on 2 January 1922 in Dallas.[22] The Praying Colonels' season of glory ended with a 10–1 record; the players and the team's followers undoubtedly had made out very nicely betting on the tiny college. Cynics pointed out that barnstorming and academics were inconsistent with educational goals unless the players were majoring in gaming.[23]

The significant increase in attendance and profits in college football in the 1920s coincided with a number of gambling incidents that appeared to do no harm to college football's popularity. While some college authorities decried the increase in betting on the sport, practical measures were not implemented to curtail it. Although some college coaches and graduate managers (later known as athletic directors) such as Amos Alonzo Stagg and Walter Camp had observed the "gambling parasite" grow with the game, decades would pass and a number of scandals would erupt before college officials and federal and state legislators would finally implement measures that made sports bribery of amateurs a violation federal or state law: In 2000, because of widespread gambling among college athletes, the NCAA changed its rule on gambling to state, "Any athlete who wagers on his or her own institution or his or her own team is permanently ineligible without the option of appealing."[24]

During the 1919 football season, a sign was posted at Dartmouth College stating that its opponent had fifteen thousand dollars to back its team. Dartmouth president Ernest Martin Hopkins reported that a college investigation revealed that the offer had been made by two individuals who had recently tampered with the fixed 1919 World Series.[25] Cornell graduate manager of athletics Romeyn Berry told the *New York Times* that gambling constituted "as strong a menace to college football as [to] professional baseball." Berry warned Cornell students about betting on the upcoming game against Dartmouth at the Polo Grounds and hinted about the possibility of Cornell players "selling the game to professional gamblers." Cornell's team had practiced behind closed doors all season, and coach Gil Dobie had forbidden his team from running through its game signals at the school's home stadium, Schoelkopf Field. Instead, signal drills took place in the baseball batting cage, away from spectators, including the serious gamblers who were known to attend practices.[26] Berry's observations and warning would characterize the nature of the comments about this aspect of college football until six decades later, when college players would be routinely penalized for violating NCAA rules regarding gambling on sports.

During the 1920s, college football players on opposing teams commonly collected money before games, with the victorious team taking the loser's pot. The night or day before a game, the players would meet for dinner and wager on the game's outcome, making side bets on who would gain the most yards, catch the most passes, or score the most points. Gipp, Notre Dame's all-American halfback and a skilled pool and poker player, had resided for a time in South Bend's Oliver Hotel, a luxury establishment known for high-stakes gambling. Gipp reportedly collected $2,100 before the 1920 Army game. At halftime, with Notre Dame losing, Rockne caustically asked Gipp whether he had "any interest in the game." Gipp responded, "Look Rock, I've got $400 bet on this game and I'm not about to blow it."[27]

By all accounts, Gipp was an outstanding all-around athlete, gambler, and nonstudent. While at Notre Dame, he played on semiprofessional and industrial football teams for money and supplemented his income by playing pool, poker, and dice. He frequented a South Bend bar, Hullie and Mike's, and was a regular at the Oliver and LaSalle Hotels, playing pool and cards with some of the best hustlers from Chicago. Gipp consistently backed up his statement, "I'm one of the finest freelance gamblers ever to attend Notre Dame." His roommate and friend, Arthur "Dutch" Bergman, recounted that Gipp never gambled with other students and that shooting craps paid his way through the university. Stated Bergman, "I've seen him win $500 in a crap game and then spend his winnings buying meals for destitute families. No wonder he was idolized by South Bend townies."[28] The descriptive labels sportswriters bestowed on Gipp included the Wild Horse of Notre Dame, Rockne's Golden Boy, and perhaps most accurately, Notre Dame's Cool Gambler.[29]

When Rutgers traveled to Atlanta to play Georgia Tech in 1921, the Scarlet Knights' graduate manager of athletics, William P. Garrison, described to the sports editor of the *Atlanta Constitution* how professional gamblers had pestered the visitors' players, coaches, and managers for information and opinions about the Rutgers team. According to Garrison, the gamblers descended on the squad immediately after their arrival in Atlanta and were observed in the stands up to game time: "Every touchdown, every penalty, every move of a player meant something to somebody's pocketbook, to be accompanied by the cheers of the winners and curses of the losers."[30]

The gambling parasite was not confined only to major football programs. At the 1921 conference of the Central Intercollegiate Association, an organization of athletic programs at African American colleges, held in Hampton, Virginia, representatives reported that betting among players, students, and spectators along the sidelines had become a common problem. In some instances, game officials were attacked when calls went against the bettors. Players reportedly were betting their entire summer earnings, and students and spectators were wagering hundreds of dollars.[31]

During the 1920s, the Golden Age of Sports had spawned a number of football programs that increasingly ignored academics. The formation of the NCAA and regional conferences did little to stem the excesses of the football establishment. In its 1924 report, the Carnegie Foundation for the Advancement of Teaching surveyed the athletic practices of thirty-three institutions, primarily in the South. Its findings included increases in commercialization and gambling, especially when football games were played at off-campus sites such as Yankee Stadium, where only a small percentage of the spectators were students. The organization condemned alumni who bet on their alma mater and cautioned that greater damage to the sport would occur if professional gamblers looked to college football as a place to do business.[32]

Five years later, the Carnegie Foundation released another report that cited gambling as a problem in college football but offered no practical measures to curtail it.[33] A likely reason for this failure is that the NCAA was not invited to participate in the Carnegie group's three-year study. The report concluded that the primary defect in college athletics was commercialism. The report's author, Howard Savage, devoted most of the study to football, as basketball and other sports had gained little spectator interest by the late 1920s. College officials, including coaches, responded with a mixture of denial, support, and silence.[34] Many athletic officials asserted that college football was funding their schools' entire athletic programs, an assumption that was tenuous at best but was used for years to support constant increases in football budgets.

The Carnegie report and its reception illustrated that the hypocrisy in college sports, especially in college football, would continue on a grander scale and that college athletics would resist investigation and change. It also sent a message to athletes that colleges would employ virtually any means possible—legal or illegal—under the guise of amateurism to operate programs that closely resembled professional teams, including ignoring the actions of players who bet on themselves. Bribe offers and other gambling-related incidents were more than likely not reported to the media. The reason was simple enough: Destroying the myth that Frank Merriwell (the turn-of-the century model for Clair Bee's Chip Hilton) had constructed about college football would risk the money the sport was generating. Savage placed the responsibility for operating a clean athletic program squarely on the shoulders of college presidents, who by the late 1920s were increasingly losing control of athletics to coaches such as Knute Rockne and Fielding Yost as well as to alumni and booster groups.

In a satiric reply to Savage's report, Dr. Harry Pritchard, former president of MIT and founder of the Carnegie Foundation, proposed in a 1932 *Atlantic Monthly* editorial that intercollegiate horse racing be substituted for football. Pritchard conceded that the college football could not remain pure and rationalized his proposal by stating that horse racing "would release for the pursuit of studies the player 'now strongly inclined to feel that he is entitled to some of the swag' and curb the 'bootlegging alumnus' ready to finance and subsidize the young athlete by dark and devious methods." He went on to propose that reputable colleges establish breeding farms in Kentucky and Virginia and suggested that the study of horse racing be made a major undergraduate requirement. He recommended that students be allowed to bet on the races because "a horse race has the extra advantage over football because the whole audience can understand what is happening."[35]

The Great Depression reduced the funding for major college football programs but increased the amount of gambling on college football games. Many individuals who began as bootleggers during Prohibition (1919–33) used their profits to enter the gambling business. Parimutuel betting on horse racing was legalized in the early 1900s as many state legislatures sought a portion of the profits, and the sport flourished until the beginning of World War II.[36] An estimated $360 million was bet in 1930 inside racetracks, with a staggering $2 billion or more bet on the same races through legal and illegal bookies. By 1936, the nation's gambling bill had risen to $6.5 billion as many people attempted to recoup their losses from the 1929 stock market crash by wagering. More than $3 billion was reportedly bet on sports pools, policy and number games, and lotteries.[37]

During the 1930s, coaches and college officials increasingly assailed the adverse affect of illegal gambling on college football's attractiveness to spectators. University of Washington coach Jimmy Phelan asserted in 1933 that large sums of money were bet on college football games in Seattle. No doubt shocking football purists, Phelan indicated that he had deliberately kept the margin of victory down in some games his team won as a means of outwitting bettors and causing them to lose money. Stanford coach Tiny Thornhill echoed Phelan's allegations by indicating that large gambling rings in the San Francisco Bay area had approached coaches and game officials to manipulate games.[38] In 1935, Professor Philip O. Badger, chair of the board of athletic control at New York University, decried the predicted death of collegiate football in ten years because of commercial broadcasts, excessive drinking at games, and the growth of gambling, which, he said, "if allowed to go unchecked may create havoc and also disorderly conduct at games." And in a statement that would be repeated over the next seventy-five years involving commercialized basketball, football, and gambling, he announced, "There is no panacea or formula for doing the job of rationalizing intercollegiate athletics in a university or college. . . . All that is needed is common sense."[39]

University of Pennsylvania coach Harvey Harman reported that his players had been approached in 1933 by gamblers to act as selling agents for racketeers backing pools.[40] In 1935, prominent coaches would become strange bedfellows with gamblers, using radio and newspapers to feed the gambling mania that according to John DeGroza, president of the American Football Institute, "was undermining the game." Coaches predicted the outcome of games, inviting numerous telephone calls to athletic departments seeking vital betting-related information. Particularly disturbing from the results of a nationwide survey sponsored by the institute was the "alarming increase of betting by high school students."[41]

Football pools became popular in the 1930s because they were inexpensive and theoretically offered bettors the opportunity to apply their knowledge about which teams to pick. Unlike baseball pools, where selecting the number of wins by a team in a series was difficult to handicap because teams greatly varied in performance, the football pool card required that a bettor select a minimum of five out of nine games without any losers or ties. Popular on college campuses, the cards provided bettors with the illusion that if they consistently studied the teams' performance, their chances of winning were increased. But the pool sellers selected the nine most competitive games, where upsets were most likely to occur, skewing the odds in the bookmakers' favor and making the payouts about one-third of what they should have been. Colleges occasionally would clamp down and arrest students who were distributing the cards. A 1936 editorial in the *Saturday Evening Post* asserted that every Saturday, millions of dollars changed hands in college football pools and that "professional gamblers are now brazen enough to get their information from the players themselves and from undergraduates working on college newspapers."[42]

Growing U.S. prosperity after World War II institutionalized a number of illegal practices that would chronically afflict college basketball and football. Whereas for college basketball, the main such practice was the fixing of games, for college football, it was soliciting athletic talent by providing under-the-table payoffs. Of course, not all highly skilled young athletes were academically qualified for football programs "that the university could be proud of."[43] Hence, academic fraud also became endemic as schools sought to attain national rankings, generate revenue, and ensure that wealthy boosters would continue to give money to athletic programs.

Betting on college football was estimated at one hundred million dollars in 1946, with about five million dollars riding on that year's Army–Notre Dame "Game of the Century" alone.[44] So much gambling and ticket scalping took place at the game that officials at the institutions suspended the series after the 1947 game, fearing that their players might consort with professional gamblers. Irish coach Frank Leahy and Father John H. Murphy, one of the institution's top administrators, discussed of the problem of gamblers appearing in hotel lobbies in cities where the two teams were quartered, presumably to offer bribes to players.[45] Other teams likely also faced this problem.

Officials at Notre Dame and Army probably were influenced in their decision to suspend the series by the attempt to bribe New York Giants running back Merle Hapes and quarterback Frank Filchock to throw the 1946 National Football League championship game against the Chicago Bears at the Polo Grounds. Alvin J. Paris, owner of a New York novelty shop and self-styled playboy, had befriended Hapes and Filchock, paid them softening-up money, and invited them to a number of parties before attempting to bribe them. The offer was uncovered the day before the title game, leading to a meeting involving Filchock, Hapes, New York City mayor William O' Dwyer, NFL commissioner Bert Bell Jr., and other officials. Filchock denied the attempted bribe, while Hapes admitted it. The officials concluded that no bribe had taken place and the game could proceed, with Filchock allowed to play but Hapes not. Possibly as a consequence of nervousness and boos from the home crowd, Filchock threw six interceptions, and the Bears won, 24–14. At Paris's trial, Filchock admitted that he had lied at the mayor's meeting, and both he and Hapes were indefinitely suspended from the NFL for "conduct detrimental to the league."[46] Hapes would not play professional football again, while

Filchock enjoyed a stellar career in the Canadian professional league and was hired in 1960 as the head coach of the Denver Broncos of the fledging American Football League.

Also in 1946, U.S. attorney Michael J. Walsh alleged that a nationwide gambling syndicate had employed scouts to attend practices of all the major college football teams. The information furnished by the scouts was the basis for odds and points set on parley cards that were sold to the public. Walsh also reported that gamblers had been seen taking bets below the stands at college football games. Walsh estimated the gambling syndicate's profits at twenty-five million dollars, a figure the Chicago Crime Commission secretary described as "conservative."[47]

Other reported attempts to rig college football games corroborated Walsh's observations. In 1952, three University of Maryland football players were offered a bribe to win the upcoming LSU game by less than the 21-point spread. Louis A. Glickfield, a junior who had previously been cut from the team, offered a thousand dollars to center Tom Cosgrove, four hundred dollars to guard Frank Navarro, and one hundred dollars to key ball handler and quarterback Jack Scarbath. Maryland easily defeated LSU 34–6, and Glickfield was convicted of attempted bribery, fined a thousand dollars, and ordered to serve eighteen months in prison.[48]

One of the most notable gambling scandals in college football history involved famed Alabama coach Paul "Bear" Bryant and former Georgia coach James Wallace "Wally" Butts. The scandal threatened the squeaky-clean myth of college football, especially in the South and especially as embodied by Bryant, one of the myth's chief promoters. It would lead to widespread media coverage, the involvement of a prominent national publication, and a landmark libel case that reached the U.S. Supreme Court.

At the time of the scandal, Bryant was in his fifth season coaching the Crimson Tide, and his program was on the upswing, having been ranked No. 1 in the nation in 1961. Butts, however, was in the midst of a downward spiral both personally and professionally. In December 1960, he had been asked to resign from the head coaching position at Georgia despite a 1959 record of 9–1, a Southeastern Conference title, and a win over Big Eight champion Missouri in the Orange Bowl. He would be allowed to retain his position as director of athletics until 30 June 1963 to maximize his pension benefits. The pressure for his resignation came largely from athletic boosters unhappy over his resistance to changing his offense to a wide-open style, his personal financial problems, and his sexual indiscretions, which involved frequenting nightclubs with young women, drinking excessively, and taking out-of-town trips, some at the university's expense, with a young mistress.[49] Butts's successor as the Bulldogs' head coach was former Georgia player John Griffith, who had been Butts's youngest assistant. Griffith publicly stated that there would be no connection between Butts and the new football regime, and the university president informed Butts that the university's football program was off-limits to him. During the 1961 season, Butts, frustrated by his demotion and unable to maintain the lifestyle to which he had become accustomed, publicly hinted that Griffith and his staff were not obtaining optimal performances from their players. The relationship between the former coach and Griffith deteriorated.[50]

On the morning of 13 September 1962, nine days before the Georgia-Alabama game at Legion Field in Birmingham, Butts visited the offices of Atlanta public relations firm Communications International, which was owned by one of his friends. While there, Butts placed a telephone call to another friend, Chicago beer distributor and heavy college football gambler Frank Scobey. After completing his call to the gambler, Butts then called Bryant in Tuscaloosa.

At precisely that moment, Atlanta insurance executive George P. Burnett was attempting to call a friend who worked at Communications International. The phone connection proved difficult to establish. During one of the attempts, Burnett heard an operator come on the line and say, "Coach Bryant is out on the field, Coach Butts, but he is on his way to the phone. Do you want to hold, or do you want him to return the call?" Butts replied that he would hold. Burnett stayed on the line and listened. When Bryant came on the line, Butts said, "Hello Bear," to which Bryant responded, "Hi, Wally, do you have anything for me?"[51] Bryant's question piqued the curiosity of Burnett, who knew that the Crimson Tide and Bulldogs would play each other in nine days and surmised that Bryant was expecting the call and that it was for his benefit.

Burnett listened as Butts gave Bryant detailed information about Georgia's team that Bryant would find useful against the Bulldogs. Burnett also heard Bryant ask Butts a number of questions to which the ex-coach responded, "I don't know," followed by Bryant asking, "Can you find out for me?" Butts responded, "I'll try." The conversation lasted a little over fifteen minutes and concluded with the two football figures arranging to talk again the next Sunday; Bryant indicated that he would call Butts at home, which he did. Burnett's seven pages of notes about the overheard conversation included information about Georgia's offensive schemes and defensive tendencies, the type of slot formations Georgia was planning to use, pass or run plays to be used in various formations, the possibility of a quick kick, which running back would go in motion, pass patterns run inside the twenty-yard line, and some of Georgia's defensive tendencies, such as free safety Woodward committing very aggressively on running plays. Butts also suggested that Georgia did not overshift the defensive line and linebackers to match a formation's strength or to the wide side of the field when the ball was on a hash mark.[52]

Bryant's team overwhelmed the Bulldogs 35–0; Georgia never got closer to the end zone than Alabama's 45-yard line, and that was only on the last play of the game; the Bulldogs' offensive production totaled 37 yards rushing and 79 yards passing. The Crimson Tide had been favored by between 14 and 17 points, so bettors choosing Alabama and the spread won their bets handily. Did Butts share information with Bryant to ensure that he or any of his gambling associates would win their bets?[53] Or had Scobey urged Butts to call Bryant, promising him business advice and a loan? (At the time of the game, Butts was reported to have lost money on investments, borrowed money from one of his gambler friends, and been on the verge of insolvency.)[54] The information from Butts might have helped Bryant avoid a season-opening upset that could derail his quest for another No. 1 ranking. Also, it was widely believed that Bryant sought to win games by more than the point spread. For example, later that season, trailing Georgia Tech 7–6 but with possession of the ball and in range for an easy field goal, Bryant elected to try for a first down in hopes of later scoring a touchdown. The pass failed, and Alabama lost the game. Bryant's decision might have been motivated by the desire to win by more than the point spread.[55] Bryant's style of winning by large margins benefited Alabama's wealthy boosters, some of whom bet heavily on the games.[56]

Burnett's notes remained at his home until January 1963, when he decided to share them with Bulldogs football supporter Bob Edwards. Edwards became enraged and arranged for Burnett to show the notes to Griffith, who said, "This looks like our game plan. I figured someone had given our game plan to Alabama. This game was like a couple of others; we were stymied—couldn't get anything going."[57]

In February 1963, Butts was shown the notes in a meeting at the law office of Cook Barwick, the University of Georgia's legal counsel. Also present were SEC commissioner Bernie Moore, University of Georgia president O. C. Aderhold, and J. D. Bolton, University of Georgia treasurer and ex-officio chair of the Georgia Athletic Boosters. According to James Kirby, who has written a convincing account of the Butts-Bryant scandal in *Fumble: Bear Bryant, Wally Butts, and the Great Football Scandal*, Butts did not seem surprised or emotional when shown the notes, nor did he deny that the conversation occurred. His only comment was, "Mr. Burnett and you gentlemen have placed the wrong interpretation on this conversation and on the notes that Mr. Burnett was supposed to have taken." Over the next two hours, Butts tiptoed around the issue by not referring to the notes again, reiterating that he would never harm the University of Georgia, and quickly changing the subject from the Burnett notes to coaches' common practice of talking to one another about teams and strategies. Kirby, then a law professor at Vanderbilt University, had been hired by Moore to monitor the legal proceedings that would surely occur if Burnett's notes became public. Butts was in friendly territory at the meeting: None of those present asked him whether he had shared valuable football information with Bryant because he was gambling on the game; whether he had passed information to a gambler with whom he had associated; whether he had shared the information to solve his financial problems or in hopes of returning as Georgia's head coach if Griffith failed. The following day, Butts resigned as athletic director, three months earlier than planned.[58]

Later on the day of the February meeting, Burnett met with Moore; Bill Hartman, an Athens businessman and close friend of Butts; Aderhold; and Jimmy Dunlap, chair of the board of regents of the University of Georgia. Hartman asked, "Mr. Burnett, don't you think you overheard two coaches talking about football in general?" Burnett responded that Butts had asked no questions about Alabama's team. Dunlap then said to Burnett, "We have a complete record of your financial situation and bad checks." Burnett was stunned. He had indeed passed bad checks, but he left the meeting believing that Butts's supporters would publicize the matter, embarrassing Burnett and his family.[59]

From this meeting, Burnett went directly to the office of Pierre Howard, his close friend and attorney. Howard advised Burnett to sell the story to sportswriter Frank Graham Jr., who had flown to Atlanta to pin down a rumor that an incriminating conversation between Butts and Bryant had taken place. Burnett had previously rejected the idea of selling the story, but he then sold it to Graham for five thousand dollars.[60]

Also in late February 1963, University of Alabama president Frank A. Rose asked Bryant to write him a letter about the phone call Bryant was said to have made to Butts on Sunday, 16 September, as indicated in Burnett's notes. Writing on 28 February, Bryant said that he had made three calls to Butts (including the one mentioned by Burnett, which lasted for sixty-seven minutes) before the Alabama-Georgia game and that Butts had given him specific coaching points on passing routes, along with a tip that allowed Alabama to defeat Tennessee later in the season.[61]

When Clay Blair assumed the reins as editor of the *Saturday Evening Post* in 1962, its twelfth consecutive year of losing money, Blair immediately commanded his staff to make the magazine "informative, crusading, and hard hitting with articles that are timely and mean something." In January 1963, as the Butts-Bryant story was developing, Blair wrote a memo to the *Post* staff that used the term "sophisticated muckraking" to describe the *Post*'s editorial policies and cited the six pending lawsuits against the magazine as proof that "we are hitting them where it hurts."[62]

In the midst of the *Post*'s transformation, sportswriter Furman Bisher of the *Atlanta Constitution* wrote an article about brutality in college football that was published in the *Post*. Bisher labeled Bryant's style of "smash mouth football" as evidence that the college game had gone haywire. The article was prompted by a serious injury suffered by Chick Graning, a Georgia Tech player who was knocked unconscious while covering a punt in a game against Alabama on 18 November 1961, suffering facial injuries that the Georgia Tech team physician described as "the worst he had ever seen in athletics." The article quoted Auburn coach Ralph Jordan as saying that the reason his team was taking up "this new hell-for-leather, helmet-busting, gang tackling style of football" was that since Bear Bryant came back to Alabama, "it's the only game that can win."[63] In early January 1963, Bryant sued for the *Post* for libel in federal district court, naming Bisher and *Post* parent company Curtis Publishing as the defendants.

While communicating with Burnett's attorney, the *Post*'s lawyers became aware of the Butts-Bryant call and pushed the magazine's editors to publish the story. Graham, a freelance sportswriter and a former editor at *Sport*, would write the story. Graham, a Columbia graduate in the early 1950s, had become disenchanted with college basketball after observing the sport's 1951 fixing scandal. Graham had also been privy to horror stories about college football coaches from many of his colleagues at *Sport*. Graham flew to Atlanta, met with Pierre Howard and Milton Flack, a friend and Burnett adviser who had seen the notes, and then interviewed Burnett. Graham had also wanted to interview John Carmichael, Butts's friend and Burnett's business partner, who had also seen the notes, but Carmichael declined, preferring not to become involved in any story excoriating Butts and Bryant.[64]

Post sports editor Roger Kahn (who later wrote *The Boys of Summer*) assigned Bisher to investigate the veracity of Burnett's notes. Bisher spent a day in Athens, Georgia, interviewing Griffith, trainer Sam Richwine, and receiver Mickey Babb and then relayed his notes over the phone to Graham in Brooklyn. Graham quoted Bisher's interviews in the article, and after Bisher read the story and recommended no changes, the article was rushed into print without the normal legal review. The article was published in the 23 March 1963 issue of the *Post* under the title, "The Story of a College Football Fix."[65] One week later, Butts sued the *Post*'s parent company, Curtis Publishing, for libel.

National reaction to the story varied: The conversation between Butts and Bryant had little effect on the score of the game; the *Post*'s financial difficulties had caused it to bypass normal editing and research on the story; the legal and financial fallout from the story would be disastrous for the *Post*. In April 1963, *Sports Illustrated* published Burnett's notes. The notes were divided into nineteen items; unnamed experts, including Butts and other coaches, were asked to evaluate each item for its usefulness in allowing the Crimson Tide to prepare offensive and defensive game plans that would virtually guarantee a lopsided win over Georgia. The experts dismissed twelve of the items as "containing no information that was secret or that any well-coached team would not be prepared to expect from its opponents." Three items were assessed as "harmless opinion," three were labeled "meaningless," and one was described as "foolish." The experts admitted that Butts's sharing of two items was "indiscreet" but felt that Alabama probably would not have needed the information.[66] Not mentioned in the article was the possibility that Butts could subsequently have given Bryant other information that was more valuable to Alabama, especially if Butts was able to obtain the answers to the questions Bryant asked during the call overheard by Burnett.

Two days before the *Post* article was published, Georgia governor Carl Sanders ordered the state's attorney general, Eugene Cook, to conduct a full investigation to determine whether the Butts-Bryant phone call violated any state law and whether the participants could be subject to criminal prosecution. Butts had campaigned against Sanders in the 1960 governor's election; Sanders opposed Butts's continuation in the post of the university's director of athletics. The attorney general concluded his investigation in two weeks, finding that no criminal laws had been violated but that "the information given by Butts to Bryant in advance of the September 22, 1962, Alabama-Georgia game was unethical, improper, and unsportsmanlike and that furnishing of such information might well have vitally affected the outcome of the game in points and margin of victory."[67]

Cook discovered that Butts had passed a lie detector test that was administered by an unqualified private detective, and the results were recorded by a galvanometer that was not recognized by either the American Academy of Polygraph Examiners or the Academy of Scientific Interrogators. Bryant had passed a polygraph test given on an older polygraph by a public prosecutor whose name could not be found among the members of these professional organizations. Burnett had passed two polygraph tests, including one administered by Major G. Ragsdale, director of the Georgia Bureau of Investigation, who had fifteen years' experience as a polygraph operator and was the president of the American Academy of Polygraph Examiners. After the media reported the results of Butts's and Bryant's polygraph tests without any comment about their unreliability, Burnett's attorney countered by suggesting that the three central figures in the case submit to questioning by attorneys after ingesting a truth serum, though that idea was not pursued further.[68]

Cook also conducted a three-hour interview in which Griffith described how Burnett's notes related to his team's game plan. Griffith and nine of his assistant coaches then signed a statement:

> After viewing the alleged notations made by George Burnett while listening to an alleged telephone conversation between Wallace Butts and "Bear" Bryant on September 13, 1962, it is my opinion, as one of the coaches of the University of Georgia football team, that if such information was given to Coach Bryant before the opening game of the season, it conveyed vital and important information with respect to the offensive and defensive plays, patterns, and formations that could have been of value to the University of Alabama football team, and could have affected the outcome of the game on September 22, 1962.[69]

The attorney general also discovered a 6 March 1963 letter Bryant had written to Rose in which the coach gave another version of his conversations with Butts, contradicting what Bryant himself had written just a week earlier. Bryant claimed that the sharing of football information as recounted by Burnett did not take place. He wrote that Butts had called to inform him about several rule changes made during the summer of 1962 and that they had discussed how these changes made various Alabama defenses illegal and might cause all-American linebacker LeRoy Jordan to be ejected from games. Bryant claimed that Butts had also informed him that Georgia players might be injured if they ran certain plays against certain Alabama defenses, something the coaches ostensibly wanted to avoid—hence the follow-up phone call on Sunday to discuss the plays in more detail. Bryant wrote that he changed his defenses to avoid losing Jordan, to avoid injuring Georgia players, and to ensure that Alabama's defenses were legal under the new rules. Bryant also wrote that he had asked the SEC's head of officials to come to Tuscaloosa to interpret the legality of the modified defenses after the conversation with Butts. Rose then wrote to University of Georgia president O. C. Aderhold recounting the substance of what Bryant had written about the two (not three) phone calls between him and Butts.[70]

Cook saw Bryant's letter as proof that Butts and Bryant had discussed specific offensive and defensive plays and formations. The letter also exposed contradictions in Bryant's story—in addition to the differences in the accounts Bryant wrote on 28 February and 6 March, he had also previously stated that the head SEC official visited Tuscaloosa one week before the 13 September phone call. Cook concluded that Burnett had in fact overheard the conversation and that Bryant had not disclosed its true nature.[71]

Butts's suit against the Curtis Publishing Company would be brought to trial in Atlanta's U.S. District Court for the Northern District of Georgia in August 1963. The cause of action alleged that the article was false in its accusations of a fix and was published recklessly and maliciously. Butts demanded five million dollars in punitive damages and five million dollars in general or compensatory damages. The publishing company's response said in part that "the statements complained of . . . are true."[72] Following the advice of University of Georgia legal counsel Cook Barwick, the publishing company hired Atlanta lawyer Welborn Cody, who had recently successfully defended ABC in a libel suit. Butts's attorney was ex–Notre Dame football player and University of Georgia law school graduate William Schroeder, who had coached Georgia's freshman football team while in law school.

During the trial, Schroeder cleverly elicited testimony from Bryant, Griffith, two Georgia assistant coaches, and three Alabama players that seriously attacked the value of the notes. The Georgia player and athletic trainer interviewed by Bisher for the article took the stand and denied the statements attributed to them. Four Georgia players testified that they had scrimmaged the Thursday before the game; two key Georgia players were injured and the rest had been "leg weary for the game."[73] The *Post*'s key participants—Graham, Kahn, managing editor Davis Thomas, and Blair—submitted testimony via deposition, and the jury viewed their failure to appear as an insult.[74]

Cody's defensive strategy was to attack Butts's character, establish a link between Butts and gambler Frank Scobey, counteract Bryant's credibility, and emphasize the accuracy and value of Burnett's notes. Six highly placed men connected to the University of Georgia testified that Butts's character was "bad and not believable under oath."[75] The most incriminating aspect of Butts's phone calls to Scobey was their pattern: no calls in April or May 1962, five in June, two in July, four in August, and fourteen in September. In 1957, Scobey's gambling habits were publicized during the federal prosecution of his bookie when he testified that he had bet as much as fifty thousand dollars per year on college football games and as much as two thousand dollars on one game. Butts had known Scobey well for years and must have known the magnitude of his friend's gambling. Cody attempted to discredit Bryant's testimony by calling to the stand Rose, the University of Alabama's president and the author of a letter to Aderhold, Rose's counterpart at Georgia, substantiating Bryant's 28 February recollection of the calls between him and Butts; on the stand, however, Rose repudiated his letter to Aderhold and testified that it did not accurately reflect Bryant's conversations with Butts. Cody also had two Georgia assistant coaches testify to the value of Burnett's notes, especially in the first game of the season.

According to court observers, the trial was a comedy of errors and a mismatch between the two attorneys. Schroeder cleverly employed the distinction between a "bettor's win" (winning by beating the point spread) and a "team win" (winning by any margin). He led the jury to believe that if a fix did occur, it likely involved only the game's outcome, not the point spread, and that the overwhelming victory, or team win, by the far more talented and better-coached Alabama proved that the conversation Burnett overheard had no effect on the game's outcome. Cody did not respond that the conversation could just as easily have ensured that Alabama would defeat Georgia by exceeding the spread, nor did he argue that no one knew before the game how convincingly Alabama would win, so knowledge of selected Georgia strategies could have been invaluable. Schroeder also argued that "there are no secrets in football" and elicited testimony from coaches to support that assertion. Yet Cody did not respond with the fact that teams practiced in closed facilities and took pains to conceal their strategies. Cody also failed to exploit the contradictions between Bryant's 28 February and 6 March letters. Nor did Cody pursue Rose when he repudiated his letter to Aderhold, even though when Cook had asked Rose about the letter, Rose had handwritten on the letter, "The substance of my letter is accurate and correct."[76]

The twelve-man jury deliberated for only one hour before unanimously finding that the *Post* article "was full of inaccuracies and misquotations and showed terrible carelessness in preparation, to be dealing with such serious accusations."[77] The ex-coach was awarded sixty thousand dollars in general damages and three million dollars in punitive damages, though the judge later found the latter amount excessive and reduced it to four hundred thousand dollars. The *Post* appealed the verdict to the U.S. Fifth Circuit Court of Appeals and filed two motions in the trial court based on the discovery of new evidence (documents subpoenaed for the Bryant suit) and the enactment of a new libel law (the Supreme Court had ruled that malice needed to be proven by a plaintiff to prevail in a libel case). The trial judge refused to grant a new trial, as did the Fifth Circuit (by a margin of two to one).[78] The *Post* filed an appeal with the U.S. Supreme Court, where it again lost when Chief Justice Earl Warren voted to affirm the trial court's finding. The case, *Curtis Publishing Co. v. Butts* (1967), remains a landmark in libel law.

Bryant's suit seeking $10.5 million in damages from the *Post* for the article about his coaching style and brutality of play was scheduled for early 1964 in Birmingham, Alabama. Before the trial began, Bryant's lawyers, Winston McCall and Harry Pritchard, along with the University of Alabama's president, Rose, urged Bryant to settle the case out of court. In preparation for Bryant's trial, the *Post*'s lawyers had taken depositions and subpoenaed records from Bryant's and Rose's files, most likely in an effort to avoid the errors and omissions Cody had made in Butts's trial. Bryant had also indicated that the events were adversely affecting his family, as the litigation could drag on for years and Curtis had hired private investigators to unearth damaging information from Bryant's past. The two sides reached an agreement on 5 February 1964, with Bryant receiv-

Wally Butts, Georgia's former football coach, was investigated by Georgia attorney general Eugene Cook for allegedly passing strategic football information to Alabama's Bear Bryant before the schools' 1962 game, a 35–0 Crimson Tide victory. The Cook investigation confirmed much of the veracity of a *Saturday Evening Post* article that reported that Butts's "finances and gambling were linked to passing information" to an upcoming opponent's coach. Nevertheless, an Atlanta judge awarded Butts sixty thousand dollars in general damages and four hundred thousand dollars in punitive damages after he sued the *Post*'s parent company for publishing "false accusations recklessly and maliciously."

ing a settlement of $320,000 before taxes and netting $196,000—far less than the $10.5 million for which he had sued but enough for Bryant and his supporters to claim vindication.[79]

Sportswriters and the press widely reported that the jury verdict in the Butts case and the *Post*'s settlement with Bryant vindicated college football. The NCAA and SEC imposed no sanctions on Bryant or Butts. Even if Butts and Bryant had lost their cases, however, the scandal might have embarrassed the sport but would not have stopped its transformation into a multi-billion-dollar business. The scandal also highlighted the fact that Division I college presidents and other officials were nearly powerless in their dealings with renowned football and basketball coaches and wealthy boosters.

College football absorbed illegal gamblers in 1962 and continues to do so today: A recent estimate put the volume of illegal betting on the sport at between sixty and seventy billion dollars per year.[80] Gamblers constantly seek information from players, coaches, and individuals connected with teams—doctors, trainers, and boosters. Could inside information passed along in, for example, a coach's weekly newsletter for elite football boosters be today's equivalent of that telephone call overheard on the morning of 13 September 1962?

SIX
COLLEGE BASKETBALL'S INCURABLE DISEASE

The 1961 Basketball Scandal

Corruption in college basketball became more rather than less pervasive after the 1951 scandal as many major colleges continued with their self-imposed mandate to provide professionalized entertainment for the American public. Critics of college sports viewed the fixing of basketball games as a by-product of the corruption that had become endemic in the sport. The 1951 scandal marked the point where the public began to accept betting scandals in college sports as no different from recruiting violations or subsidizing players. When media voices asked why colleges did not reform their athletic programs, college sports' apologists placed much of the blame on individual players and on increasingly brazen and unscrupulous gamblers. Game fixing continued unabated.

After escaping Judge Saul S. Streit's stinging criticism of college basketball programs implicated in the 1951 scandal, Columbia head basketball coach Lou Rossini must have felt a sense of relief. His star player, future all-American sophomore Jack Molinas, had just led the Lions to an undefeated season, and 1951–52 seemed just as promising. But during that season, Molinas would continue his career as one of the master fixers in the history of college sports. And, like Adolph Rupp, Nat Holman, and Clair Bee, Rossini would do his part, consciously or subconsciously ignoring the signs.

In a February 1952 game at Holy Cross, gambler Joey Hacken, a longtime friend of Molinas's, appeared at Columbia's bench just before tip-off. Hacken would certainly have been noticeable, as he was usually unshaven and dressed in a long, frayed overcoat with one or two newspapers stuffed in a pocket. Hacken covertly signaled to Molinas that the spread favored Holy Cross by 2½ points. At the first timeout of the game, Molinas spotted Hacken subtly gesturing to him from the drinking fountain. Molinas left the court to get a drink and was informed by Hacken that the point spread now favored Holy Cross to win by at least 4 points. What coach allows a player to saunter away from a timeout to meet with a character like Joey Hacken? Rossini, a New York City native, would seem to have been particularly able to guess what Molinas's unsavory friend was up to. With the score tied in the last few seconds of regulation, Rossini directed Molinas to set a screen on a teammate's man, freeing him to shoot the possible winning field goal. As the ball left the shooter's hand, Molinas jumped and raised his arm, slightly brushing the ball. The shot did not go in. In the timeout before the overtime began, Rossini asked, "What was that all about, Jack?" Molinas said that he turned into the man he screened and had to jump, trying to avoid being called for an offensive foul. Columbia lost by 5 points in overtime, and Molinas and Hacken each won ten thousand dollars.[1] Rossini's inaction contributed to Molinas's increased fixing of games, which would not be discovered until 1961. If Molinas had been tailed or his phone wiretapped in 1952, his meetings and conversations with Hacken and other gamblers would likely have been uncovered.

St. John's coach Joe Lapchick faced the same predicament as Rossini. Lapchick had been one of the nation's best players in the 1920s with the

Original Celtics and was known for his impeccable honesty, fairness, and unflinching respect for basketball. He took over as St. John's head coach in 1936, left to coach the NBA's New York Knicks in 1947, and returned in 1956, inheriting two seniors, Michael Parenti and William Chrystal, who had been manipulating final scores since their 1954–55 sophomore season. Lapchick had run a clean program in his first tenure at St. John's, and he was unable to believe that two of his players were fixing games. Rated No. 8 in a preseason poll, the Redmen lost two preseason games, one to 11-point underdog Utah and another to BYU. These losses were followed by rumors that Parenti and Chrystal were fixing games with Molinas's friend, Hacken.[2]

Newspaper writers and bookies confirmed to Lapchick that at least two of his players were fixing games, and Gus Alfieri, a sophomore on the team, and his teammates also reported the chicanery to the coach. And Lapchick was assuredly acquainted with fixing in basketball: The Original Celtics were known to rig games by keeping the score close while winning the first game of a two-game series. After placing bets on the second game, they would win handily and leave town. As one professional recounted, "It wasn't fixing in those days, it was survival."[3] Yet Lapchick chose not to initiate an investigation into Parenti and Chrystal—an investigation that, as in the case of Molinas, would likely have reduced the scope of the coming scandal and prevented many of its disastrous effects. After Hacken was arrested in March 1961 and the two St. John's players were exposed, Lapchick offered rationalizations that were stunningly similar to those made by coaches in 1951. It was as if basketball had contracted a disease that lay hidden for a decade, growing more dangerous until it finally required the state and federal governments to attempt to treat it.

Before the opening of 1957–58 NBA and college basketball season, Molinas was introduced to St. Louis bookie and gambler Dave Goldberg. Molinas had been the Ft. Wayne Pistons' first choice in the 1953 NBA draft but was indefinitely suspended from the league in January 1954 for betting on games; in 1957, he was playing in the Eastern Basketball League

Former New York Knicks coach Joe Lapchick returned to coach St. John's in 1956 and could not bring himself to believe that two senior players had been routinely fixing games since their sophomore season. Despite confirmation by players on the team, newspaper writers, and bookies that William Chrystal and Michael Parenti were doing business with noted fixer and Jack Molinas associate Joey Hacken, Lapchick chose not to act.

and had passed the New York state bar. Goldberg suggested that Molinas begin fixing college basketball games and selling the fixed games to gamblers or backers, who could bet as much as three hundred thousand dollars on one game. At the time, Goldberg was fixing college basketball games with former Big Ten and Missouri Valley Conference referee John K. Fraser.[4] Molinas agreed to the idea. Hacken, Aaron Wagman, and Joe Green joined the alliance of fixers. Wagman and Green were pool sharks with visions of becoming high-level fixers and gamblers. Wagman had been a Stevens Concessions Company manager at Yankee Stadium, and Green had been an outstanding basketball player at New York's Taft High but lacked the credits to graduate. Former Brooklyn College basketball captain Dave Budin later joined the group.[5]

Molinas and his group had planned to begin rigging and selling games during the 1957–58 season, but they had to address several logistical issues first: What criteria should be used in deciding which players were likely to fix a game, and how should they be recruited? Possible criteria included a player's family background, skill, ability to control a game, need for money, personality weaknesses, willingness to sacrifice individual or team fame for money, susceptibility to influence if set up with a prostitute, and interest in clothes and cars. After likely targets were identified, the players would have to be contacted and softened. The actual mechanics of conducting the fix would have to be established. A cadre of backers or gamblers would also have to be created to finance player payoffs and to spread money (make bets) among illegal and legal bookies throughout the country to help hide the rigging.[6]

The Molinas group used various softening strategies. One was for Molinas and Green to meet targeted players in neighborhood or summer games and give them money, buy them lunch or dinner, or arrange a party with liquor and women. Another way was for one or two of the fixers to travel to a college town such as Tuscaloosa, and over lunch or dinner and after sensing a player's interest in fixing, offer him a bribe. Players who agreed to fix games could be paid to recruit other players. Molinas and the alliance also hired college students to ask players about their interest in rigging, communicate with players who had agreed to fix specific games, and relay information from the fixers to the players and vice versa.[7]

The fixers and players usually established a code language in which to communicate. For example, Molinas began one telephone conversation with an Alabama player by saying, "We'll go less than four o'clock. But if it falls one, two or three o'clock, you figure on a double. You'll end up with thirty fruits instead of fifteen." Molinas was suggesting that the player had the choice of dumping the game ("we'll go less than four o'clock") or making sure that Alabama won by one, two, or three points ("but if it falls one, two, or three o'clock"). If Alabama won by three or fewer points, the payoff would be doubled ("you figure on a double"). The player in this conversation responded, "That's wonderful. I'm a hell of a fruit eater."[8]

Since betting lines were usually not set until just before game time to maximize the amount of gambling, one of the fixing crew members might have to be at the game to inform the cooperating player which way to manipulate the final score. Discreet visual signals would be passed between the fixer and the player. Fixers would also call players before games from a variety of public or private phones to lessen the chances of a wiretap.[9]

Those who wanted to buy fixed games included organized crime members and high-stakes gamblers such as Goldberg and his associate, Steve Lekemetros (Steve Likos), from St. Louis; Philip La Court from Boston; Ralph Gigante from New York; and Norman "Lefty" Rosenthal from Chicago. Rosenthal had been betting on sports since his teen years in the bleachers at Wrigley Field. Attracting the attention of organized crime because of his ability to handicap, or set the line, for certain sporting events, he was hired to operate a bookie operation in Cicero, just west of Chicago. Rosenthal's organized crime contacts and other bookies liked the idea of betting on rigged college football and basketball games. If Rosenthal bought a fixed game, he would call another bookie and bet ten thousand dollars on five different teams, with one of the games fixed. He would call another bookie in a different city and reverse all the bets except for the one on the fixed game. He might call ten bookies in ten cities, balancing five against five on the four honest games but betting a total of one hundred thousand dollars on the fixed game.[10] Rosenthal also did a substantial business with bookies who wanted to lay off bets—that is, to ensure that equal money was bet on both teams in a game that was not fixed. A bookie could equalize the amount bet by adjusting the betting line to bring in more money on one team, or he could bet enough with another bookie to balance the stakes.[11]

The actual fixing of games proved rife with missteps, suspicion, and betrayal. When Joe Green approached Brown University star player Jerry Alaimo before the 1957–58 season, Alaimo not only turned Green down but called the Manhattan district attorney's office and reported the bribe attempt—but he did so anonymously to avoid being subpoenaed to testify and to preserve his own health and that of his family. Players might agree to fix a game but then decide to play the game straight, or they might fix a game and take the money but try to give it back or contend that it was payment for advice. The fixers would sometimes stiff (double-cross) the players. In one game, Columbia star Fred Portnoy was to ensure that Columbia lost by at least 8 points; the Lions lost by 9. But Green told Portnoy that the spread had been 13 and did not pay Portnoy for his efforts. In a subsequent game, Portnoy was to ensure that Columbia lost by more than the spread. When Portnoy led Columbia to a 3-point lead at the end of the first half, Green was waiting for him and angrily asked, "What do you think you're doing?"[12] Columbia won the game, and Portnoy was not paid. Backers would also threaten or refuse to pay if they believed the fixers had double-crossed them. In one suspected double-cross, Goldberg and Lekemetros summoned Wagman, Green, Hacken, and Molinas to a Pittsburgh hotel. After questioning the men separately, everyone except Molinas was allowed to leave. Molinas was hung by the ankles off the balcony of the seven-story hotel for several minutes as he shouted to the gamblers' henchmen, "You can't do this to me! I'm Jack Molinas!"[13] Members of the fixers' group also double-crossed each other. Molinas paid Green to spy on Wagman; Wagman and Green decided to leave the group because Molinas had not paid them all the money he owed. Two fixers might be working with different players in the same game, or fixers might lie about fixing games or sell games that were not fixed.

If the bettors lost money, the consequences for the players could be severe. In 1958, St. John's star Alan Seiden lost his potential NBA career when fixer Dave Budin mistakenly told Molinas that Seiden would fix a game, and Molinas sold the game to Rosenthal, who lost a substantial sum. Molinas blamed Seiden to save Budin's life. The St. Louis Hawks then mysteriously benched Seiden from the beginning of his rookie season, and he quit the NBA out of frustration. Seiden's teammate, Tony Jackson, was barred by the NBA for failing to report a bribe offer. A North Carolina State player reported feeling a gun in his stomach after a final score was not what a gambler had paid for.[14] And when the performance of Mississippi State's Jerry Graves in one game caused a group of backers to lose money, they dispatched a thug to teach him a lesson. Detectives from New York district attorney's office tailing the thug made sure he knew he was being watched, and he left Mississippi without harming Graves.[15]

In response to the college sports gambling scandals of the late 1950s, New York representative Kenneth B. Keating urged Congress in 1958 to pass a bill to prevent gamblers from plying their trade on college campuses. He also urged the passage of a federal law banning the use of any communications facility, such as telephone, telegraph, or radio, to transmit gambling information across state lines. Keating believed that bookies would overwhelm college and professional football, basketball, and baseball. An estimated ten billion dollars a year was bet with bookies on these sports, earning the bookies a healthy one billion dollars in commissions. But little action would be taken until three years later, when attorney general Robert F. Kennedy began aggressively to investigate and prosecute organized crime. The scandals continued throughout the nation.

Most of the players arrested for fixing games in the 1951 scandal had hidden their money to avoid suspicion. But players who fixed games later in the 1950s had every intention of spending the money they earned. Gary Kaufman, a star basketball player from the College of the Pacific in Stockton, California (renamed University of the Pacific in 1961), was handsome, suave, and had plenty of women, a new red Corvette, and lots of money. As a basketball camp counselor in the Catskills in the summer of 1959, Kaufman made a lasting impression on thirteen-year-old Dave Leveton. One day Kaufman informed Leveton and his fellow campers that a former NBA player who was "down on his luck" would be visiting the next day and that they should be nice to him. Molinas appeared as expected and helped Kaufman with basketball instruction and drills. Three years later, when Molinas was arrested in May 1962, Leveton learned the truth about Kaufman's "coolness": the money, the new Corvette, and the women were earned by fixing games, and Kaufman was now testifying against Molinas to protect himself. The assassination of President John F. Kennedy in 1963 was for many of Leveton's generation the end of innocence, but for Leveton, the rude awakening came a year earlier as his basketball hero was revealed to be a criminal.[16]

In March 1959, radio newscaster George W. Barrett, former managing editor of the *Peoria Journal*, reported that between twenty thousand and thirty thousand dollars per night was being bet on college basketball in the city. Called before a grand jury, Barrett indicated that the betting lines were set nationally and that similar betting occurred in Springfield,

Illinois, and elsewhere in the state. Barrett testified that Hacken had given softening money to Bradley University players Alphra Saunders and Jim Robinson, but there was no evidence to support Barrett's allegation. When Hacken was arrested in March 1961, he did not confess to rigging Bradley's games, since it could not be proven.[17]

On 21 December 1959, Edward H. Sebastian, a dentist from Pittsburgh suburb of McKees Rocks, was arrested for attempting to bribe Pitt players Dick Falenski and John Fridley. The players had been offered half of any winnings, assistance with entry into Pitt's dental school, where Sebastian had taught, and the purchase of an auto at a reduced price. Fridley met with the dentist twice, and Falenski joined him at a third meeting. Sebastian explained to investigators that the purpose of the meetings was to encourage the players to seek dental treatment. He was sentenced to between eight months and three years in prison.[18]

In March 1960, officials at Cincinnati's Xavier University reported receiving an anonymous phone call from New York warning that a "fix was on" in a game against the University of Dayton. The caller, later revealed to be *New York Journal* sportswriter Jimmy Breslin, indicated that a bookmaker in Newport, Kentucky, across the river from the Cincinnati Gardens, where the game was to be played, had told him that so much money was being bet on underdog Dayton that bookies suspended betting on the game. In an upset, Dayton defeated Xavier 91–82. After the game, it became clear that the heavy betting was caused by rumors of injuries on the Xavier squad; the game was not reported to have been rigged.[19]

That same month, NYU played West Virginia University, led by Jerry West, in the opening round of an NCAA regional semifinal in Raleigh, North Carolina; the regional winner would play in the Final Four in San Francisco. With seconds left in an overtime and NYU leading by one point, West drove for the basket, closely guarded by Tom "Satch" Sanders. As West attempted a jump shot over Sanders's outstretched hand, NYU sophomore Ray Paprocky left his position and jumped, blocking West's view of the basket and causing him to miss. NYU went on to defeat Duke in the regional final and earn a spot in the NCAA finals. After the Duke game, NYU head coach Lou Rossini held forth at a party about how his team had won the two games. One of the listeners was Bob Quincy, sports editor of the *Charlotte News*. Quincy told Breslin, who was also at the party, "We got a mess down here. There's been something the matter all season long. I just can't get at it yet. The state bureau of investigation is on it. They won't tell me anything. If you happen to hear anything up North you let me know and if I hear anything down here I'll let you know. Sure as we're here there's trouble." On the plane trip back to New York, Breslin sat next to Ray Paprocky. The Queens native told Breslin that he was unsure of the future because his wife was pregnant and the money she earned and his basketball earnings of $150 per month might not be enough after the baby arrived; also, he could not work during or after the basketball season because he needed to catch up on his studies. Breslin cautioned him, "Well, whatever the hell you do, don't take any money on this basketball thing." When Paprocky asked, "What do you mean?" Breslin stated, "I mean don't take money to blow a game. They're doing it you know." "Me," responded the player, "never! I don't know anything about that stuff." A week earlier, Paprocky had accepted a thousand dollars from Hacken to throw the game against West Virginia, but during the heat of the game he forgot about the fix and played to win.[20]

The story of Connie Hawkins and Roger Brown, two of the best players in the history of New York's Public School Athletic League, shows the extent and effect of abuses in college basketball recruiting. Hawkins had received more than a hundred recruiting offers, including one where the recruiter told Nat Mazer, Boys High School assistant basketball coach, that Mazer "could put all the offers in the pile with the best on top, and [the recruiter] would top the best one." Although Hawkins was unable to complete a high school curriculum, he was admitted to the University of Iowa in the fall of 1960. When asked by a sportswriter why Iowa had accepted Hawkins, an admissions officer credited "a successful testing program" but could not explain how the testing program could predict that Hawkins would be able to complete a college curriculum.[21] Brown had graduated from Brooklyn's Wingate High School but was unqualified to enter a four-year college; nevertheless, the University of Dayton accepted him in 1960. Both players had met Hacken and Molinas while in high school. During the summer of 1960, they were furnished money, women, and the use of Molinas's convertible.[22] Brown was expelled from Dayton after his freshman year for admitting that he had received money from Molinas.[23] Hawkins was expelled from Iowa as

Former Oregon defensive back Michael Bruce points a finger at Norman "Lefty" Rosenthal at the witness table in September 1961 before the Senate committee investigating organized gambling. Bruce testified that Rosenthal was one of two gamblers who offered him five thousand dollars to intentionally lose a 1961 game against Michigan in Ann Arbor. The other gambler was Dave Budin. The gamblers had previously pled no contest in a North Carolina court for offering NYU's Ray Paprocky a bribe to dump a March 1960 NCAA semifinal game between NYU and favored Jerry West–led West Virginia. NYU won by one point in overtime.

a consequence of his association with Molinas. Neither Hawkins nor Brown ever rigged a college basketball game, but both were barred from entering the NBA for accepting money from Molinas.[24] The Indiana Pacers of the new American Basketball Association (ABA) signed Brown in 1967; in eight years, he averaged 17.4 points and led the Pacers to three ABA titles. After playing for the Harlem Globetrotters and in the ABA, Hawkins was cleared of any involvement in the 1961 scandal and became a Hall of Fame player in the NBA.[25] In the 1972 ABA finals, Brown dueled one-on-one with the New York Nets' Rick Barry. Asked who won the matchup, former Pacer coach Slick Leonard answered, "It's hard to say who won the duel, but we won the series. Now Rick's in the Hall of Fame and nobody remembers Roger."[26]

The 1961 gambling scandal was more than a New York City phenomenon. The dogged pursuit by New York County district attorney Frank Hogan of individuals who conspired to fix sporting events in 1951 uncovered scandals in basketball, boxing, and harness racing. When Hogan ran for other political offices, opponents cited his ambition to move up the political ladder as the reason for his aggressive pursuit of sports rigging.[27] The reality was that if other prosecutors had investigated fixing in sports as thoroughly as he did, the documented instances of manipulating final scores in college football and basketball would have been significantly greater than what was reported. The feigned or real naïveté of college officials and the NCAA regarding game fixing showed that both groups were more interested in presenting an appearance of vigilance and reform to the public than in crafting a solution to the problem. Exposing the unsavory aspects of basketball's corruption and gambling's menace risked the profits that commercialization generated. The frequent reporting of attempted fixes in cities other than New York was reason enough to believe that the manipulation of final scores was widespread.

In early December 1960, University of Detroit player Charles North reported to his coach, Bob Calihan, that a casual friend, Mike Siegel, had written him a letter inviting him to join a resort basketball team to make some fast money. Calihan passed the letter to athletic director John Mulroy, who labeled the letter "ambiguous" and said that it justified no further action. North gave a second letter from Siegel to Calihan, who warned North that the outside activity suggested by Siegel was not permissible.[28] Calihan gave that letter to Mulroy as well, but no action was taken. In retrospect, it is clear that the athletic director and coach should have informed the police. North and Siegel had several conversations that North claimed to have reported to the university, though the university denied knowledge of the conversations. North and teammate John Morgan met Siegel and Yonkers attorney Charlie Tucker at a Detroit restaurant in early December 1960. At the meeting, the two players were asked to fix four games during the 1960–61 season. After initially balking, they agreed fix the upcoming game against Ohio State. After returning to the restaurant to collect the agreed-upon one thousand dollars each for rigging the game, the fixers quickly exited, believing they had been set up after spotting off-duty policemen eating dinner. The university immediately dismissed the two players.[29]

By the 1950s, the Big Ten conference had refined sports boosterism to such an extent that even an academically renowned institution as Northwestern University was eager to demonstrate that a successful basketball program was needed to facilitate the pursuit of scholarship. Arthur Hicks had been an outstanding Chicago high school player, but his grades were too low to attend college, though more than fifty major colleges were willing to admit him. In the fall of 1957, he enrolled at Northwestern, but after two quarters, officials asked him to leave. While visiting New York, Hicks met Hacken, who offered ample softening money. Seton Hall then accepted Hicks for the fall of 1958, and while there, he met Henry Gunter and introduced him to Hacken.[30]

In explaining his decision to fix games in an interview with *Sports Illustrated*, Hicks recounted that gamblers had sensed that the highly commercialized environment of college basketball had taken the fun out of the game for the players. And when a player lost his passion for the game and respect for his coach, he was vulnerable to the advances of gamblers. According to Hicks, gamblers knew that black players at certain colleges were not socially accepted. For Hicks, a lavish gambler-hosted party with plenty of women convinced him and more than likely other players to join in the rigging. Also, Hicks overheard teammates in a dormitory room discussing an upcoming game with an opponent they were easily supposed to defeat saying, "Tomorrow we got an easy game, so we won't be giving the ball to the niggers."[31] Hicks had also heard racist remarks from spectators, and his teammates' attitudes made him more receptive to the idea of rigging games. Hicks asserted, "The gambler becomes the most reliable person in your life. He replaces the coach."[32] The gambler to whom Hicks referred was Hacken.

Hicks agreed to lose a game during the 1959–60 season to heavily favored Cincinnati by more than 12 points. However, after overhearing the Cincinnati players bragging about demolishing Seton Hall, his competitive instincts kicked in, and he played to win. His team lost by 8, under the spread. After the game, a man unknown to Hicks walked up to him and said, "You black sons of bitches lost a lot of money for us tonight—$100,000. If I don't see the money by Friday, you won't see Saturday." After that incident, Hicks purchased a pair of snub-nosed .38s. When recounting how his play affected the final score, Hicks described a fast break where he was the center man with the ball with two teammates on the wings. At the moment when he decided to pass, he whipped the ball too far in front of one of the wings and out of bounds. Hicks admitted rigging losses to Duke and Dayton during the 1960–61 season, along with least five other games. His tally of fixed games did not coincide with the six Seton Hall games Hogan reported rigged that season. After the Dayton game, the same man who had threatened Hicks after the Cincinnati game failed to appear with the money. Hicks found him in a bar the next morning; the fixer tried to stiff him. Putting his .38 to the fixer's head, Hicks quickly received his money.[33]

Hicks and Gunter were two of the first players apprehended by New York detectives at Seton Hall's South Orange, New Jersey, campus on 17 March 1961. After the two were picked up, teammate Al Senavitis was asked to clean out the pair's room. He found eight hundred-dollar bills behind a baseboard and a man's Persian lamb coat in the closet. Since Senavitis had been close to both players, he decided to visit them in New York, where they were being held in protective custody, to ask why they had rigged games. The New York detectives did not allow him to see them. Senavitis later said that he had not spotted the fixing at the time even though he was one of the team's best players, but after hearing that Hicks had rigged games, Senavitis said that if he had "thought fix" when the playing lapses occurred, the rigging would have been evident.[34]

In March 1961, St. Joseph's of Philadelphia was practicing for its opening game in the NCAA Final Four in Kansas City. The team had compiled a 24–4 record and was to play Ohio State in the semifinals. One of the players on the team appeared to be sleepwalking and distracted during practice. "Everybody looks good but Majeski," said the faculty athletic moderator, the Reverend Joseph M. Geib, as the practice ended. He added, "I don't know where his mind is, but it certainly isn't here." Head coach Jack Ramsey, who had been irritated all season with Majeski's uneven play, remarked, "Some days he seems to stand around and do nothing at all." Majeski had recruited teammates Rich Egan and Vince Kempton to rig games during the season. Majeski's father had died when he was a sophomore, and his widowed mother had suffered a heart attack. Egan had two small sons, and his wife had suffered a miscarriage before the 1960–61 season. And Kempton needed money for a reason that he would not disclose—presumably gambling debts.[35]

Before the team was to leave for Kansas City, Ramsey expressed his concern about the soon-to-be-uncovered rigging scandals. "If one of my players were ever involved, I'd quit," he said. "You watch them and watch them, but you can't know all the people they meet. What's more, nobody can tell me when a player is shaving points. Nobody!" St. Joseph's lost to Ohio State, but the following evening, the team defeated a talented Utah team led by all-American center Billy McGill in four overtimes. Perhaps feeling that he had betrayed his coach and teammates during the season, Majeski played his heart out in the Utah win and led the team to a third-place NCAA trophy. Later in March, Geib and Ramsey would have their answer about Majeski's sleepwalking and erratic play. The arrests of Hacken and Wagman would reveal that Majeski, Egan, and Kempton had rigged three games with Wagman. All three would be expelled from the college. Egan, who had been drafted by the Philadelphia Warriors, and Kempton, drafted by the New York Knicks, were barred for life from the NBA. St. Joseph's moment in the sun would not last long, as the team was stripped of its third-place NCAA finish.[36]

Other players who rigged games echoed Hicks's point that fixers possessed an uncanny ability to sweet-talk players into going along with the schemes. University of North Carolina player Lou Brown noted that the New York County district attorney's detectives had psychologically profiled Wagman's partner, Joe Green. Green was not fond of money; he lived cheaply and was unmarried, so he did not fix games for financial gain. The detectives viewed him as angry at the basketball establishment because he could not qualify to enter a college. He had been an outstanding New York City basketball player but had failed to graduate from high school. They saw fixing games as his way of satisfying his anger and righting a misperceived injustice. Green had admitted to Brown that he was ashamed of his role in bribing players.[37]

According to the detectives, Wagman's primary motive for fixing games was his desire to gain power over successful athletes by getting them to agree to accept bribes and manipulate final scores. The detectives believed that this temporary control over players made him feel superior to them, like a coach. His sales pitch was to tell players that fixing had gone on for years in college basketball without detection. To rig a game, all they had to do was to pass the ball out of bounds at the right moment, kick the ball, miss a rebound, palm the ball, get called for traveling, or play loose defense. Mistakes made at the beginning of a game were less suspicious than those made during the closing minutes. And they should always watch the clock and the score. Wagman's pitch also included a true story about a fixer's team that was favored by 2 points. The player was to ensure his team won or lost the game by 1 point. With two seconds left and the fixer's team losing by 1 point, he drove for the basket, scored, and produced a 1-point victory for his team.[38] The point shaver became a campus hero. So, it was possible to win three times: the game, the money, and adulation of a team's followers.

Wagman and University of Florida student Phil Silber were arrested in Gainesville on 24 September 1960 for attempting to bribe Florida fullback Joe McBeth in a game against Florida State. Wagman told Florida police that Budin was in Ann Arbor, Michigan, trying to bribe University of Oregon defensive back Michael Bruce, whose squad was to face off against the University of Michigan the following day. Budin had teamed with Norman Rosenthal in the attempted bribe. They offered the defensive back five thousand dollars if he could enlist Oregon quarterback Dave Grosz and promised Bruce a hundred dollars per week for the rest of the season if he kept them informed about the Oregon team's physical status. Rosenthal left Michigan before the police arrested Budin for registering at the same hotel as the Oregon team under a false name.[39] Wagman pled guilty to the Florida bribe charge and received a five-year jail sentence and a ten-thousand-dollar fine. He was freed on a twenty-thousand-dollar bond while he appealed the court's decision. During that time he agreed to cooperate with the New York district attorney's office and testify against Molinas at trial. He also identified Green and Hacken as members of the fixing alliance. Soon after Wagman's arrest in Florida, Hogan's detectives began to wiretap the fixers' phones and follow their activities. Molinas was confident that he could not be arrested unless players he bribed turned against him. And Wagman, Green, and Budin ultimately cooperated with Hogan's office and implicated him.

On 17 March 1961, detectives from Hogan's office arrested Wagman and Hacken for offering bribes to basketball players from the University of Connecticut and Seton Hall University. Connecticut lost a game to Colgate by 12 points in which the spread favored the winners by 11. Bookies, correctly sensing a fix, had suspended betting on the game; Wagman and his backers won their bets, which had already been placed. Former Alabama players Jerry Vogel and Dan Quindazzi acted as the go-betweens in the fix, along with Connecticut football player William Minnerly. Wagman, whom Hogan labeled a "master fixer," had obtained a passport, prompting detectives to arrest him before he could leave the country.[40] Wagman was also indicted for attempting to bribe New York County detective David Campbell. Molinas paid Hacken's twenty-thousand-dollar bail. The Connecticut players involved in fixing were identified as Bill Cross, Pete Kelly, and Jack Rose.

Hacken was charged with bribing Seton Hall's Hicks and Gunther in their loss to Dayton at Madison Square Garden on 9 February 1961. The betting line initially favored Dayton by 6 points. When a large amount of money was bet on Dayton to exceed the spread, bookies suspended betting. A *New York Times* report hinted at a possible fix when a writer observed, "Seton Hall provided little more than a group of undergraduate straight men for Dayton. There was considerable hilarity and the outclassed Pirate quintet always was the butt of the joke. The South Orange forces were caught looking the wrong way time and again as the Flyers breezed past them for uncontested shots."[41]

After his arrest, Hacken offered a gambler's perspective on what made young college basketball players willing to risk their futures: "I'm funny, but I used to admire a kid when he'd turn me down." But, he continued, "Every kid did it for a simple reason: cash money. They thought they could make a fortune of money on basketball. The colleges already spoiled them. The colleges gave these kids money and deals. In other words, the kid got into college on a fix. So, why shouldn't they fix games too? Look! You could say I'm bad. All right I'm bad!" Hacken went on, "But, what about the colleges? Are they clean? They're in this just as deep as me. Only I have to do time in jail. The colleges, all they have to do is go out and get a new team."[42]

Jack Molinas was arrested on 18 May 1962, on three bribery charges and two counts of attempted subornation of perjury. Fourteen players were indicted: Thomas Falentino and Billy Reed of Bowling Green University; Gary Kaufman and Leroy Wright of the University of the Pacific; Salvatore Vergopia and Leonard Whalen of Niagara University; Leonard Kaplan of the University of Alabama; Donald Gallagher, Stanley Niewierowski, and Anton Muehlbauer of North Carolina State University; and Richard Hoffman, Michael Callahan, Larry Dial, and Robert Franz of the University of South Carolina. This group included fewer than half of the fixers; among the omissions were Ed Bowler of La Salle; Michael Parenti and William Chrystal of St. John's; Bill Cross, Pete Kelly, and Jack Rose of the University of Connecticut; Richard Egan, Frank Majeski, and Vince Kempton of St. Joseph's; Hank Gunther and Arthur Hicks of Seton Hall; Fred Portnoy of Columbia; Ray Paprocky of NYU; Jerry Graves of Mississippi State; Terry Litchfield of North Carolina State; and Edward Test and Richard Fisher of the University of Tennessee.[43]

Twelve coconspirators were named, including Molinas's partners, Hacken, Wagman, and Green. Also named were gamblers Frankie Cardone and Morris Heyison from Pittsburgh, Dave Goldberg and Steve Lekemetros from St. Louis, Norman Rosenthal and Anthony Di Chiantini from Chicago, and New Yorkers Ralph Gigante, Charles Tucker, and Paul Walker. Ralph Gigante's brother, Vincent "The Chin" Gigante, had been previously acquitted on a charge of attempting to murder Mob boss Frank Costello. Well-known gambler Philip La Court of Boston also would later be indicted as a coconspirator. Green and Wagman accepted a plea bargain in which they would receive suspended sentences of three to five years if Molinas was found guilty at trial; they were sentenced on 24 May 1962.[44]

Molinas's trial began on 30 October 1962, before New York Supreme Court justice Joseph Sarafite, a former prosecutor known for issuing severe sentences. Wagman spent seven days on the witness stand and seemed pleased that his testimony might be instrumental in convicting Molinas. Other witnesses included players Billy Reed, Gary Kaufman, Leroy Wright, and Len Kaplan. Reed's testimony included sites, dates, and payments for rigged games. An incriminating tape recording of Molinas coaching Reed to lie to a grand jury was played, as was a tape recorded in Kaufman's home in which Molinas threatened to kill Kaufman if any of the fixers were implicated in the rigging. Fred Schaus, coach at the University of West Virginia and a former NBA Ft. Wayne Pistons player, also testified for the prosecution. Schaus stated that Molinas's play with the Pistons was so uneven that it generated suspicions of fixing.[45] After calling thirty witnesses and presenting sixty-two exhibits that included conversations between Molinas and the players he bribed, the prosecution rested. The trial then recessed until 3 January 1963 because the judge was ill.

According to Charley Rosen, Molinas's attorney, Jacob Evseroff, believed that Molinas could have won his case if he had testified on his own behalf. But he did not take the stand, probably because of how much he knew about the Mob and its connections to sports gambling; he would undoubtedly have been asked about his relationship with members of organized crime. Evseroff commented, "That was the only time I ever saw Jack lose his nerve." Molinas also did not accept Evseroff's suggestion that he present the closing argument.[46] The main thrust of Molinas's defense was to present character witnesses to illustrate that he was incapable of committing the acts with which he was charged. On 8 January, Molinas was found guilty on all counts.

On 11 February, Judge Sarafite sentenced Molinas to between five and seven and a half years in prison for bribing Bowling Green's Reed; the subornation of perjury charge carried the same sentence, and the two sentences were to be served consecutively. Molinas would be eligible for parole after six years and eight months, two-thirds of his minimum sentence, were served. Before the trial, he had refused the prosecution's offer of a six-month jail term if he agreed to plead guilty and forfeited his attorney's license. On appeal, Molinas's jail term was reduced to between seven and a half and twelve and a half years. Hacken received seven and a half to eight years, Green six to seven, and Tucker a suspended sentence. Wagman would serve five to ten years for the attempted football fix in Florida. There is no court record that Ralph Gigante served time in prison. Goldberg, Lekemetros, Heyison, Cardone, and Walker would be indicted and tried in North Carolina. La Court received a sentence of two to five years and Budin a suspended sentence. Dave Budin's son, Steve, became a pioneer in offshore gambling, booking sports bets from the United States. Budin was also involved in his son's business, and both were indicted and convicted for violating the Federal Wire Act in 1998. Dave Budin received a sentence of house arrest and probation, while Steve Budin was ordered to pay a substantial fine.[47] Recruiter-players Louis Brown, Jerry Vogel, and Daniel Quindazzi received suspended sentences and lengthy probation.

After two years in Attica, Molinas informed District Attorney Hogan's office that he had knowledge of fixing at harness racing tracks in Yonkers, Roosevelt, and Monticello. An NBC News program named Molinas as the informant who touched off an investigation into the suspected infiltration of organized crime into the harness racing industry. Writing about fixing inquiry in the *New York Times*, Charles Grutzner reported that Molinas "has been giving information about racing that fits in surprisingly well from what has been learned from outside sources." Molinas also had knowledge of a check scam in which Hogan was interested. When Molinas returned to Attica, his status was changed to "informant," and he was isolated from the inmate population and placed in protective custody.[48]

Molinas left Attica in 1968 after fifty months in jail. In 1970, he moved to Los Angeles, where he became involved in selling pornography, loan sharking, fraud, gambling, and bookmaking. In one of his last business ventures, he walked away from his debts in a fur business that was a front for the Mob. His partner was found beaten to death, and Mob emissaries demanded that Molinas pay his debt. Molinas believed that the Mob would not kill him as long as there was a chance that he could pay. Either he was wrong, or the Mob had already concluded that he would not pay: On 3 August 1975, as Molinas and his former girlfriend, Shirley Marcus, admired the late-night view of the downtown Los Angles skyline, truck thief turned Mob hitman Eugene Connor shot Molinas in the back of the head, killing him instantly.[49]

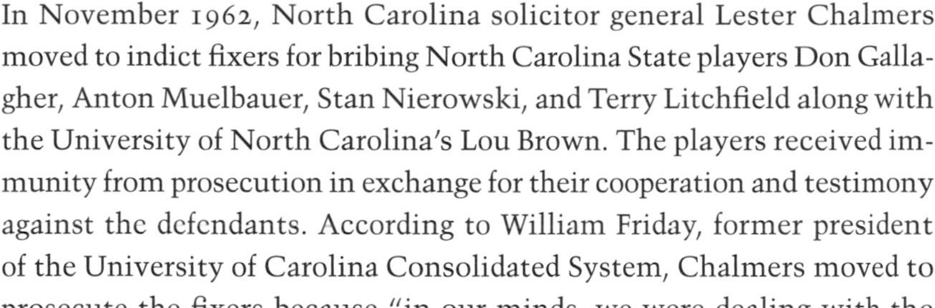

In November 1962, North Carolina solicitor general Lester Chalmers moved to indict fixers for bribing North Carolina State players Don Gallagher, Anton Muelbauer, Stan Nierowski, and Terry Litchfield along with the University of North Carolina's Lou Brown. The players received immunity from prosecution in exchange for their cooperation and testimony against the defendants. According to William Friday, former president of the University of Carolina Consolidated System, Chalmers moved to prosecute the fixers because "in our minds, we were dealing with the protection of human life of an innocent college kid that, because he had exceptional skills, had gotten all his fame, forces were preying upon these young men that were bigger than they could handle."[50] The North Carolina state prosecutions were nearly unique in that they targeted the actual fixing of games rather than perjury, fraud, or some other crime.

After a 31-point loss to rival North Carolina in February 1961, North Carolina State basketball coach Everett Case was sure at least three of his players—Muehlbauer, Niewierowski, and Litchfield—were rigging games. He immediately asked the director of the State Bureau of Investigation to investigate.[51] Case remains the only coach of a major college program on record to report suspected players to the authorities.

The Wake County grand jury returned its first set of indictments in September 1961, naming Joe Green, Dave Budin, Joey Hacken, and Aaron Wagman along with Charles Tucker, Bob Kraw, and go-betweens Louis Barshak and Michael Siegel.[52] The following January, the grand jury indicted Dave Goldberg, Steve Lekemetros, Morris Heyison, Frank Cardone, Jake Israel, Paul Walker, and Peter Martino.[53] Walker, Wagman, and Greene pled guilty in exchange for testifying against the others indicted. Cardone and Heyison avoided trial by fighting extradition from Pennsylvania. Goldberg was convicted and sentenced to five years in prison and fined twenty-one thousand dollars; Lekemetros received the same amount of jail time and a fine of nine thousand dollars. The two men also received suspended three-year sentences for each of sixteen and fourteen counts, respectively, and were ordered to pay fines and court costs; they unsuccessfully appealed their case all the way to the U.S. Supreme Court. Walker was sentenced to eighteen months. Barshak and Siegel received three-year suspended sentences. Wagman received a suspended sentence of three to five years contingent on his serving five to ten years in Florida for the football bribe; Green received the same sentence contingent on serving five to ten years in New York.[54] Hacken was to serve his sentence in New York.

The final tally for the 1961 basketball scandal included at least thirty-one players from twenty-two colleges who fixed games. At least nine players received money from fixers or gamblers but were never convicted of crimes.[55] Eight go-betweens were prosecuted, and two players were shown to have received bribe offers without reporting them.[56] It is almost certain that far more individuals were involved than these numbers reflect: students working with fixers on campuses, players who were offered bribes but did not report them, and gamblers whose discreet participation went unprosecuted.

In writing about the 1961 scandal, many authors have attributed it solely to Jack Molinas.[57] It is true that his compelling background and his outsized personality, flair, brazenness, and criminal genius were key elements of the story. Yet it is also true that the scandal would have occurred without him. As in the 1951 scandal, coaches and college authorities ran professionalized sports operations, recruiting players not qualified to be students, paying them to play, and ignoring obvious signs of rigging, all to win championships and national rankings and in the process earn money for themselves, their institutions, and their boosters. In this environment of hypocrisy and corruption and widespread popularity of gambling and organized crime, a scandal was inevitable.

The 1951 college basketball scandal became etched in memory as a defining event similar to professional baseball's Black Sox Scandal of 1919. As rigging of games continued on a grander scale throughout the

1950s and early 1960s, basketball's apologists crafted an image of the sport as being too pure to be destroyed by the actions of a few bad apples. The 1961 scandal was quickly explained away and forgotten. College football and basketball would continue their professionalization, maintaining their position as two of the most corrupt sports in the United States.

SEVEN
WINNING IN SMALLER WAYS

The 1978 Boston College Scandal

College basketball prospered after the 1961 scandal as the ignominy of fixing was buried in the public's consciousness by the turmoil of the 1960s and the rise of the UCLA basketball dynasty under John Wooden. From 1963 to 1975, UCLA won ten of twelve NCAA titles, including seven consecutive titles and eighty-eight straight games. Coach Wooden's middle America values, devout Christianity, and skillful coaching, combined with racially integrated teams and a winning formula of precision, teamwork, and stability, provided a counterpoint to the racial, countercultural, and political unrest of the times. Racism came to the forefront in college sports in the 1960s as gambling, professionalization, and corruption receded. In one example, racial turmoil engulfed the sports programs at Texas Western University (renamed the University of Texas at El Paso in 1967) after its basketball team defeated Adolph Rupp's all-white Kentucky team for the 1966 NCAA championship by playing the entire game with black players. Coach Don Haskins received death threats; many white athletes at the university resisted the integration of sports. The UCLA Bruins, however, portrayed college basketball as clean and uncorrupted, a place where whites and blacks were literally on the same team.

In reality, UCLA's dynasty forced other basketball programs to spend large sums of money to recruit outstanding players. Boosters were increasingly providing this money. The UCLA program's benefactor was Sam Gilbert, a wealthy contractor who befriended the Bruin players, often providing them with financial handouts.[1] Wooden later professed "tunnel vision" regarding Gilbert's giving money to the UCLA players.[2] Gilbert's support of the UCLA basketball program was hardly a secret among basketball cognoscenti, and it led to many accusations from other coaches and athletic directors that the NCAA's enforcement was selective.[3]

One program that produced a minor scandal during the 1960s—and sent more players to the NBA than any other college during that decade—was Jesuit-run Seattle University. Seattle U attained national recognition during the Elgin Baylor years of the mid- to late 1950s. In January 1965, the FBI alleged that two Seattle players, Peller Phillips and Charlie Williams, were asked to influence the final score of their 22 January game against the University of Idaho. The fixers included Leo Casale and Frank Polito, both of Chicago. Casale attempted to recruit a reluctant Phillips, who rejected the offer, fearing for his life, but Phillips did take $130 from Casale and gave $50 to teammate L. B. Wheeler. Williams, an all-American, did not receive any money but was present in the room when the incident occurred. The game was not fixed, as Seattle coach Bob Boyd played Phillips and Williams very little in the second half, and the Chieftains won the game but failed to beat the spread. The players were charged, but the charges were dropped because the prosecution believed its case was weak; all three were expelled from the university. Casale was convicted and served six months in prison.[4] Williams was barred from the NBA despite the fact he had received no money and was declared innocent of all involvement—his only mistake was not reporting the incident to his coach. He later became an all-star in the American Basketball Association.

In the 1960s, payoffs to athletes overshadowed gambling and fixing, at least in the minds of the athletic establishment and NCAA. As the gaming industry expanded in the 1970s and became a source of revenue for many local and state governments, the presence of organized crime increased. The scandal involving three Boston College players and a number of individuals connected to organized crime reminded college officials that basketball games in the 1970s were just as likely to be fixed as they had been in the 1940s.

The 1978–79 Boston College basketball scandal was uncovered by accident. On 27 April 1980, Henry Hill, a convicted extortionist, thief, and Mob associate, was arrested in New York for narcotics trafficking, immediately bonded, and then rearrested as a material witness in the 11 December 1978, Lufthansa robbery at New York's JFK Airport. The Lufthansa robbery involved an estimated $5,000,000 in cash and $875,000 in jewels—the largest cash robbery committed up to that time in the United States. The heist became the subject of two television films, *The Ten Million Dollar Getaway* and *The Big Heist*, and was a key plot in the movie *Goodfellas*, which featured Ray Liotta as Hill. Hill had long been associated with James "The Gent" Burke and Paul Vario, a capo in the Lucchese crime family. Burke had allegedly masterminded the Lufthansa heist and had been recorded telling Vario that Hill needed to be killed because of his knowledge of the Lufthansa heist and other thefts at JFK.[5]

Hill entered the federal witness protection program to save his life and the lives of his wife and children. In July 1980, while still in the witness protection program, Hill informed one of the prosecutors, Boston College alumnus Ed McDonald, that he had visited Boston to meet with two Boston College basketball players to fix games before the 1978–79 season. The FBI spent the next year collecting evidence before indicting two Pittsburgh brothers, a Pittsburgh drug dealer, three organized crime figures, and two players from the 1978–79 Boston College basketball team. A third player involved in fixing was not indicted; Hill was also not indicted, as he agreed to testify during the trial of the indicted individuals, and the FBI still hoped for his aid in retrieving the money stolen from Lufthansa.[6]

In 1963, Boston College, located on the western edge of Boston in an area known as Chestnut Hill, hired Hall of Fame player Bob Cousy to resurrect its moribund basketball program. In 1964, the college earned its first NIT invitation; three more NIT appearances followed. The Eagles appeared twice in the NCAA Tournament and in 1969 played Temple for the NIT championship. Despite its loss in the NIT final, the team was ranked in the national Top 10. Before the 1977–78 season, the college hired Tom Davis as its head coach and Kevin Mackey as his assistant.

The players involved in the scandal were Jim Sweeney and Rick Kuhn; Ernie Cobb was linked to the scandal but was never proven to have participated. Sweeney, a senior point guard and playmaker, had been an all-state high school basketball and baseball player from Trenton, New Jersey. Kuhn was a part-time starter from Swissvale, Pennsylvania, who had spent two seasons as a pitcher in the Cincinnati Reds' farm system and had been brought to Boston College by coach Bob Zuffelato, Davis's predecessor, from a junior college near Pittsburgh. Cobb, the team's captain and leading scorer, was a high school standout from Stamford, Connecticut. The fixers were Rocco Perla, a high school friend of Kuhn's; Rocco's brother, Tony, a school librarian and part-time drug dealer; Paul Mazzei, a drug dealer from Pittsburgh; and Henry Hill.[7]

The fixing scheme was hatched after Hill and Mazzei were released from the federal penitentiary at Lewisburg, Pennsylvania, on 15 July 1978. Hill had served six years of a ten-year sentence for extortion in connection with the Lucchese crime family; Mazzei had received a five-year sentence for selling LSD in Pittsburgh. The two had become friends in prison and had planned to set up a drug distribution operation in Pittsburgh after their release. When Mazzei met Kuhn in Pittsburgh, Mazzei proposed that he, the Perla brothers, and Hill make money by rigging Boston College basketball games, with Kuhn as their lead fixer on the team.[8]

For money, connections, and muscle, the fixers turned to the Lucchese crime family, one of the nation's largest and deadliest crime syndicates. Burke's "witness elimination" program had been responsible for killing all but seven of the individuals who had knowledge of the Lufthansa theft. Burke liked to gamble on sports, and he could not refuse the prospect of making easy money from fixing. He would give the money to finance the operation to Hill. Mazzei would collect the money from Hill and pass it to Tony Perla, who was to wire it directly to Kuhn or give it to Rocco Perla for distribution to Sweeney and Cobb. Similarly, the point spreads for fixed games would go from Burke to Hill, to Mazzei, to the Perlas, and finally to Kuhn prior to each game. Before the fixers could begin, the scheme needed the approval of Lucchese capo Paul Vario and Richard Perry. Both approved of the plan. Perry, known as Richie the Fixer, had coached a number of amateur teams in New York City, was considered a shrewd judge of basketball talent, and was the Lucchese family's adviser involving the illegal gambling business.[9]

Kuhn and Sweeney had been friends at Boston College on and off the court. Sweeney met Kuhn's friends Tony Perla and Henry Hill at Boston's Logan Airport Hilton; Mazzei waited in the lobby. Hill told Sweeney he was a "perfect front," a scholar-athlete no one would suspect of shaving points or dumping games. He also told Sweeney that extremely powerful men in New York were backing the operation and that it could be extremely financially rewarding for him. According to David Porter, Sweeney's reaction to Hill's pitch was, "I couldn't believe this was happening. I felt confusion, like, what am I doing here? I can't believe I'm having this conversation." Hill called Mazzei in to close the deal by acting as a "muscle man from New York." Mazzei played his part, saying, "Listen, you guys understand what you have to do, throw the ball out of bounds, double dribble. . . . [Y]ou know better than I do." Mazzei said the players would be paid twenty-five hundred dollars for each game that was successfully fixed. He also suggested they needed to get Ernie Cobb, the team's leading scorer, in on the scheme to make it work. At this point, Sweeney thought, "What if [I] said no? Could I leave the hotel? What about Kuhn and my teammates if I agreed to take part in the fixing? How about Henry's powerful friends in New York? Would they threaten my family in Trenton? What if I agreed to cooperate and informed Coach Davis?"[10]

According to Hill, Kuhn and Sweeney knew Hill had the connections for "betting money" (to be spread around on other games that were not fixed to deflect attention from bets on rigged games). Hill described Sweeney as "a businessman like me" who "wanted thirty-five hundred a game, but settled for twenty-five hundred." Hill said that the two players also wanted to ensure that he would get their bets down and talked as if they were seasoned bettors: "The thing that got me was they were familiar with the betting, they knew about spreads, they were not dumb kids. They knew how to shave, because when I tried to explain it to them, they said, Naw, we know all about that shit." Hill said that Sweeney pulled out a wallet-sized schedule and circled the games they could fix, and Hill gave both players five hundred dollars before they left the hotel room; by accepting it, they violated an NCAA precept by taking money from a known gambler. Sweeney said Hill told them, "Don't make matters difficult for yourselves, or we can make matters difficult for you."[11]

The first game to be fixed was against Providence on 6 December 1978 at Roberts Center, Boston College's cracker box arena. The spread favored Boston College, starting at 7 points and then moving to 9 points. The Eagles needed to win by less than 9, but they won by 19, a loser for the bettors. Kuhn had assured Tony Perla before the game that both he and Sweeney were set to rig the game, but when Kuhn told Sweeney about the fix, Sweeney said he was playing to win and was not part of the scheme. After the game, the fixers were not happy, but since they had lost only five thousand dollars, according to Hill, they would overlook the unsuccessful fix.[12] The fixers believed they needed Cobb and starting center Joe Beaulieu if they expected to win future fixed games. Kuhn later stated that Sweeney told him that Beaulieu might be interested in joining them, a statement that is plausible but highly unlikely. Rocco Perla was enlisted to obtain Cobb's participation in the upcoming game against Harvard at the Boston Garden.[13]

Boston College covered the 12-point spread against Harvard on 16 December 1978. According to Hill, Sweeney did his part by throwing the ball out of bounds three times, but he scored 18 points, and his overall execution did not point to rigging. Kuhn fumbled the ball out of bounds, then fouled a player in the act of shooting and allowed him to get a rebound and make a 4-point play. Hill said that the game was "good for him and his people" and that he made fifteen thousand dollars (five thousand of which he gave to Rocco Perla for the players), Burke made about ten thousand dollars, and Perry fifteen thousand.[14] Yet Hill's accounting of these amounts varied. He testified at Kuhn's trial that he gave Tony Perla three thousand dollars to give to Kuhn after the game, while the other two thousand was to be given to Kuhn early the following week. On another occasion, Hill said that he and Mazzei went into the locker room after the game and gave Kuhn three thousand dollars and said, "Here's three thousand, you'll get another two Monday or Tuesday."[15] Mazzei said he gave either Rocco Perla or Hill fifteen hundred dollars, and then Kuhn got three thousand dollars in the locker room. Kuhn said that Rocco Perla gave him only five hundred dollars at his apartment.[16]

Cobb's performance against Harvard was below normal, as he scored 12 points and committed seven turnovers. Rocco Perla alleged that he gave Cobb's girlfriend, Laverne Mosley, one thousand dollars after the game. Cobb admitted at his 1984 trial that he received money after the game but said he believed it was for giving information to Perla about Boston College's first game of the season against Stonehill College. Cobb's story illustrates the vulnerability of young athletes without much money. He had worked extremely hard since his junior high school years to overcome academic deficiencies and then play at Boston College, and he dreamed of an NBA career. Accepting money from Rocco Perla after the Harvard game, if uncovered, would prevent him from ever playing in the NBA. Like Tony Jackson, Connie Hawkins, Roger Brown, and others, Cobb had broken no law, but he had committed a crime in the eyes of the NBA.[17]

Sweeney shared his angst about shaving points and dumping with roommate Mike Maycock, a Boston College football player. Sweeney confessed his involvement in fixing games to Maycock but said he was playing to win. Maycock immediately arranged for himself and Sweeney to see athletic director Bill Flynn, a former FBI agent, but Sweeney decided not to report the rigging of games to Flynn.[18] Sweeney knew that the college would probably expel him, Kuhn, and any other players whose involvement in rigged games could be corroborated. If Sweeney had approached Flynn, he probably would have requested a complete FBI investigation that would have turned up at least one fixed game involving Sweeney and might also have exposed his organized crime connections. Sweeney later explained that he did not approach Flynn because the two men did not have a strong relationship—probably true but not sufficient. More likely, the real reason was greed, balanced by the fear of Hill and Mazzei and the other mobsters involved.[19]

Before heading to Hawaii's Rainbow Classic, Boston College played two games on the West Coast. During the trip, the spending habits of Kuhn, Cobb, and Sweeney drew attention from their teammates. Sophomore Chris Foy explained, "I got on the plane and Kuhn's got on this full-length leather coat, and Cobb's got the biggest boom box I've ever seen."[20] After losing to St. Mary's of California in Los Angeles, the Eagles faced UCLA at Pauley Pavilion two days before Christmas. Boston College was a 13–15 point underdog; the Eagles lost by 22. Hill won between twenty-five thousand and thirty thousand dollars on the game.[21] Perry, Burke, and the other gamblers probably won much more.

The fixing of the UCLA game exposed suspicion and distrust among Sweeney, Kuhn, and Cobb, and their manipulation of the final score was so clumsy as to be nearly obvious. Kuhn, the recruiter, knew that Sweeney was fixing the game, but he did not know whether Cobb was uninvolved in the fixing, working independently with Perla, or working with some unknown gambler. Sweeney believed that Cobb was secretly working with Kuhn and denied asking Cobb to rig the game. The other members of the team desperately wanted to beat powerhouse UCLA, but the Bruins were ahead by 15 at halftime and increased their lead to 19. With nine and a half minutes left in the game, however, BC closed to within 6. According to senior Tom Meggers, at that point Cobb stopped shooting. In his 1984 trial, Cobb said that Sweeney stopped pushing the ball up the court and virtually ignored him on offense; during the game, Cobb argued with Sweeney over this matter and was benched.[22] Sophomore Chris Foy supported Cobb's version of the events in a statement to the FBI. Foy also said that he suspected that Kuhn was rigging the game, but there is no record that Foy or any other players reported it to Coach Davis.[23]

Davis said that his team played erratically during that season because of his aggressive coaching style. If so, why not change his style? He indicated that he was aware of rumors of fixing and that he and Flynn discussed them but dismissed the possibility.[24] Flynn stated that he did not recall any such conversation with Davis. Brad Holland, who played guard for UCLA in the game and later coached at San Diego State, used film of the game to caution his players against consorting with gamblers. Holland said, "When I heard about them shaving points, I went back and looked at the tape. You could pick some stuff up. A guy bouncing the ball off his leg . . . making some ridiculous fouls away from the ball."[25] It is highly likely that Davis and Mackey viewed the same tape after the game, yet no accusations were brought, nor were any investigations begun. Davis later testified that he failed to see any unusual play during the entire season. Echoing Rupp, Holman, Bee, and other coaches whose players rigged games, Davis preferred to admit ignorance rather than risk his coaching career.

Returning from Hawaii, Boston College easily defeated crosstown rival Northeastern, then lost to a strong Rhode Island team by 13 points on 10 January 1979. Boston College would have lost by a larger margin had it not been for freshman Vin Caraher, who played his heart out at the end of the game, scoring 15 consecutive points. The final point spread had been Rhode Island by 15; the 2-point differential cost Hill and his other bettors a great deal of money. After the game, Hill screamed at Kuhn over the phone, "If you're not gonna do what you're supposed to do, if you're not gonna live up to the deal you made, just forget about it. I'll walk away from it now. Just don't make me blow another twenty-five to fifty thousand. Now I gotta bet twice as much to get even for the last game." Hill said he was going to "lay down the law" and warned Kuhn that he could not play basketball with broken fingers.[26]

The fixers had won two games (Harvard and UCLA) and lost two (Providence and Rhode Island); it was never made clear whether the fixers had won or lost money in total at this point. Hill's anger and his statement that they were ready to throw in the towel seems to indicate that they were not ahead by much. Hill said Kuhn insisted that they keep the scheme going and promised big paydays for the gamblers. If Hill is to be believed, Kuhn and Sweeney were happy to be fixing games and earning money. Kuhn probably passed Hill's threat on to Sweeney, Cobb, and Beaulieu. Since Beaulieu was not indicted in the fixing and there is no indication that he participated, it is possible that Kuhn lied to the fixers that Beaulieu was rigging and pocketed the money intended for him.[27]

Boston College's 10-point win over the University of Connecticut on 17 January beat the 5-point spread and yielded a win for the players and bettors. Against traditional rival Holy Cross three days later, the opening line favored Boston College by 5 but was reduced to 2 before the game.[28] The Eagles won by 2, resulting in a push—neither a win nor a loss for any bettor who chose either team. Hill alleged that Kuhn, Sweeney, Cobb, and Beaulieu rigged the final of the Colonial Classic on 27 January between Boston College and Connecticut and that he won thirty-five thousand dollars on the Eagles' 1-point win.[29] However, no one was ever charged with fixing this game, and Hill's allegation remains unproven.

By this time, many bookies suspected that Boston College games were being rigged and stopped taking bets on them.[30] Some bookies adjusted the point spread to create more pushes; some wanted to know which games were fixed so they could also cash in.[31] Legal bookies in Nevada contacted David Cawood, assigned by NCAA executive director Walter Byers in 1978 to enforce the NCAA's gambling rules, and informed him of suspicious activity involving Boston College games.[32] Cawood reported this information to Flynn, who told Cawood that he had made every effort to substantiate the rumors but found no evidence of fixing involving the team. In *Unsportsmanlike Conduct: Exploiting College Athletes*, Byers devoted three pages to gambling's influence in college sports. He did not describe any NCAA efforts to address the game fixing despite the 1951 and 1961 scandals and the rumors that it was still happening. He wrote that "point shaving and fixing are threats to which colleges are most vulnerable and to which they give occasional attention. This is not due to lack of concern but a sense of helplessness about how to deal with the problem successfully."[33] If it were true that the NCAA under Byers lacked the knowledge and mechanisms to address the problem, why not seek the expertise of the federal, state, and local law enforcement agencies? Byers's silence represents yet another acknowledgment that "cash cow hypocrisy"—looking the other way as the money rolls in—is the critical factor behind corruption in college sports.[34]

Kuhn and the fixers wanted to make sure that Cobb was participating in their scheme. By the Fordham game on 3 February, Sweeney would admit to being "locked in to the fixing" and would be involved for the rest of the season.[35] Boston College beat Fordham by 13, covering the 10-point spread and making the bettors happy. Cobb made seven out ten field goals, hit all of his free throws, handed out seven assists, and committed only one turnover—not the play of someone shaving points. Appearing at a booster function after the game, Sweeney told Perla that he had missed a free throw late in the game because he "looked at the rim and saw a pair of cement shoes. I figured I'd better miss."[36]

Three days after beating Fordham, Boston College played St. John's at Alumni Gym in New York. Hill claimed that the game had been rigged. Kuhn said that Sweeney and Cobb had rejected his offers to rig the game, but his veracity was by now questionable. The spread started with St. John's by 9 points, but it went up to 12 as more money was bet on the Redmen. St. John's won by 9, a push for the bettors who chose St. John's at 9 but a loss at 12.[37] For Cobb, who was playing in front of his family and his high school coach, Herman Alswanger, the game was a disaster: he scored 6 points (four free throws and one field goal), committed seven turnovers, and fouled out. Coach Alswanger said about the game, "I kept saying, why aren't they passing to him? He never gets the ball. Even at the end of the game, he almost took the ball out of bounds himself and took it downcourt. [It seemed like] there were no set plays for him. He had wanted to beat St. John's so bad."[38] Hill alleged that his poor play had earned Cobb twenty-five hundred dollars, but Cobb was never charged with rigging the game. After the game, Hill again offered to stop the fixing operation, and Kuhn again refused, saying that the next game against Holy Cross would be a big payday. Hill again reminded Kuhn about the broken fingers, although he did not testify at Kuhn's trial about this comment.[39]

The Holy Cross–Boston College game in Worcester on 10 February was expected to be close because of the intense rivalry between the two institutions. Hill believed, no doubt with reassurances from Kuhn, that

Cobb, Sweeney, and Kuhn would lose the game by more than the 7-point spread. Sweeney fouled out of the game after playing 21 minutes; Kuhn finished the game scoreless. Announcer Marv Albert described Cobb's play early in the game as "forcing his shots" and playing "out of control." With 1:25 remaining in the game and Boston College behind by 8 points, Hill and Burke had popped the champagne corks and were preparing to celebrate. But the Eagles pulled within 2 of Holy Cross, and Cobb's last shot, which would have tied the game, barely missed. Boston College lost by 2 points.[40] Burke allegedly lost fifty thousand dollars on the game and Hill twenty-five thousand. After the game, the team learned that a death threat had been made against Cobb three days earlier.[41]

Hill told *Sports Illustrated* that the players talked him and the other fixers into rigging the Eagles' NCAA New England regional tournament game against Connecticut, but he told a grand jury in July 1981 that the game was not rigged.[42] Playing its worst game of the season, Boston College lost by 17 points.

After the season, in the spring of 1979, Sweeney was awarded the Frances Pomeroy Naismith Award as one of the best basketball players in the country under six feet tall; he was also selected as an academic all-American and a finalist for a Rhodes Scholarship. The current Boston College media guide, however, does not mention Sweeney's awards. Cobb was selected as the first pick in the sixth round by the Utah Jazz but was cut during training camp. He later tried out with the New Jersey Nets, but they did not sign him. As was true for many other players before him, the NBA's inflexible position on signing players with even a hint of involvement with gamblers seemed to be the rationale.

The fixing scandal hit the newspapers in January 1981, and on 16 February, Hill's article, "How I Put the Fix In" (for which he was paid ten thousand dollars) appeared in *Sports Illustrated*. In late July 1981, James Burke, Paul Mazzei, Tony Perla, Rocco Perla, and Rick Kuhn were indicted by a federal grand jury in the Eastern District Court of New York on charges of racketeering and conspiracy in connection with rigging Boston College games against Providence, Harvard, UCLA, Fordham,

St. John's, and Holy Cross.[43] Mazzei was already in jail on a federal drug conviction, and Burke was in jail for a parole violation.[44] Both had been convicted because of Hill's testimony. Peter Vario and Ernie Cobb were later indicted. Cobb's lawyer, David Golub, reportedly believed that prosecutor Edward McDonald was too lenient in allowing Sweeney complete freedom from prosecution, saying that "a lot of people said [McDonald] identified with Sweeney. I thought it was very inappropriate that a former white guard at Boston College did not prosecute a white guard, and a black guard was [prosecuted]. I thought it looked very bad."[45]

The trial of Burke, Mazzei, the Perlas, and Kuhn began on 27 October 1981. Before the trial, Judge Henry Bramwell ruled that any statements Hill made on the witness stand that contradicted what he said in his *Sports Illustrated* article could be impeached.[46] Hill was the prosecution's first witness; the four defense attorneys demolished his five days of testimony, revealing gaps and inaccuracies in his memory, detailing his past crimes, impugning his credibility, and exposing contradictions with his statements in the *Sports Illustrated* article; they also came close to revealing a past sexual indiscretion.[47] Fortunately for prosecutor McDonald, his other witnesses rehabilitated most of Hill's testimony.

Sweeney admitted to receiving five hundred dollars from Kuhn but testified that he repeatedly refused Kuhn's entreaties to rig any games and claimed that he did not report Kuhn's bribery attempts out of fear for his and Kuhn's lives.[48] The defense argued that Sweeney should have been indicted because he admitted receiving money, had been dishonest when he did not inform Davis and Flynn about the rigging, and had lied to the FBI when first questioned.[49] Kuhn's attorneys then moved for a dismissal of the charges against him, arguing that he had been the target of selective prosecution and had been denied equal protection under the law.[50] Judge Bramwell denied the motion. Barbara Reed, Kuhn's ex-girlfriend, offered incriminating testimony against him, including his conversations about point rigging, his sudden acquisitions of large amounts of cash, his meetings with Rocco Perla and Hill, his joking with Sweeney about deliberate miscues in games, and his statement that Boston College was trying to "win in smaller ways."[51] She testified that she relayed the point spread to Kuhn for the second Holy Cross game and, most damagingly, that Kuhn had threatened to kill her if she ever went to the police with knowledge of the fixing operation.[52] Joe Beaulieu testified that Kuhn attempted to enlist him in the fixing scheme with drugs on more than one occasion and that he refused the offers. FBI agent James Byron agent testified that Kuhn voluntarily and without any coercion admitted his role in the alleged fixing of three games, though he was not asked about fixing the Providence, UCLA, Fordham, or St. John's games. The prosecution also offered several days' testimony against the other defendants. In his closing argument, McDonald argued, among other things, that Hill had no motivation to lie because if he did, he would lose his guarantee of immunity and would find himself at the top of Burke's witness elimination list.[53]

On 16 November 1981, the defense began by subpoenaing Douglas S. Looney, who had coauthored Hill's *Sports Illustrated* article. Looney testified that he wrote what Hill told him, with some exaggerations, and stated that Hill read the story before publication and confirmed its veracity.[54] John Yarmosh, Burke's bookie, who had known Hill and Burke for many years, rebutted Hill's assertion that Hill and Burke met Yarmosh and another bookie at a restaurant to discuss the fixing scheme. Edward Medo, a former Las Vegas bookie, testified that he did not recall any abnormal betting on Boston College games during the 1978–79 season. Davis testified that none of the miscues committed by Kuhn, Sweeney, or Cobb appeared out of the ordinary. The defense attorneys closed by stating that Sweeney should have been indicted. They pressed the fact that the FBI had no notes or tape recordings of its interview with Kuhn, and that Agent Byron had reported only three rigged games, not the six that the prosecution charged in the indictment.[55]

On 23 November, the jury found the defendants guilty on all counts. Late the following January, Bramwell sentenced Burke to twenty years in prison and a fine of thirty thousand dollars, Tony Perla to ten years in prison, Rocco Perla to four, and Paul Mazzei to ten. On 5 February 1982 Bramwell sentenced Kuhn ten years in prison.[56] Kuhn's sentence was the longest given to any individual convicted of fixing a game in college basketball history. In sentencing Kuhn, the judge stated that an argument "can be offered that a substantial term of incarceration imposed on this defendant will be recalled in the future by another college athlete who may be tempted to compromise his performance."[57] In April 1984, Bram-

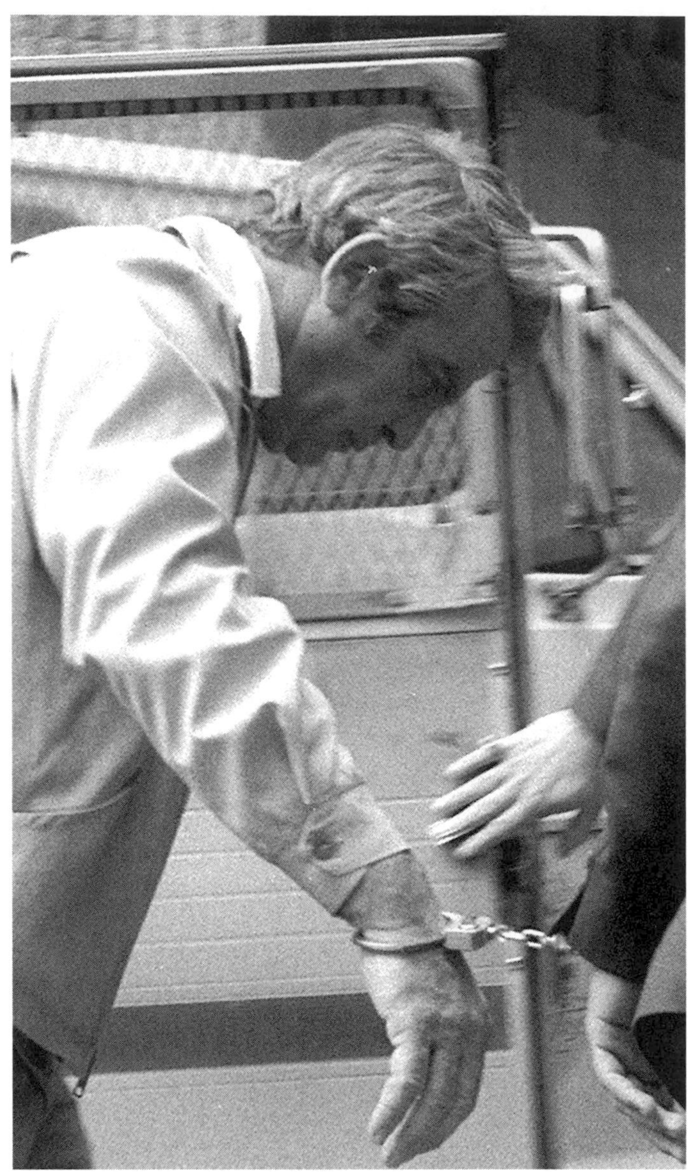

James "The Gent" Burke is led handcuffed from a law enforcement vehicle in 1979. The suspected mastermind of the $5.8 million Lufthansa heist at Boston's Logan Airport and a notorious New York gangster, Burke operated a "witness elimination" program that killed nearly all the participants in the airport theft. In November 1991, he was tried and convicted on charges of racketeering and conspiracy in connection with rigging six Boston College games. He died in prison.

well reduced the sentences of all the defendants: Burke from twenty to twelve years; Kuhn and Tony Perla from ten to four and six years, respectively; Mazzei from ten to eight years; and Rocco Perla from four years to time served and five years' probation. He was released immediately.[58]

Ernie Cobb was indicted in June 1983 by a federal grand jury in Brooklyn on charges of taking bribes for the Harvard, Rhode Island, and Fordham games. The charges carried a maximum five-year prison term and a ten-thousand-dollar fine. Because Cobb steadfastly refused to accept a plea bargain, his trial was delayed nine months. After Tony Perla admitted to meeting with Richard Perry and Peter Vario (Paul's son) at the Aqueduct Racetrack in New York in November 1978 to plan the fixing, Vario and Perry were added to the Cobb indictment, reportedly because the prosecutors theorized that to prosecute Cobb alone would appear to be an inefficient use of the legal system.[59] The Cobb trial began in March 1984. The Perla brothers, Kuhn, Mazzei, and Hill agreed to testify for the prosecution in exchange for reduced sentences.[60]

On 23 March 1984, the jury unanimously acquitted Cobb and Vario. The verdict had been expected due to the weakness of the prosecution's case. The witnesses who testified to Cobb's involvement in the rigging of games were not able to avoid contradicting their testimony from the previous trial: for example, Tony Perla had testified in the case against Kuhn that the UCLA and second Holy Cross games had not been fixed, but the prosecution had alleged that they had. Cobb's attorney also established that Cobb believed that the money he received after the Harvard game was payment for information he gave to Rocco Perla to bet on the Stonehill game.[61] Hill's testimony contradicted his statements in the Kuhn case, and Kuhn egregiously lied about what he had confessed to during his trial. One FBI agent who testified for the prosecution admitted on the witness stand that he was unfamiliar with point shaving and assumed that if Cobb received any money from gamblers, it implied he was guilty of fixing a game; the other FBI agent testified that Cobb claimed to have played his best against Stonehill and Bentley and refused an offer to rig a third game. Also, the prosecution changed the charge from that in the indictment—that Cobb took bribes in the Harvard, Rhode Island, and Fordham games—to the accusation that Cobb accepted bribes in the Stonehill and Bentley games. Probably most damaging to the prosecution was Cobb's honest, believable presence and testimony on the witness stand. Stated juror George Simaras, "We knew he took the money, but did he take it knowing he had done something wrong? It's a matter of whether Ernie knew what he was doing." Another juror said, "We all felt in the end that [the gamblers who set up the scheme] were trying to set him up by getting him used to taking money."[62]

Perry fled to Canada, was arrested as he attempted to reenter the United States, and pled guilty when threatened with Hill's testimony. Perry was fined five thousand dollars and sentenced to a year's probation and time served days after his arrest. After moving to Las Vegas, he would be prohibited from entering the state's casinos and spent fifteen months in jail on tax evasion. Perry was deeply involved in the scandal that led to the resignation of UNLV basketball coach Jerry Tarkanian in 1992; Perry sat in NCAA-assigned floor-level seats when UNLV appeared in the 1990 Final Four and was photographed in a hot tub with three UNLV players in 1991. That a convicted gambler of Perry's notoriety could gain such access to college basketball speaks volumes about the NCAA's inability to control game rigging in college sports.

The Boston College scandal illustrated that even after decades of investigations and prosecutions, gamblers and fixers could still use vulnerable college athletes to manipulate the outcome of games. These players were willing to expose themselves to danger and to compromise their futures for relatively small sums of money. The NCAA's failure to investigate gambling in the late 1970s reinforces the view of critics who argue that the organization's primary goal has been to convince the public that college sports are uncorrupted by professionalization and commercialization. Not until 1996 did the NCAA appoint a full-time person to direct enforcement of gambling and agent infractions, and not until 2000 was an athlete barred from participating in NCAA-sponsored activities as

Three former UNLV basketball players drink beers in a Las Vegas hot tub with convicted gambler Richard "The Fixer" Perry. Pictured (left to right) are Moses Scurry, Perry, Anderson Hunt, and David Butler. The players were members of the Rebels' 1990 NCAA championship team. Perry had previously been convicted for his role in the 1978–79 Boston College scandal and was the gambling adviser for New York's Vario crime family.

a consequence of sports betting.[63] The disgrace the scandal brought to Boston College would be quickly forgotten as the institution continued to use its basketball and football programs to increase income and prestige. Less than five years after the final sentences were handed down to the Boston College perpetrators, scandals at other major universities would demonstrate that corruption in college basketball remained as wide and deep as ever.

EIGHT

STUDENT-ATHLETES AND CAMPUS BOOKIES

Basketball Scandals of the 1980s and 1990s

In 1975, University of Alabama football coach Paul "Bear" Bryant clearly enunciated his view of the role of athletes at a major university:

> I used to go along with the idea that football players on scholarship were "student-athletes," which is what the NCAA calls them. Meaning a student first, an athlete second. We were kidding ourselves, trying to make it more palatable to the academicians. We don't have to say that and we shouldn't. At the level we play the boy is really an athlete first and a student second. He's there as an emissary of the school, paid with a scholarship to perform a very important function. He represents the students, the administration, the alumni, everybody. Sometimes before millions of people, the fact that he's a student, the second part of the deal, is the only meaningful way we have to pay him.[1]

This view was also widespread in college basketball. As Peter Golenbock showed in *Personal Fouls: The Broken Promises and Shattered Dreams of Big-Time Basketball at Jim Valvano's North Carolina State,* academically unqualified basketball players entering a four-year institution were thrust into an environment in which they were supposed to be like any other student but quickly realized that they had been "paid with a scholarship to perform a very important function." Colleges recruited and paid thousands of dollars in scholarships to top players to fill arenas, win games, and advance to the NCAA tournament, appearing on television as many times as possible, on any night of the week, notwithstanding college courses, breaks, or holidays.

At the same time, gambling became increasingly accepted among college students. Since wagering on college sports was illegal in all states except Nevada, shady bookmakers reaped immense sums from the public's interest in betting on college football and basketball. By the early 1980s, the NCAA relied on the federal, state, and local governments to enforce and prosecute gambling-related crimes because the association, along with the conferences and colleges' athletic establishments, found it impossible to prevent game fixing. Most coaches had convinced the public that it was impossible to detect the rigging of basketball games, a viewpoint that only encouraged anyone wanting to fix games. A new generation of college student gamblers on sports would contribute to the decades-old scourge of game rigging, leading once again to federal and state investigations and prosecutions.

The 1985 Tulane basketball point-shaving scandal can largely be explained by the university's quest to return to a level of athletic prominence it had once held in the SEC. The Harvard of the South wanted to emulate colleges such as Duke, Vanderbilt, Stanford, and Rice, which had earned high marks for their athletic programs without compromising their academic reputations. However, Tulane's athletic programs were losing money, and the university could not afford to recruit nationally prominent athletes. To get the best athletes yet shield its reputation, the university reinstated physical education as a major in the University College, a continuing-studies division that was designed to serve part-time and adult students. Scholastic Aptitude Test (SAT) scores required for acceptance in University College were 200 points lower than the campuswide average, and the college was a source of faculty resentment. Eighty percent of the university's football and basketball players were enrolled there.[2]

During the 1984–85 basketball season, four of Tulane's starters fixed two games and planned to fix a third. The players included potential first-round NBA pick John "Hot Rod" Williams, who enrolled with SAT scores close to the minimum of 200 in English and approximately 270 in math, half the average of students in the College of Liberal Arts and Sciences.[3] Other players involved included senior forwards Jon Johnson and Clyde Eads, sophomore point guard David Dominique, and senior reserve guard Bobby Thompson.[4]

The plan to fix games was hatched when Eads approached Tulane student Gary Krantz to purchase cocaine. Within two weeks, their conversations turned to fixing. After Krantz proposed that Eads and Johnson rig the Southern Mississippi game on 2 February, the players approached Williams, who readily agreed and recruited Dominique. Two other Tulane students, Mark Olensky and David Rothenburg, joined the scheme.[5] Tulane covered the spread of 10½ points, winning 64–63. The players soon turned their attention to fixing the game with highly ranked Memphis State University. Johnson drew Roland Ruiz, a New Orleans bookie, into the effort. The players' task was to lose the game by more than the 6-point spread, and they succeeded, going down 60–49.[6] When talk arose about rigging the upcoming Louisville game, the players refused, going on to defeat their rival 68–56.

The five players' exploits were uncovered in early March 1985 through careless talk by some of the players and a tip to the New Orleans district attorney. Eads and Johnson confessed in exchange for immunity, which set the stage for the first arrests. Rothenburg, Olensky, and Krantz pled guilty to lesser charges and were fined and given suspended sentences. Thompson was fined and given five years' active probation.[7] Dominique pled guilty to a lesser charge of misdemeanor theft and received a three-month suspended sentence, three months of unsupervised probation, and a fine. Craig Bourgeois, a campus and bookie runner, pled guilty to misdemeanor gambling and received a six-month suspended sentence, one year of nonreporting probation, and a fine. Ruiz pled guilty to misdemeanor gambling and was sentenced to a six-month suspended sentence and fined. After two trials in which the defense attacked the credibility of the testifying participants, Williams was acquitted of all five sports bribery charges.[8] He became a star in the NBA, playing for Cleveland, Phoenix, and Dallas for thirteen years. Tulane's president, Dr. Eamon Kelly, disbanded the basketball program in April 1985. In 1988, Tulane's board of administrators voted to reinstate basketball for the 1990–91 season.

The Tulane scandal revealed an alarming trend in which students and athletes were gambling in association with bookies on college campuses. Former mobsters such as Michael Francese and Bill Jahoda were invited to warn college athletes away from gambling, and convicted players attempted to convince their audiences that gambling could destroy a person's life just as quickly as any other addiction. Despite these efforts, the problem of college students and athletes gambling on sports became pandemic over the next twenty-five years.

When Arizona State's 1993–94 point shaving scandal came to light in 1997, it was perhaps no surprise that the school's head coach was Bill Frieder, who had never made a secret of his taste for hitting the tables in Las Vegas. Frieder had left the University of Michigan six games before the team won the NCAA championship in 1989. His leaving could not have been better timed, as Michigan soon uncovered a series of wrongdoings involving its basketball program. Frieder's substantial salary at Arizona State included larger bonuses for increases in attendance hikes and tournament wins than for graduation rates.[9] In return for its investment, the institution received a trip to the Sweet Sixteen, a point shaving scandal, and a number of off-court problems that included credit card fraud and sexual assault.

The players implicated in the point shaving scandal were guards Isaac Burton and Stevin "Hedake" Smith. Smith began placing bets on NFL games in November 1993 with his friend, campus bookie Benny Silman. The association with Silman led to a meeting with Chicago gambler and investor Joseph Gagliano in which Smith asked for one hundred thousand dollars for each game fixed, though he ultimately accepted considerably less. Silman did not inform Smith that a larger group of Chicago gamblers were backing the bets on the games. The fixers planned to rig games in which Arizona State was favored by a large margin. Smith, who was usually assigned to guard an opponent's highest scorer, would shave points by allowing his man to score.[10]

The first game selected for rigging was against Oregon State on 27 January 1994. The Sun Devils were favored by 14½, but Silman wanted to win by less than 6 in case the spread went down before the game. Silman suggested that another player would be needed to carry out the fix. Smith recruited Burton, telling him he could make two thousand dollars by manipulating the final score and giving him half that amount up front. The Sun Devils led by 13 points at halftime, but in the second half, Smith gave the man he was guarding room to shoot, and Oregon State cut the lead in half. Arizona State won by 6 points, with Smith scoring 39 points. He received ten thousand dollars for rigging and made another ten thousand by betting on his team to cover the spread; Burton collected thirteen hundred. No one suspected that the final score had been rigged.[11]

The University of Oregon game on 29 January was the next to be rigged. Arizona State covered the 6-point spread, and Burton received two thousand dollars and Smith eighteen thousand. After the game, Smith purchased seven thousand dollars in jewelry, clothes, and shoes; gave his mother his car; and placed a down payment on a $28,000 sports car. He then lost ten thousand dollars to Silman betting on his own team in a nonrigged game.[12]

For the University of Washington game on 5 March, Smith and the fixers grew greedy: Smith was slated to earn $20,000 for shaving points and $20,000 for betting on Arizona State to cover the spread of 11 points. Gagliano reportedly bet $1,400,000 legally and illegally on the game, carrying $1,000,000 in a duffel bag to Las Vegas. So much money was bet on the underdog Huskies on the day of the game that Ron Asher, head of enforcement for the Nevada Gaming Board, labeled the betting "amateur hour."[13] A Las Vegas point setter called the Pac-10 office in Walnut Creek, California, to report the possibility of a fixed game; the Pac-10 official notified Arizona State athletic director Charlie Harris just before the game. Arizona State scored its first field goal twelve minutes into the game and led by two at the half. Coach Frieder blasted the team at halftime and told them that he was going to ask a Portland Trailblazer scout in the stands to leave. Fearing that a subpar performance might jeopardize his chances of being drafted, Smith played hard in the second half, and the Sun Devils won by 18. Smith lost $40,000 and the three betting groups lost more than $1,000,000.[14]

After the game, another gambler, 400-pound Sean Puopolo, who lost seventy-five thousand dollars on the game, robbed Silman and Smith at gunpoint of at least three thousand dollars. Smith promised Puopolo that he would receive the rest when Smith received the bonus he expected for signing with an NBA team. At ten o'clock that evening, Coach Frieder summoned all the players to the Arizona State basketball arena. Bluffing, Frieder told them that the FBI believed there had been point shaving in the Washington game. He said that he knew the identity of the players involved and asked them to voluntarily step forward. Neither Smith nor Burton did so. The FBI did not question Smith at that time about the Washington game, and the rumors of fixing stopped. Smith ended the season as Arizona State's all-time leading scorer. When he was not selected in the June 1994 NBA draft, Smith believed it was because league officials believed the rumors of his point shaving at Arizona State. He played three seasons in the Continental Basketball League and in professional leagues in Argentina, France, and the Philippines. In March 1997, the Dallas Mavericks signed him to two ten-day contracts and expressed an interest in having him attend their training camp. But Smith learned from friends that the FBI was closing in on him, so he turned himself in. The FBI also had enough evidence to indict Silman, Burton, and the Chicago gamblers.[15]

Frieder was forced to resign in September 1997 after eight seasons that saw the point shaving scandal as well as other incidents of player criminality and a mediocre won-loss record. Silman received forty-six months in prison. Joseph Gagliano was sentenced to fifteen months in prison, three years' parole, and one hundred hours of community service and was fined six thousand dollars. Burton was sentenced to two months in prison, six months of home detention, and three years' probation; he was also fined eight thousand dollars and ordered to complete two hundred hours of community service.[16] Smith received a prison sentence of one year and a day, three years of probation, and an eight-hundred-dollar fine and was prohibited from gambling in any form.[17] The alleged conspirators placed more than sixty-one bets topping one million dollars in what the FBI identified as a major sports gambling scandal. The NCAA and the college athletic establishment continued to call the campus gambling problem an isolated one: According to James Rund, Arizona State's interim vice president, "to characterize [the scandal] as a student gambling ring is an exaggeration and probably an inaccurate depiction of the circumstances."[18]

In the 1994–95 Northwestern basketball scandal, two players—guard Kenneth "Dion" Lee and center-forward Dewey Williams—accepted money from Brian Irving and former Notre Dame soccer player and football place kicker Kevin Pendergast to dump games against Wisconsin, Penn State, and Michigan. Matthew Purdy was also named as an unindicted coconspirator. Northwestern campus bookie and former football player Brian Ballarini was charged with accepting bets from other Northwestern athletes, including Lee.

The scandal had its roots in gambling by student-athletes. In the fall of 1994, more than two dozen Northwestern athletes, including two women, regularly bet on college and professional sports.[19] In December, after the university conducted an investigation, Lee, a senior, admitted his role in the betting and was suspended for six games. At the beginning of the season, coach Ricky Byrdsong implemented changes that he believed would motivate Lee to improve on his previous season's performance, such as calling Lee "Kenneth" instead of "Dion," his nickname since childhood, and changing the number he wore. Lee resisted these changes, believing that the coach was humiliating him, and their relationship deteriorated. In January 1995, Ballarini threatened Lee with bodily harm if Lee did not pay two thousand dollars he owed from losing bets on NFL games. To pay his debt, Lee began conspiring with Pendergast, a star athlete turned compulsive gambler and Chicago bartender, to rig Northwestern games for the rest of the season. Northwestern beat the 14-point spread in its 15 February 1995 loss to Wisconsin. One week later, Northwestern lost to Penn State by 30 points, again beating the 14-point spread. The Wildcats failed to beat the spread against Michigan on 1 March, losing by 17 points rather than 25. Teammate Dan Kreft stated that "all the players [on the team] knew [Lee and Williams] were gambling, but we never imagined they were shaving points"; moreover, according to Kreft, "no one was going to go to the coaches and tell them." Lee "never showed any outward signs of a particular need of having received some kind of financial reward. And, he was fun to play with, always upbeat, I always thought he was trying to win."[20]

The fixing of games came to light after Northwestern suspended Lee for gambling on college and professional sports. Suspecting that Lee may have been involved in game fixing, the U.S. attorney's office and the FBI began what would become a three-year investigation. Ballarini cooperated, which led Lee to admit to the FBI that he had dumped games.[21]

In November 1998, Pendergast was sentenced to two months in prison, and Irving, Lee, and Williams each received one month. All four were placed on two years' probation after their prison terms ended. In an agreement with the FBI and NCAA, Lee and Pendergast were to give antigambling talks at colleges for five years. Purdy was not sentenced, but when his involvement with Lee and Williams became known, he was dismissed from an assistant coaching position at California State Polytechnic University, Pomona. In return for cooperating with the investigations, Ballarini escaped jail time, receiving a sentence of three years' probation, three months of electronic monitoring, two hundred hours of community service, and five years of speaking to college students about the dangers of gambling. Ballarini, who came from a wealthy suburban background, was not fined, since he had fifteen thousand dollars in credit card debt.[22]

Lee, who came from a working-class background, graduated from a highly regarded public high school, and entered Northwestern with a solid academic record, was quoted in the *Chicago Sun-Times* as saying that "anyone who believes that there were just two people involved not to mention the racial thing of two African-Americans, are fools. Everyone knows it's bigger. We were the scapegoats. It ain't no secret."[23]

Dion Lee was right: Gambling by students and athletes on campuses had become widespread. In 1993, Phoenix police seized two hundred betting accounts that belonged to students at Arizona State University; from August 1993 to February 1994, an average of $120,000 a month was wagered by this ring.[24] At the University of Georgia, a student ran a betting operation from an apartment until he quit in early March 1994 because his student clients owed him and his partners $10,000; two other students continued the operation with 170 clients, a quarter of them betting nightly. The operation made about $4,000 on basketball on a good weeknight and about $10,000 on a busy Saturday.[25] And police in Nutley, New Jersey, uncovered a student-run gambling operation at Nutley High School that handled single bets as high as $1,000 and used strong-arm tactics, violence, and kidnapping to persuade losers to pay up. One prosecutor commented, "The operation was sophisticated and exactly mirrors an adult-run organized crime bookmaking business."[26] Campus gambling would outrun law enforcement, campus athletic officials, and the NCAA, and would predictably lead to more game fixing scandals, most notably involving college football.

NINE

A CONTINUING NIGHTMARE

Gambling and Fixing in College Football, 1990–2010

In 1992, Congress passed the Professional and Amateur Sports Protection Act (also known as the Bradley Act, after its sponsor, Senator Bill Bradley), which made sports betting illegal in all states except Nevada, Oregon, and New Jersey.[1] The act sought to preserve the purity of athletic competition and to protect athletes by outlawing betting on high school, collegiate, and Olympic events. However, in the subsequent two decades, betting on sports has become a more serious problem than drug or alcohol abuse in educational institutions from elementary schools to college campuses. Included in this alarming trend are bookmaking operations run by between one and fifty students on college campuses.[2]

Because gambling has become so widespread in this country, most people do not take seriously the legal ban on sports betting. Results released by the NCAA in May 2004 illustrated that 35 percent of male and 10 percent of female college athletes had gambled in the past year. Among the twenty-one thousand athletes surveyed, 1.1 percent (231) of the football players reported taking money for playing poorly, 2.3 percent (481) had been asked to influence the game's outcome because of their gambling debts, and 1.4 percent (294) admitted altering their performance to change the game's final score. The range of problems related to college students' gambling include murder, drug addiction, depression, attempted suicide, and academic failure, and parents have felt the need to step in to pay their children's gambling debts.[3]

Football and basketball programs at U.S. colleges and universities generate billions of dollars annually. The athletes responsible for producing the money, publicity, and national rankings can legally receive no more than an annually renewable scholarship that pays for tuition, room, meals, and books, plus a small amount for incidental expenses. The unfairness of the situation has led to under-the-table payments and other gifts, usually from boosters. Athletes from low-income families can play for a college for four years and not have money to buy clothes, a personal computer, or school supplies; do their laundry; pay transportation expenses; go on dates; travel home for vacations; obtain non-sports-related medical or dental care; or even call home.[4]

The significant number of college athletes gambling on sports may result in part from the restrictions on the money athletes receive from scholarships, but no data back up this hypothesis. Many examples over the past two decades, however, do show that increasing numbers of student-athletes who incur gambling debts have chosen to pay off these debts by manipulating final scores.

Boosters at the University of Florida, in their desperation to win SEC titles in football and basketball, became so egregious in violating NCAA precepts that speculation was rampant that the football program would receive the death penalty, as had Southern Methodist University in 1983. When Florida sought a new president in 1983, its applicant pool numbered 357; six years later, after the resignation of president Marshall Criser, only 67 people applied for the job. One of the three finalists for the position, Malcolm Gillis, a Florida alumnus and dean of Duke's graduate school, withdrew his name and cited as the primary reason "fundamental and longstanding" problems in intercollegiate athletics. Adding to these problems in the Florida football program were the numbers of players wagering on sports, including betting on their own team. In October 1989, starting quarterback Kyle Morris and his backup, Shane Matthews, were suspended for one year for betting on sports with student bookies in Athens, Georgia. Two walk-ons, quarterback G. A. Mangus and receiver Brady Ackerman, were also removed from the team, presumably for gambling. An anonymous letter sent to athletic director Bill Arnsparger describing the betting of Morris and Matthews "wasn't real detailed, but it did have facts," according to Arnsparger. "The writer knew what he was talking about." Morris had indicated that he believed that the Georgia bookies "handled a lot of action from a lot of students."[5]

In the late spring of 1992, Rhode Island state police uncovered a student-run gambling ring at the University of Rhode Island and at Bryant College, a nearby private business school. This ring appeared eerily similar to organized crime, as it included bookmakers, runners, toll-free numbers, and enforcers for collecting debts. Since September 1991, the group of students had generated income of one hundred thousand dollars per week from gamblers, including student-athletes. Two University of Rhode Island basketball players were dismissed from the team for gambling on college and professional games.[6]

Despite the increasing number of suspensions, removals from teams, and undoubtedly unreported incidents of athletes gambling, college football players increasingly took calculated risks to gamble on sports. On 10 July 1995, University of Maryland senior quarterback and potential all-American Scott Milanovich was suspended for eight games (reduced to four on appeal) for gambling on college sports; three other players were also suspended, including star receiver Jermaine Lewis, who was barred for one game.[7] The message from the NCAA was that gambling by college athletes would not be tolerated, but that message went unheeded on many occasions.

At a news conference in early December 1998, a week after the sentencing of the participants in the 1994–95 Northwestern University basketball scandal, Scott R. Lassar, U.S. attorney for the Northern District of Illinois, announced the indictment of four Northwestern football players on charges related to game fixing during the 1994 season. The players included leading rusher Dennis Lundy, wide receiver Chris Gamble, and cocaptain Michael Senters. Also indicted later was Gregory Gill, a former Wildcat football player who had graduated in 1993. Lassar stated at the news conference that "these four defendants fumbled their opportunity to participate in intercollegiate athletics and maintain the integrity of athletic competition. . . . Then, they fumbled again and again when they had the obligation to come clean and testify truthfully before a grand jury."[8]

The four-year federal investigation of the football players was connected to the investigation of the Northwestern basketball players for game fixing and the arrest of former Wildcat football player–bookmaker Brian Ballarini. From the fall of 1993 to late 1994, while he was a reserve quarterback, Ballarini accepted wagers on a regular basis from approximately fifteen individuals, including both male and female athletes at Northwestern. In at least two games, Lundy, Senters, and Gamble placed bets with Ballarini on Northwestern to lose by more than the point spread. Ballarini accepted wagers on credit and allowed individuals to defer paying a losing bet until after their next bet, in effect loaning them money to place bets. He also imposed a surcharge, or vigorish, of 10 percent on losing bets.[9]

Lundy was charged with three counts of perjury for giving false testimony to grand juries. In a game against the University of Iowa on 12 November 1994, Northwestern had the ball on Iowa's 1-yard line in the third quarter, behind by 22 points. Lundy had bet that the Wildcats would lose by more than 6 points; if Northwestern scored, the deficit would be cut to 15 with plenty of time left. Lundy fumbled the handoff, and Iowa recovered and went on to win by 36 points. A year later, on 2 November 1995, Lundy testified before the grand jury that he "got hit on the arm real good and the ball just came out."[10] Film replays, however, showed that he had not been touched on the play. Lundy's teammates were aware of his gambling habits, and many of them resented his attitude.[11] Cornerback Rodney Ray, suspecting that the fumble had been intentional, confronted Lundy in a heated exchange overheard by an assistant coach. University officials began an investigation, and head coach Gary Barnett suspended Lundy for the last game of the season, against Penn State. Lundy was also charged with falsely denying that he bet with Ballarini and an unnamed individual that Northwestern would lose by more than the spread against Ohio State on 1 October 1994 and against Notre Dame on 3 September 1994. The final indictment against Lundy charged him with giving false testimony about the allegation that he regularly placed bets with Ballarini on college and professional sports.[12] In early May 1999, after pleading guilty to the perjury charges, each of which carried a maximum penalty of five years and a $250,000 fine, Lundy was sentenced to one month in jail and two years of probation, his sentence reduced because he provided evidence against the other three Wildcat players and because he had begun speaking to athletes at other colleges about the dangers of gambling.[13] He stated that gambling "started kind of innocent. I kind of got into it. I would win one day. I would lose the next. Winning and losing. It overrode anything else I was doing. It just kind of swallowed up my life for two years."[14] He warned other athletes, "You don't want to end up where I am now."[15]

Wide receiver Chris Gamble was charged with two counts of perjury for allegedly giving false testimony to grand juries. A native of Marietta, Georgia, an upscale suburb of Atlanta, Gamble had become addicted to gambling, whether at Las Vegas casinos, at kitchen-table poker games, or on riverboats. On 28 September 1995, he falsely denied betting with at least two other Northwestern football players that the team would lose by more than the point spread to Ohio State; Northwestern played an outstanding game and lost by 2 points instead of the spread of 24, costing Gamble his five-hundred-dollar bet.[16] Other teammates were aware that players were betting against their own team on the game.[17] On 24 July 1997, Gamble falsely denied that he bet several times a week on college football during the fall of 1994 and that he paid 10 percent interest on each losing bet to Ballarini.[18] He accepted a plea bargain on all charges. At his sentencing, prosecutors revealed that he had been involved in introducing Northwestern basketball player Kenneth "Dion" Lee to Kevin Pendergast, who was instrumental in the university's 1994–95 basketball scandal. Gamble was sentenced to two months in prison and three years' probation, and he agreed to speak to athletes at other colleges about his negative experiences with gambling.[19]

Cocaptain Michael Senters, the team's fastest player, leading kick returner, and star receiver, was charged with perjury for giving false testimony to a grand jury about his involvement in placing a five-hundred-dollar bet against his team in the 1994 Ohio State game and about his knowledge that Gamble was betting against the Wildcats in the same game. He also falsely denied placing bets with Ballarini on college and professional sports and that he had personal knowledge of the campus relationship between Ballarini and Gamble.[20] At sentencing, the perjury charge was dropped if he remained trouble-free.

Ex-football player Gregory Gill was charged with falsely testifying that at least one year before the internal university gambling investigation began, he did not have firsthand knowledge that one or more current football players were placing sports wagers with Ballarini. He also falsely testified that beginning no later than the fall of 1993, he had not placed bets with Ballarini, and he denied being aware that Ballarini was booking sports bets. He also denied that from August through November 1994, he discussed sports betting with Ballarini in phone calls placed by Ballarini to his phone.[21] Gill also falsely denied that from at least 1993 through late 1994, he placed bets on college and professional sports with Ballarini for which he paid a 10 percent fee on losing bets; that from at least 1993 through late 1994, he was aware that Ballarini accepted bets; and that during this period, he regularly called Ballarini to place bets. He also denied being aware that one or more of his former teammates had bet that the Wildcats would lose to Ohio State in 1994 by more than the published point spread.[22] Gill was fined five thousand dollars and received probation.

A fifth Northwestern football player, cornerback Dwight Brown, was later indicted for perjury for giving false testimony to a grand jury about placing bets with Ballarini in 1993 and 1994 and about knowing nothing about betting by a roommate. There was no evidence that Brown bet on games when he was a player. He was sentenced to thirty days in jail.[23]

Ballarini cooperated with both the basketball and football investigations and received three months of home electronic monitoring and three years of probation. He was also ordered to speak to athletes about the perils of gambling.[24] Michael Stemberk, an associate of Ballarini's who also cooperated with the investigation, received six months of home probation and three years' probation.[25]

Northwestern administrators and Coach Barnett responded to the football scandal in the time-honored tradition of denial dating back to Nat Holman and Clair Bee. The key difference was that where the players coached by Holman and Bee fixed games to get money to support their families, pay for lavish lifestyles, or other non-gambling-related reasons, the Northwestern players largely used the money to pay off gambling debts to the same people who paid them to fix games. For many of these athletes, gambling and associating with bookies and gamblers had consumed their lives. Still, Barnett stated that "the stain is on the individuals. It's not on us or the school."[26] In 1994, Barnett assuredly knew that his career would have been terminated by any hint that he or his staff of at least eight assistant coaches had even considered that the four players might be rigging games. Although team members suspected or knew about the gambling, Barnett and his coaching staff somehow maintained ignorance. The following year, Barnett would be labeled a "miracle man" as Northwestern posted a 10–1 record that would earn the university a Rose Bowl trip for the first time in forty-seven years.[27] In 1998, he left Northwestern for the University of Colorado, where his program would be accused of illegal recruiting using escort services and prostitutes and conducting parties fueled with alcohol and where a number of women accused football players of rape.[28] In 2004, Barnett was temporarily suspended for his insensitive comments about placekicker Katie Hnida, who alleged that she had been raped by a teammate. In December 2005, he was forced to resign and accepted a three million-dollar buyout.[29]

Northwestern may well have been a "gambling haven," the phrase used by Ballerini's attorney at his client's sentencing. However, it was not the only college campus where serious gambling could lead to extortion, threats, beatings, and academic and financial failure.[30] The temptation for student-athletes to gamble and incur large debts would only increase.

* * *

On 6 November 1996, thirteen members of the Boston College football team were suspended for placing bets with bookies on professional and college sports, including bets against their own team. Rumors of betting had come to a head after the Eagles lost to Syracuse on 26 October by a score of 42–17, when the team heard that sophomore running back Jamall Anderson and defensive end Marcus Bembry had bet that their team would lose by more than the spread.[31] Although neither player had been in a position to affect the outcome of the game, many on the team were shocked, among them co-captain Omari Walker, who reported the rumors to head coach Dan Henning.[32]

Henning called a team meeting and asked anyone who had bet on sports to stand up. No one did. In their 31 October game against the University of Pittsburgh, 11-point favorite Boston College lost, 20–13. After the game, Henning again challenged any player involved in gambling to stand up. Again, no one did. Two days later, Henning asked the team's four cocaptains to try to find out who the gamblers were. Henning also alerted athletic director Chet Gladchuk about the situation, and he in turn informed Middlesex County district attorney Thomas Reilly. At a team meeting without the coaches, twenty-five to thirty players admitted to betting, but no one admitted to betting against the team. The cocaptains later met with the players again; after this meeting, Reilly formally interviewed five players suspected of having bet against the team.[33]

An official investigation was begun. Reilly returned to the campus on 3 November with a team of investigators and, with the players' cooperation, rounded up a number of student bookies from whose lists they identified thirteen football players who had placed bets of between $25 and $5,000 on a variety of sports. The players who bet against the Eagles in the Syracuse game wagered $200 and $250 and won their bets.[34] Following the football season, Gladchuk and Henning resigned.

The Middlesex County district attorney brought no charges against any of the thirteen suspended players. On 15 July 1997, the NCAA ruled that five of the players could return for the 1997 season: one was suspended for the first four games, two others for the first two, and the remaining two were eligible immediately. The exact amount of money and frequency of betting among the players were not disclosed. Another player who petitioned the NCAA for reinstatement of his eligibility for

In November 1996, thirteen members of the Boston College football team were suspended when Middlesex County district attorney Thomas Reilly rounded up several campus bookies whose lists of bettors who had wagered on college and professional sports included two Boston College players who had bet against their team. A more serious revelation uncovered an association between campus bookies and New York City organized crime member James C. Potter, who was also arrested.

the upcoming season suffered a career-ending injury in spring practice. Three players lost their scholarships, and four of the seven remaining players who were suspended had graduated.[35]

In January 1998, Boston College announced that eight seniors involved in illegal bookmaking on campus would be suspended for one year and would not be allowed to complete any coursework toward their degrees. Approximately twenty other students (none football players) had been identified as participating in illegal gambling activity on campus and faced possible disciplinary action. The student bookmakers reported taking in an average of five thousand dollars a week, with student bets as high as sixteen hundred dollars.[36]

A more serious revelation associated with the scandal was its apparent connection with organized crime. In January 1997, Flushing, Queens, resident James C. Potter was arrested for organizing and promoting gambling, using the telephone for gaming purposes, and conspiring to organize and promote gambling. His employee, Timothy J. Doheny, was charged with organizing and promoting gambling and conspiring to organize and promote gambling. Reilly's investigation disclosed that Doheny, of Newton, Massachusetts, took bets and made payoffs at Mary Ann's, a student hangout near the Boston College campus frequented by many Eagle football players, and Potter's associates traveled to and from the campus to collect money from student bookies. One student bookie who owed Potter four thousand dollars was severely beaten; his father paid off the debt. The investigation also uncovered student bookies at nearby Bentley College. In July 1997, Potter, Doheny, and four other individuals were indicted, and all were convicted in February 1998.[37]

In an effort to stem the tide of gambling by student-athletes, the NCAA in 2000 changed its rule on gambling to state, "Any athlete who wagers on his or her own institution or his or her own team is permanently ineligible without the option of appealing."[38] The effectiveness of this rule would be apparent only two years later.

Florida State sophomore Adrian McPherson became the Seminoles' starting quarterback after the team's 34–24 loss to Notre Dame on 26 October 2002. Over the next three games, he led the team to a 3–0 record, demonstrating that he had a promising—and lucrative—future in the National Football League. On 18 November, two days after leading his team to victory against North Carolina, McPherson stole a blank check from an auto accessories shop in Tallahassee and wrote it out for thirty-five hundred dollars to his friend Melvin Capers Jr., who cashed it and gave McPherson all the cash except thirty dollars. McPherson used the money to pay off gambling debts.[39] He admitted the theft to the Florida State coaching staff a day before the game at North Carolina State. The coaching staff allowed him to play, he performed poorly, and the Seminoles lost 17–7. Head coach Bobby Bowden removed McPherson from the team a week later. Investigators discovered that McPherson had been gambling on college and professional football games since his freshman year. He was arrested on 27 November for illegal gambling and grand theft.[40]

McPherson's jury trial on charges of illegal gambling began in June 2003. Two of his closest friends, Capers and Otis Livingston, testified that McPherson had bet on the Internet and with bookies and detailed his extravagantly compulsive gambling.[41] The jury deadlocked on the gambling charge; if McPherson had been found guilty of betting on Florida State's games, he would have been declared permanently ineligible to compete for an NCAA institution. A month after the trial, McPherson pled no contest to the second group of charges of theft, forgery, and gambling. His sentence included ninety days of work camp, thirty months of probation, and fifty hours of community service, and he was ordered to pay four thousand dollars in restitution. McPherson successfully completed all terms of his probation and avoided a criminal record.[42] Derek Delach, a former Florida State student through whom McPherson placed bets, was convicted of four misdemeanor gambling charges and ordered to pay $452 in court costs, attend ten sessions of Gamblers Anonymous, and spend thirty days picking up trash while wearing prison clothes, and he was placed on probation for two years.[43]

McPherson played in the Arena Football League for one year before he was selected in the fifth round of the 2005 NFL draft by the New Orleans Saints. He was subsequently injured by a cart driven by the Titans' raccoon mascot, placed on injured reserve, and released by the Saints in 2007. He was signed by the Montreal Alouettes of the Canadian Football League in May 2008, and he appeared on the team's roster in May 2012.[44]

In December 2002, the Florida State Police Department, Tallahassee Police Department, and the Florida Department of Law Enforcement investigated McPherson's and other students' betting at Tallahassee-area colleges. They questioned thirty individuals, confiscated computers, and subpoenaed cell phone records, credit card transactions, and bank statements. They placed the entire Florida State baseball team under oath and asked the players to fill out a questionnaire about their own and other athletes' sports betting.[45] The resulting eight-hundred-page report, released in the spring of 2003, substantiated the charges against McPherson and questioned the integrity of the Florida State athletic department, where administrators admitted to hearing rumors about McPherson's betting before the 2002 football season. Associate athletic director Robert Minnix was chastised for not turning over to the Florida State University police information that was reported to him about McPherson's gambling, debts, and credit card thefts. Sworn testimony indicated that football manager Jeff Inderhees had reported to director of football operations Andy Urbanic that McPherson had stolen a credit card belonging to Inderhees's girlfriend; Urbanic responded by warning Inderhees not to commit slander against McPherson.[46]

McPherson was so consumed by gambling that he consciously risked a multi-million-dollar future in the National Football League to place relatively small bets with bookies on college and professional sports. The Florida State University athletic department proved less than willing to investigate or address McPherson's compulsion and the widespread gambling by other athletes, demonstrating once again that integrity can take second place to winning games and collecting substantial revenues at the professionalized upper level of NCAA sports.

On 6 May 2009, three former University of Toledo football players and three former Toledo basketball players were indicted in the U.S. district court in Detroit on a number of charges for fixing games for two Detroit-area gamblers. Former Toledo football players Adam Cuomo, Quinton Broussard, and Harvey McDougle Jr. and basketball players Keith Triplett, Anton Currie, and Kashif Payne were alleged to have schemed with gamblers Ghazi Manni and Mitchell Karam to influence the outcome of basketball and football games from December 2004 through December 2006.[47] A fourth basketball player, Sammy Villegas, reached a plea agreement with the federal government and was not indicted. The gamblers had bet approximately $407,000 on seventeen Toledo basketball games between November 2005 and December 2006. No football games were listed on the indictment as part of the alleged rigging. Other charges included using interstate telephone facilities to communicate with the six players and to place bets.[48]

During the 2005 football season, the Las Vegas lines on Toledo's football games moved by 2 points or more on seven games, and each time the bettors who caused the changes won their bets. These line changes became so suspicious that the Nevada State Gaming Control Board investigated two games, but officials found no casino violations and closed the investigation in December. Kenny White, the chief operating officer and head oddsmaker at Las Vegas Sports Consultants, revealed that in 2004, Toledo and another Mid-American Conference team he declined to name drew heavy betting. During the 2005 season, the unusual pattern stopped with the other unnamed team, but not with Toledo. As White's suspicions grew, he watched tapes of all of Toledo's games during the 2004 and 2005 seasons: He and others "couldn't pinpoint a single coach or player, or official. But, we knew something was happening there." White filed verbal reports with the Nevada Gaming Commission and NCAA in the summer of 2006 and believed that the bettors won big. "If they were giving a kid $10,000 to sit a game out, they were probably betting $100,000. . . . I bet if we tracked the roots, it wasn't one guy. Probably 100 people were in on this knowing what the right side was going to be in those games."[49]

On 8 December 2010, a federal prosecutor in Detroit reported that at least four of the athletes charged in the University of Toledo fixing scheme in late 2009 would plead guilty. The four included Cuomo, McDougle, Broussard, and Currie. On 12 January 2011, Cuomo pled guilty, as did McDougle six months later. Broussard was expected to plead guilty in August 2011. Sentencing of all guilty athletes was delayed until after all remaining defendants had been tried. As part of the plea agreements, the athletes agreed to cooperate in the trials of the other defendants. Prosecutors continued to work on plea agreements with gamblers Manni and Karam and former players Triplett and Payne. The former athletes who have pled guilty could face up to five years in prison and a $250,000 fine. Cuomo has admitted to hatching the gambling scheme with Manni.[50]

Because major college gambling scandals have become less frequent in recent years, most followers of college football and basketball seem to feel that when it comes to rigging games, college players cannot be bought at any price. However, college coaches, athletic administrators, and players know that the next rigging scandal is no further away than a wiretap on an individual involved in a criminal act. On 12 April 2011, the FBI and federal authorities announced the indictment of University of San Diego basketball star Brandon Johnson, the team's all-time leader in points and assists; Thaddeus Brown, a San Diego assistant in 2006–7; and Brandy Dowdy, a former University of San Diego and University of California, Riverside, player. Seven others were named. Among the allegations were charges that Johnson accepted a bribe to influence a February 2010 game and recruited another player to influence a January 2011 game. The individuals were charged with conspiracy to commit sports bribery, conducting an illegal gambling business, and distributing marijuana.[51] The FBI had discovered the game fixing in the course of investigating the marijuana distribution ring.

Predictably, the college establishment, including the NCAA, administrators, and coaches, expressed shock, dismay, and disbelief that a rigging scandal could occur at a small Catholic university in the Big West Conference. The rationale presented by college authorities in the 1990s when three members of the Northwestern basketball team were charged with deliberately losing games was, "If it can happen at Northwestern, it can happen anywhere."[52] Today, that rationale should be, "It happened at San Diego, and it's happening somewhere else, too."

AFTERWORD

When the Cost of Winning at All Costs Is Too High

In a November 2010 *ESPN: The Magazine* poll of a sample of college basketball players, one in four stated that they would consider winning by less or losing by more than the point spread in the face of a 40-point blowout.[1] After nearly a century of gambling scandals, major college basketball and football remain rife with social and economic influences that guarantee that more game fixing scandals will occur.

Gambling has become fully integrated into the U.S. entertainment industry. Betting on college and professional sports is just as accepted as voting for a contestant on a televised talent competition, buying a lottery ticket, paying a monthly fee to play an online video game, or guessing which movie will win an Academy Award. Television and radio networks, newspapers, and websites admiringly publicize the vast sums involved in professional sports, from players' multi-million-dollar salaries to owners' billion-dollar contracts with television networks, as well as in college sports—coaches' salaries, merchandising revenue, and television contracts secured by the NCAA, the conferences, and individual programs.

The professionalization of college sports has coincided with increased urbanization, the widespread development of youth sports at the earliest ages, improvements in communications and transportation technology, and easy availability of capital resources. Spectators seeking excitement in college sports emphasize heroic achievement over aesthetic expression and individual success over that of the team in the belief that success in college sports is consistent with educational values. Yet major college sports programs are unique in that their perceived control rests in the hands of the sponsoring institution and the NCAA. Theoretically, the NCAA, in concert with athletic administrators and coaches, ensures that athletes obtain a useful education and are not exploited. The reality is that in the college sports programs where gambling scandals have been documented, the primary goal of the programs has been to maintain power and increase revenue production. The benefactors have been the athletic administrators and coaches, who in many cases earn salaries exceeding the college's highest-paid nonathletic faculty and administrators. The revenue flows not only from ticket sales, broadcasting, and merchandising but also from wealthy individual boosters and corporate sponsors who influence changes in sports practices such as creating the Bowl Championship Series in college football and March Madness in college basketball.

Major college football and basketball programs spend more than half a billion dollars every year to produce teams that will garner a share of media, booster, and sponsor largesse. Athletic departments include large staffs for coaching, advertising, media, recruiting, academic tutoring, and strength training and conditioning. Their state-of-the-art training and playing facilities are surpassed only at the professional level. Athletes who enter this environment are quick to note that their year-round efforts pay for everything, but many of them persist in hopes of a professional career. Their chances are slim: For example, only one in forty college football players will play in the National Football League. College athletes who have spent the majority of their lives preparing for professional careers may be vulnerable to the entreaties of gamblers after realizing that their hopes are in vain. Student gamblers and student bookies are nearly ubiquitous on college campuses, making it inevitable that some athletes will succumb to the lure of rigging games.

Yet the NCAA and colleges continue to respond as if gambling scandals simply fall out of the sky, unwilling to acknowledge the danger until a major scandal exposes it. Although college basketball was tainted by rigged games beginning in the 1930s, the college establishment did not begin to view the problem with alarm until 1951, when the scale of the scandal was no surprise to any insider (except perhaps the major coaches involved). Ten years later, a scandal twice as large showed that fixers had made much greater progress in rigging games than the NCAA had made in preventing it. Destroying the myth of amateur college athletics proved very costly for the players in 1951, with harsh punishments and a lifetime of being scourged in the court of public opinion. With only a few exceptions, the colleges and universities involved ignored and dismissed the dangers of professionalizing their basketball programs, and some even accelerated the process. The athletic establishment and the NCAA labeled the involved players a few bad apples, shielding their widespread corruption just as society's tolerance of gambling and hunger for sports entertainment led to increased gambling pressure and lesser penalties for rigging. That the same organization that has anointed itself the overseer of college sports would virtually ignore and fail to craft effective remedies for a problem that placed the lives of athletes in the crosshairs of organized crime is remarkable. Not until 1998 did the NCAA create a full-time position to address the gambling problem, which by then had become almost insoluble.[2] And the universe of potentially rigged games has grown: By 2000, women's basketball accounted for approximately 10 percent of college basketball betting in Nevada.[3]

Legislators at the state and federal levels have nibbled at the possibility of enacting a statute that makes gambling on college sports illegal in all states.[4] The law would seek to curb a behavior that is accepted as legal in virtually every other professional sports enterprise. And as was the case with Prohibition, driving college gambling underground would only exacerbate the demands on law enforcement, which today does not place a high priority on prosecuting illegal and legal gambling corruption in college sports.

Basketball coaches also failed to stop game rigging, variously claiming that fixing is impossible to detect and that a coach must have complete confidence in his players. Such claims enable coaches to protect their careers and reputations as well as their relationships with wealthy boosters and sponsors. Scandals certainly went unexposed and unrecorded thanks to active or tacit compliance from coaches, and when scandals were exposed, coaches took refuge behind selected sportswriters who kept the public in the dark, blamed the morality of the times and the character flaws of the players, and went to extraordinary lengths to promulgate the myth that college athletics are pure and untainted by corruption.

Since 1961, federal, state, and at times local governments have assumed the lead in investigating and prosecuting gambling in college football and basketball. Federal and state laws increasingly prohibited the bribery of amateur and professional athletes. Still, most scandals were uncovered by accident, usually in connection with the investigation of some other crime. By the 1990s, the FBI and state bureaus of investigation began to view gambling and game rigging by college athletes as increasingly connected to other student problems, including alcoholism, gambling addiction, and drug trafficking.

The fixing of basketball games reported in early April 2011 involving the University of San Diego and the University of California, Riverside, bodes ill for any institution with a professionalized football or basketball program. The easy acceptance of and access to gambling, an environment in which athletes are not paid for the enormous revenue they generate, boosters' under-the-table payoffs to players, blatant recruiting violations, academic fraud, and above all the pressure to win remain immune to reform. Budget cuts have reduced the priority of monitoring and investigating college gambling and game fixing by the FBI and other agencies, threatening the public's assurance that the games they enjoy watching are fair. The budgets of major college football and basketball programs continue to escalate, and NCAA and collegiate preventive mechanisms continue to be limited by the politicized nature of their operations. In presenting lucrative, professionalized entertainment to an insatiable public, college athletic programs have created a mandate to win at all costs. The highest cost is that game fixing scandals will continue to occur.

Notes

Introduction

1. Thelin, *Games Colleges Play*, 1.
2. Quoted in Benagh, *Making It to #1*, 238–39.
3. Quoted in Horn, *University in Turmoil*, 315.
4. Quoted in Telander, *Hundred Yard Lie*, 23.
5. Light, Rutledge, and Singleton, "Betting."
6. Quoted in Francis, "Illegal Gambling."
7. Ibid.
8. Donaghy, *Personal Foul*.

Chapter 1

1. Riess, *City Games*, 107–8.
2. Neil D. Isaacs, *All the Moves*, 31.
3. Weyand, *Cavalcade of Basketball*, 1–41; Neil D. Isaacs, *All the Moves*, 102–8; Bjarkman, *Hoopla*, 1–19.
4. Neil D. Isaacs, *All the Moves*, 149–56.
5. "Wabash Court Star Asked to 'Throw' Game," *Davenport (IA) Democrat and Leader*, 4 February 1927, 24.
6. Davies and Abram, *Betting the Line*, 41–46.
7. Quoted in Vincent, *Mudville's Revenge*, 256.
8. Ibid., 258.
9. Bjarkman, *Hoopla*, 39.
10. Ibid., 23–24.
11. Vincent, *Mudville's Revenge*, 263.
12. Ibid., 265.
13. Ibid., 39.
14. Neil D. Isaacs, *All the Moves*, 80.

15. Figone, "Gambling and College Basketball," 45.
16. Quoted in Rosen, *Scandals of '51*, 28.
17. Quoted in Vincent, *Mudville's Revenge*, 268.
18. Sifakis, *Encyclopedia of Gambling*, 211–12.
19. Budin and Schaller, *Bets, Drugs, and Rock and Roll*, 49–90.
20. Figone, "Jack Molinas," 46–48.
21. Vincent, *Mudville's Revenge*, 273.
22. Bjarkman, *Hoopla*, 341.
23. Boyle, "Brain," 34.
24. Quoted in Davies and Abram, *Betting the Line*, 9.
25. Boyle, "Brain," 34.
26. Quoted in Moldea, *Interference*, 60.
27. Jeffries and Oliver, *Book on Bookies*, 1–59.
28. Quoted in Moldea, *Interference*, 64.
29. Ibid., 61.
30. Ibid.
31. Davies and Abram, *Betting the Line*, 52–57.
32. Ibid.
33. Moldea, *Interference*, 61.
34. Kanfer, *Summer World*, 210–19.
35. Ibid., 215.
36. "Borscht Basketball: The Best U.S. Collegians Play for Catskills Resorts," *Look*, 28 August 1950, 63.
37. John Russell, *Honey Russell*, 12–13.
38. Kanfer, *Summer World*, 211–17.
39. "Oklahoma Cage Star Tells Bribe Offer by Sollazzo," *New York Journal American*, 23 February 1951, 8.
40. Robert Rice, *Business of Crime*, 251–61.
41. "I Told You So: Phog," *Peoria (IL) Journal*, 19 August 1951, 38.
42. Vincent, *Mudville's Revenge*, 274–75.
43. "You Don't Say, by Mac," *Dunkirk (NY) Evening News*, 4 April 1945, 9.
44. Ibid.
45. "I Told You So: Phog," 38.

Chapter 2

1. Quoted in "A Scandal Grows in Brooklyn," *Time*, 12 February 1945, 70.
2. "Report of the Committee on Intercollegiate Basketball to Board of Higher Education," 17 November 1952, 21, Scandals Folder, City College of New York Archives (hereafter referred to as CCNYA).
3. "Judge Blasts Coaches of Cage Fix," *New York Journal-American*, 11 November 1951, 1.
4. Parrott, "School Fires Players," 21.
5. Quoted in "Boys Warned Early in Year Coach Reveals," *Sporting News*, 8 February 1945, 21.
6. Quoted in "Scandal Grows," 70; Lunquist, "Grand Jury to Report," 9.
7. Stanley Cohen, *Game They Played*, 60.

8. Meier, "Garden Games," 10.
9. "Gideonse Tells Why Brooklyn College Is Lax," *New York Herald Tribune*, 14 March 1945, 3.
10. "Scandal Grows," 70; "Brooklyn Pay-Off Blows the Lid Off: Bribes Expose Basketball Gambling," *Newsweek*, 12 February 1945, 78.
11. Daley, "Court Scandal," 24.
12. "Scandal Grows," 70.
13. Peter V. Cacchione to Ordway Tead, 4 February 1945, Athletics Folder, Brooklyn College Archives.
14. Ordway Tead to Peter V. Cacchione, 21 February 1945, in ibid.
15. Nat Holman and Anthony E. Orlando to Dr. Frank S. Lloyd, 12 March 1945, Scandals Folder, CCNYA.
16. "Sports Bribe Bill Sent to Governor," *New York Times*, 17 March 1945, 32.
17. Wilson, "They Took the Back Door," 30.
18. Ibid.
19. Ibid., 148.
20. Ibid., 150.
21. Young, "Bee Stung by Whispers."
22. Iba, "1947 Forecast," 16.
23. Koppett, *24 Seconds to Shoot*, 67.
24. Frank, "Basketball's Big Wheel," 25, 134.
25. Sperber, *Onward to Victory*, 297–98.
26. "Let's Not Duck the Real Issue in Sports Mess," *Saturday Evening Post*, 24 March 1951, 10.
27. Leonard Cohen, "College Authorities Warned," 1.
28. "Report and Recommendations of the Board of Higher Education of the City of New York in the Matter of Charges Preferred against Nat Holman and Robert Sand," 19 February 1954, Scandals Folder, CCNYA.
29. Maude Stewart to CCNY President Harry Wright, 19 January 1948, in ibid.
30. "Gambler Testifies to Suspicion of Garden Games," *New York Times*, 25 March 1951, 1.
31. "Colleges Adopt the 'Sanity Code' to Govern Sports," *New York Times*, 11 January 1948, 21.
32. Ibid., 48; Daley, "Menace to All Sports," 16.
33. Barke and Santora, "Murphy Will Sift Charge," 2.
34. "Data Buried on Order of 'Higher Up,'" *Brooklyn Eagle*, 23 February 1951, 1.
35. Ibid.
36. McFadden, "Lonely Death," 3.
37. "New York: A Bookie in Command," *Time*, 1 October 1951, 53.
38. Grutzner, "Gross' Tale of Graft," 1.
39. "Crime: Listen to the Mocking Bird," *Time*, 19 May 1952, 40.
40. "New York: A Bookie in Command," 53.
41. McFadden, "Lonely Death," 1.
42. Grutzner, "Gross' Borrowing from Police," 1.
43. "New York: A Bookie in Command," 53; Ira Henry Freeman, "New York Police Winding Up Gross Case," *New York Times*, 7 September 1952, E12.
44. "Crime: Listen to the Mocking Bird," 53.

45. Quoted in ibid., 40.
46. McFadden, "Lonely Death," 1.
47. Ibid.

Chapter 3

1. Stanley Cohen, *Game They Played*, 62.
2. "The Fix That Fizzled," *Time*, 17 January 1949, 53.
3. Ibid.
4. Vincent, *Mudville's Revenge*, 53–55.
5. Quoted in ibid.
6. "The Press: Catching the Fix," *Time*, 5 March 1951, 44; Kase, "How Many Scandals?" 36.
7. Quoted in Rosen, *Scandals of '51*, 3.
8. "Don't Stink It Up," *Time*, 29 January 1951, 85; Berger, "Two Ex-Stars Held," 1.
9. Quoted in Berger, "Two Ex-Stars Held," 1.
10. "Sketches of Cage Scandal Principals," *New York Journal-American*, 19 February 1951, 20; "3 CCNY, 4 Others Held in Games Fix," *New York Daily Mirror*, 19 February 1951, 28; Lewin, "Hogan Blasts Garden," 28; "Probe 3 LIU Cagers," *New York Journal-American*, 19 February 1951, 1.
11. Quoted in Lewin, "Hogan Blasts Garden," 28.
12. "Cage Scandal Rocks Nation," *Pittsburgh Courier*, 24 February 1951, 26.
13. Quoted in Lewin, "Hogan Blasts Garden," 28; "Sketches of the Pulitzer Prize Winners in Journalism," *New York Times*, 6 May 1952, 24.
14. Greaves and Williams, "3 LIU Stars Confess Bribes," 1.
15. White, "Basketball Fix," 14.
16. Ibid.; Stanley Cohen, *Game They Played*, 91.
17. Keegan, "Basketball Star," 3; Feinberg, "L.I.U. Star," 1.
18. Stanley Cohen, *Game They Played*, 121–25.
19. "Hunt Up State Boro Man Who Skipped," *Brooklyn Eagle*, 26 February 1951, 6.
20. "Goldsmith, Former L.I.U. Player, Indicted in Basketball Fix Here," *New York Times*, 24 April 1951, 25.
21. "Stars Plead Guilty in Cage Fixing Case," *Chicago Defender*, 14 July 1951, 18.
22. Quoted in Rosen, *Scandals of '51*, 134.
23. Quoted in Woodward, "Basketball Betting," 14.
24. Williams, "Bank President Explains," 64.
25. "2 Ex-Dons Cagers Bare 'Dump' Bids," *New York Daily Mirror*, 2 February 1951, 36.
26. Rosen, *Scandals of '51*, 148.
27. Figone, "Gambling and College Basketball"; "TU Athletic Board to Meet Today in Basketball Scandal," *Toledo Times*, 26 July 1951, 1; Steve Senn, "Toledo Takes TU Scandal in Stride," *Toledo Times*, 25 July 1951, 18.
28. Jones, "Cagers Named," 1.
29. "Holy Toledo! Another 'Fix' Charge," *San Francisco Call Bulletin*, 27 July 1951, 12.

30. Ibid.; "Two More TU Players Named in Basketball Fix," *Toledo Blade*, 27 July 1951, 1; "TU Disciplinary Board Calls McDonald," *Toledo Times*, 27 July 1951, 15.

31. "Bradley U. Basketball Stars Admit Accepting Bribes," 1.

32. "2 'Small Fry' Held in Basketball Fix," *New York Times*, 1 August 1951, 16.

33. "Jack West Is Held in Basketball Fix," *New York Times*, 7 September 1951, 23.

34. "Benintende, Alleged Head of Cage Fixers, Arrested," *Alton (IL) Evening Telegraph*, 16 October 1951, 12.

35. "Fixer Acts to Stop Husband's 'Revolt,'" *Peoria (IL) Journal*, 26 July 1951, 1.

36. "St. Joseph's Game in Detail," *Peoria (IL) Journal*, 26 July 1951, 1.

37. Ibid.

38. "Eye More Schools in Quiz," *Chicago Daily News*, 27 July 1951, 45; "Melchiorre of Bradley, 6 Gamblers Indicted, but 3 Players Escape Basketball Fix Charge," *New York Times*, 15 September 1951, 6.

39. "Melchiorre of Bradley, 6 Gamblers Indicted," 6.

40. "3 Kentucky Greats Confess Fix," *Peoria (IL) Journal*, 20 October 1951, 1.

41. Quoted in Rosen, *Scandals of '51*, 178.

42. Nelli, "Adolph Rupp," 51–56.

43. Russell Rice, *Adolph Rupp*, 111.

44. Tony Englisis with Jimmy Breslin, "How I Fixed Big Basketball Games," *True*, 25 March 1952, 17.

45. Rosen, *Scandals of '51*, 189–91.

46. Nelli, "Adolph Rupp," 64–67.

47. Quoted in ibid., 64.

48. "Remarks of Assistant District Attorney Vincent A. G. O'Connor in Moving the Dismissal of the Perjury Indictment against William G. Spivey," 15 April 1953, 1, Basketball Folder, University of Kentucky Archives (hereafter referred to as UKA).

49. Minutes of the Meeting of the Board of Directors of the University of Kentucky Athletics Association, 2 March 1952, 6, UKA; Nelli, "Adolph Rupp," 65.

50. Murray, "Athletics' Victim," 49.

51. Albert J. Figone, "Gambling Scandals in College Basketball and the Reaction of Coaches: Powerlessness of Selective Inattention?," paper presented at the North American Society for the Sociology of Sport Conference, San Antonio, Texas, 10 November 2000; Woodward, "Basketball Betting"; "Kentucky Schedule, 1952–53," 26 January 2011, http://www.bigbluehistory.net/bb/Statistics/1952–53.html, accessed 5 June 2012.

52. "Bradley U. Basketball Stars Admit Accepting Bribes," 1.

53. "Lifting the Curtain," *Time*, 3 December 1951, 86.

54. Rosen, *Scandals of '51*, 194, 206.

55. "Lifting the Curtain," 86.

56. "Judge Forgives Three Athletes—Blasts Bradley U.," *Mt. Vernon (IL) Register-News*, 7 December 1951, 6.

57. "Sport: Degrading and Shocking," *Time*, 12 May 1952, 55.

58. Figone, "Jack Molinas," 45.

59. Ibid.

Chapter 4

1. "Football Is a Farce," *Life*, 17 September 1951, 54; "West Point Bars 90 Ousted Cadets," *New York Times*, 28 November 1951, 20.

2. "Lifting the Curtain," *Time*, 3 December 1951, 86; Mays, "Students May Have to Show Us," 21.

3. Quoted in "Basketball v. Learning (Education)," *Time*, 17 December 1951, 56.

4. "Lifting the Curtain," 86.

5. "Football Is a Farce"; "Judge Blasts Coaches of Cage Fix," *New York Journal-American*, 11 November 1951, 1; Lewin, "Has Basketball Really Cleaned House?" 12.

6. Quoted in Hobson, "How to Stop Those Basketball Scandals," 26.

7. Stanley Cohen, "1951 Basketball Scandals," S2.

8. Quoted in Rosen, *Scandals of '51*, 243, 253.

9. Clark, "Judge in Fix," 1.

10. Small, "Crafty Wizard," 23.

11. Thelin, *Games Colleges Play*, 116–27.

12. Donovan, *Keeping the University Free and Growing*, 140–44.

13. Quoted in Thelin, *Games Colleges Play*, 119–21.

14. Griffenhagen and Associates, Division of Education Studies, Report No. 7: University of Kentucky, 2 vols. (Commonwealth of Kentucky, April 7, 1947), 13, UKA.

15. Thelin, *Games Colleges Play*, 119–21.

16. Ibid.

17. H. C Willett, President, NCAA, to H. L. Donovan, 22 October 1952, 18, H. L. Donovan Papers, UKA.

18. Ibid., 115.

19. Kefauver, "I Meet the King," 30.

20. Nelli, "Adolph Rupp," 70.

21. Bjarkman, *Hoopla*, 177–79.

22. "Kentucky to Keep Coach Rupp Despite Basketball Disclosures," *New York Times*, 5 November 1952, 56.

23. Hobson, "How to Stop Those Basketball Scandals," 65.

24. Quoted in Russell Rice, *Adolph Rupp*, 112.

25. Hobson, "How to Stop Those Basketball Scandals," 65.

26. Quoted in Russell Rice, *Adolph Rupp*, 55.

27. Clark, "Judge in Fix," 1.

28. Moldea, *Interference*, 60.

29. Rice, *Adolph Rupp*, 87.

30. Quoted in Eskenazi, "Kentucky's Baron," 76.

31. "Kentucky Pledges Athletic Reforms," *New York Times*, 7 May 1952, 8.

32. H. L. Donovan to Adolph Rupp, 12 August 1952, 8, Kentucky to Keep Coach Rupp, 12 August 1952, 56, both in H. L. Donovan Papers, UKA.

33. Neil D. Isaacs, *All the Moves*, 67–68; Kenneth T. Jackson, *Encyclopedia of New York*, 13–15.

34. Stanley Frank, "Basketball's Holman: Easy Doesn't Do It," *Collier's*, 18 February 1950, 19.

35. Frank, "Basketball's Holman," 19; Rosen, *Scandals of '51*, 109, Bjarkman, *Hoopla*, 63–68.
36. Quoted in Rosen, *Scandals of '51*, 65.
37. Bjarkman, *Hoopla*, 63–68.
38. "I Just Can't Believe It: Holman," *New York Post*, 19 February 1951, 1.
39. Quoted in Gross, "Speaking Out," 46.
40. Burton, "Coaches Can Clean It Up," 55.
41. Ibid.
42. Bee, "Coach's Judgment Not Infallible."
43. Gross, "Speaking Out," 4.
44. Parker, "Judge Targets Coaches," 21.
45. Quoted in Stanley Cohen, "Game They Played," 115.
46. Quoted in Rosen, *Scandals of '51*, 105.
47. Viuker, "When Gambling Nearly Destroyed College Hoops."
48. Statement on the Cases, 1–5, Scandals Folder, CCNYA.
49. Quoted in Stanley Cohen, *Game They Played*, 91.
50. Statement on the Cases, 1–5, Scandals Folder, CCNYA.
51. Board of Education, "In the Matter of Charges Presented against Nat Holman and Harry Robert Sand," 2 March 1953, 1–40, Scandals Folder, CCNYA; "Lloyd Quits CCNY in Action Growing Out of Scandal," *Syracuse (NY) Post-Standard*, 28 May 1953, 27.
52. Board of Education, "In the Matter of Charges"; Separate Statement of Porter R. Chandler, 24 February 1954, 1–40, Scandals Folder, CCNYA.
53. "Holman Ousted at City College," *New York Times*, 6 March 1954, 1.
54. Stanley Cohen, *Game They Played*, 89.
55. Daley, "Caesar Was Ambitious," 42; Abramson, "One Man's Fight, 115.
56. "A Basketball Team That Stood Up," *Time*, 4 August 2008.
57. "Sport: LIU's Buzzer," *Time*, 15 January 1951, 76.
58. Woodward, "Basketball Betting," 76.
59. Stanley Cohen, *Game They Played*, 131–34.
60. Grutzner, "Impact of Athletics," 3.
61. White, "Basketball Fix," 14.
62. Bee, *Championship Ball*, 42.
63. Stanley Cohen, *Game They Played*, 124.
64. White, "Basketball Fix," 14;
65. "College Basketball: When Sherman White Threw It Away," Associated Press, 19 March 1980, 3.
66. Bee and Frank, "I Know Why They Sold Out," 27.
67. Ibid.
68. Ibid.
69. Bee and Jacobs, "Cage Coach," 12.
70. Quoted in Gildea, "Muckraking for a Young Audience," 14.

Chapter 5

1. Quoted in Ronald A. Smith, *Play-by-Play*, 179.
2. Bernstein, *Football*, 19, 44.

3. Quoted in Betts, *America's Sporting Heritage*, 211.
4. Bernstein, *Football*, 37.
5. Quoted in ibid., 73.
6. Betts, *America's Sporting Heritage*, 68.
7. Schmidt, *Shaping College Football*, 39–40.
8. Ibid., 69; Riffenburgh and Clary, *Official History*, 9–17.
9. McDonough et al., *75 Seasons*, 28–29.
10. Watterson, *College Football*, 151–52.
11. "Ten Notre Dame and Nine Illinois Gridiron Stars Take Part in 'Clean Out' Battle," *Hartford (CT) Courier*, 29 January 1922, Z2.
12. Schmidt, *Shaping College Football*, 68.
13. Ibid., 58–59.
14. Quoted in ibid., 56.
15. Ronald A. Smith, *Play-by-Play*, 15–17.
16. Ibid, 45.
17. Ibid, 51.
18. Powers, *Super Tube*, 32–33.
19. Schmidt, *Shaping College Football*, 45–61.
20. "Centre Conquers Harvard, 6 to 0," *New York Times*, 30 October 1921, 1; "Centre Only Team from Afar to Defeat Harvard," *Boston Globe*, 7 October 1927, 29.
21. Quoted in Ziegler, "C6-Ho."
22. Ibid.
23. Pritchard, "Substitute for Football."
24. Carlson, "Major Ramifications in McPherson Trial," 10.
25. "Dartmouth Head Sees Sports in Poor Shape," *Syracuse (NY) Herald*, 17 April 1926, 32.
26. "Calls Betting a Menace," *New York Times*, 30 October 1920, 27.
27. Cox, "Was 'the Gipper' for Real?" 130.
28. Quoted in ibid., 132.
29. Ibid.
30. "Atlanta Gambling Injures Football," *New York Times*, 31 October 1931, 43.
31. "High Standards in Athletics Is Set by Colleges," *Chicago Defender*, 21 April 1921, 11.
32. Thelin, *Games Colleges Play*, 23–24.
33. "College Sports Tainted by Bounties, Carnegie Fund Finds in Wide Study," *New York Times*, 24 October 1929, 1; Thelin, *Games Colleges Play*, 24–37.
34. Miller, *Truth about Big-Time Football*, 74–76.
35. Pritchard, "Substitute for Football," 447.
36. Schwartz, *Roll the Bones*, 337.
37. "The Press and the Gambling Craze," *Christian Century*, 24 September 1930, 1142.
38. "College Grid Gambling Not Serious: Tiny," *Oakland Tribune*, 30 January 1933, 8.
39. "Badger Predicts Death of Football," *New York Times*, 15 December 1935, 1.
40. "Football Betting Scored by Harman," *New York Times*, 30 October 1935, 26.
41. "Survey Discloses Gambling Mania Threatens to Undermine Football," *New York Times*, 29 October 1935, 24.

42. "Pig Skin Game: Football's Newest By-Product," *Saturday Evening Post*, 8 February 1936, 67.

43. "Before It's Too Late," *El Paso Herald*, 20 December 1951, 16.

44. Ibid.; "Army-Navy Game Will Be the Last for Indefinite Period," *New York Times*, 31 December 1946, 57.

45. Sperber, *Onward to Victory*, 161.

46. "Pro Careers End for 2 Giant Backs," *New York Times*, 4 April 1947, 27.

47. "College Football Games Rated by Tipsters for Benefit of Gamblers, Prosecutor Says," *New York Times*, 18 December 1946, 34.

48. "Student Accused of Attempt at Maryland Football Bribe," *New York Times*, 30 October 1952, 1; *Glickfield v. State*, No. 46, October Term, 1953, Maryland Court of Appeals Reports, Decided 10 December 1953.

49. Kirby, *Fumble*, 20–30.

50. Ibid., 48–50.

51. Quoted in ibid., 31–33.

52. Quoted in ibid., 33.

53. "Records Show Butts Had Talked with Gamblers Prior to Alabama Game," *Tucson (AZ) Daily Citizen*, 28 March 1963, 51.

54. Kirby, *Fumble*, 28.

55. Sharnik and Creamer, "Rough Day for the Bear," 43.

56. Ibid., 44.

57. Kirby, *Fumble*, 36.

58. Ibid., 47–48.

59. Ibid., 48–49.

60. Graham, "Story of a College Football Fix."

61. Paul Bryant and John Underwood, "Black Days after a Black Charge," *Sports Illustrated*, 5 September 1966, 28.

62. Friedrich, *Death Struggle*, 29.

63. Furman Bisher, "College Football Is Going Berserk," *Saturday Evening Post*, 20 October 1962, 20–21.

64. Kirby, *Fumble*, 55–58; Graham, *Farewell*.

65. Graham, "Story of a College Football Fix," 80–88.

66. "Scandalous Notes," *Sports Illustrated*, 8 April 1963, 45.

67. "Butts Is Accused of Phone Calls to Gamblers," *New York Times*, 28 March 1963, 16; "Georgia Upholds Charge Butts Gave Football Team Secrets to Alabama," *New York Times*, 3 April 1963, 53; "Butts Evidence Called Limited," *New York Times*, 9 April 1963, 80; "Says Ex-Georgia Coach Did Talk with Gamblers," *Chicago Defender*, 28 March 1963, 45.

68. "Butts of Georgia Passes a Lie Test," *New York Times*, 21 March 1963, 15; "Burnett Offers to Take 'Truth Serum,'" *Clovis (NM) Journal*, 21 March 1963, 8.

69. Quoted in Kirby, *Fumble*, 68.

70. Bryant and Underwood, "Black Days after a Black Charge."

71. Ibid., 61–72.

72. *Curtis Publishing Company v. Butts, Butts v. Curtis Publishing Company*, No. 21491, U.S. Court of Appeals, Fifth Circuit. 16 July 1965; Rehearing Denied 1 October 1965.

73. "Trippi, Jordan, Take Stand in Butts' Suit," *Rome (GA) News-Tribune*, 12 August 1963, 1–2.

74. "Butts Jury Lost Little Time Deciding on Libel," *Chicago Defender*, 22 August 1963, A32; "The Press: $3,060,000 Worth of Guilt," *Time*, 30 August 1963, 34; Robert H. Boyle, "It's Not the Money, It's the Vindication," *Sports Illustrated*, 2 September 1963, 32.
75. Kirby, *Fumble*, 123.
76. Quoted in ibid., 141.
77. "Butts Jury Lost Little Time," A32; "The Press," 34; Boyle, "It's Not the Money," *Sports Illustrated*, 32.
78. *Curtis v. Butts*, 1965.
79. Kirby, *Fumble*, 149; Bryant and Underwood, *Bear*, 219–46.
80. McCarthy, "Point-Shaving."

Chapter 6

1. Rosen, *Wizard of Odds*, 76; Keidan, "Fixer."
2. Alfieri, *Joe Lapchick*, 191–208.
3. Quoted in Jacobson, *Sports in America*, 127–28.
4. "Belatedly, Missouri Valley Conference Takes a Stand," *Sports Illustrated*, 20 May 1957, 57.
5. Lou Brown and Herbert, "I Worked with Basketball's No. 1 Briber."
6. Ibid.
7. Cave, "Portrait of a Fixer," 8, 23.
8. Quoted in Rosen, *Wizard of Odds*, 195.
9. Lou Brown and Herbert, "I Worked with Basketball's No. 1 Briber," 80.
10. Ibid.
11. Jeffries and Oliver, *Book on Bookies*, 93–109.
12. Quoted in "Ivy Tinge to Cage Fixes," *Oneonta (NY) Star*, 20 June 1961, 8.
13. Quoted in Rosen, *Wizard of Odds*, 224.
14. Ron Morris, "Scandal," 34.
15. Ibid.
16. Leveton, "Coolest Guy," 84.
17. "Betting Ring in Springfield, IL, Investigated," *Oneonta (NY) Star*, 9 March 1959, 10.
18. "Dentist Answers 'Fix' Charges," *Chicago Defender*, 24 December 1959, 28.
19. "Basketball 'Fix' Ghost Returns," *Montana Standard*, 2 March 1960, 9; "Heavy Betting Causes Suspicion," *Arizona Republic*, 2 March 1960, 44.
20. Quoted in Breslin, "Untold Facts," 223.
21. Cohane, "Irresponsible Recruiting," 84–86.
22. Wolf, *Foul!*, 87.
23. Ibid., 85–93.
24. Ibid., 127–28.
25. Frauenheim, "Flying with Hawk," 47.
26. Quoted in "A League of His Own: Former Pacers Star Roger Brown Left Behind a Legacy as the Ultimate ABA Player," *Sports Illustrated*, 17 March 1997, 18.
27. P. Miller, "Ken Keating vs. Frank Hogan—The Man with Experience," *Rochester Times-Union*, 30 August 1958.
28. Cohane, "Irresponsible Recruiting," 91.
29. "Cage Scandal Is Spreading," *Palm Beach Post*, 30 January 1961, 23.

30. "Arthur, What Did You Do?" *Sports Illustrated*, 10 March 1986, 56.
31. Quoted in ibid.
32. Ibid.
33. Ibid., 58, 56.
34. Ibid., 56.
35. Cave, "Portrait of a Fixer," 8, 23.
36. Ibid., 22, 23; "N.C.A.A. Penalizes St. Joseph's in Aftermath of Betting Scandal," *New York Times*, 16 August 1961, 65.
37. Lou Brown and Herbert, "I Worked with Basketball's No. 1 Briber," 82.
38. Ibid.
39. "Athlete Points Out Gambler at Hearing as Offerer of Bribe to Fix Game," *New York Times*, 9 September 1961, 1.
40. "Three Players Charged with Bribe Acceptance," *Troy (NY) Times Standard*, 18 March 1961, 12.
41. "2 Seized in College Basketball Bribery; Nation-Wide Fixing of Games Indicated," *New York Times*, 18 March 1961, 18.
42. Quoted in Breslin, "Fix Was On," 18.
43. Jack Roth, Molinas Indicted in Basketball Fix," *New York Times*, 18 May 1962, 64.
44. Ibid.
45. "Sudden Letdown Laid to Molinas," *New York Times*, 11 January 1961, 30.
46. Rosen, *Wizard of Odds*, 284.
47. Budin and Schaller, *Bets, Drugs, and Rock and Roll*, 24–36.
48. Grutzner, "Basketball Fixer Aids Race Inquiry," 7.
49. Rosen, *Wizard of Odds*, 409.
50. Quoted in Ron Morris, "Scandal," 34.
51. William H. Beezly, "The 1961 Scandal at North Carolina State and the End of the Dixie Classic," *Arena Review: The Institute for Sport and Social Analysis* 7 (1983): 33–52.
52. Ibid., 40.
53. "Indict 10 in Fix Scandal," *Chicago Defender*, 10 January 1962, 23.
54. "Basketball Fixer Is Given 18 Months in North Carolina," *New York Times*, 7 December 1962, 45.
55. Teitelbaum, *Sports Heroes*, 88.
56. "College Administrators Shocked by Scope of Basketball Scandal," *New York Times*, 25 May 1951, 30; Cohane, "Irresponsible Recruiting," 84.
57. Figone, "Jack Molinas."

Chapter 7

1. Chris Dufrense, "The Dark Side of the UCLA Basketball Dynasty," *Los Angeles Times*, 8 June 2010, 75.
2. "Sport: A Patron Called Papa Sam," *Time*, 25 February 1974, 78.
3. Yaeger, *Undue Process*, 41–50.
4. "Pick Casale Fix Jury," *Chicago Daily Defender*, 25 August 1965, 36.
5. Fried, "Ex-Player and 4 Are Indicted," D23; Douglas S. Looney, "The Cast of Characters in the BC Caper," *Sports Illustrated*, 16 February 1981, 14.
6. Fried, "Ex-Player and 4 Are Indicted," D23.

7. Looney, "Cast of Characters," 14.
8. Ibid., 14.
9. Figone, "1978–79 Point-Shaving Scandal."
10. Porter, *Fixed*, 11–13.
11. Quoted in Hill and Looney, "How I Put the Fix In," 22.
12. Porter, *Fixed*, 11–13.
13. Ibid., 40.
14. Ibid.
15. Ibid., 50.
16. Looney, "Cast of Characters," 14.
17. Maitland, "Basketball Inquiry Is Widened"; *Molinas v. National Basketball Association.*
18. Porter, *Fixed*, 43–44.
19. Strauss, "Witness Tells of Bribe," B18.
20. Porter, *Fixed*, 61.
21. Hill and Looney, "How I Put the Fix In," 12.
22. Ibid.
23. Stan Isaacs, "College Scandals," E2.
24. Jane Gross, "Coach Says He Investigated Shaving in '79," *New York Times*, 23 January 1981, A17.
25. Quoted in Porter, *Fixed*, 67.
26. Quoted in Hill and Looney, "How I Put the Fix In," 12.
27. Porter, *Fixed*, 70.
28. Ibid., 73.
29. Hill and Looney, "How I Put the Fix In," 12.
30. Ibid.; Gross, "Coach Says He Investigated," A17.
31. Hill and Looney, "How I Put the Fix In," 12.
32. Porter, *Fixed*, 84.
33. Byers and Hammer, *Unsportsmanlike Conduct*, 48–51.
34. Stan Isaacs, "College Scandals," E2.
35. Porter, *Fixed*, 88.
36. Quoted in ibid.
37. Strauss, "Informant Tells Court," B19.
38. Quoted in Porter, *Fixed*, 92.
39. Strauss, "Informant Tells Court," B19.
40. Porter, *Fixed*, 97.
41. Hill and Looney, "How I Put the Fix In," 12.
42. *U.S. v. Mazzei*, 700 F.2d 85 C.A.2 (N.Y.), 1983.
43. "Five Charged in Point Shaving Scheme," *Baltimore Afro-American*, 8 August 1981, 9.
44. Maitland, "Fix Suspect Indicted," B13; Fried, "Ex-Player and 4 Are Indicted," D23.
45. Porter, *Fixed*, 138–39.
46. *United States of America, Appellee, v. James Burke, Anthony Perla, Rocco Perla, and Richard Kuhn, Defendants-Appellants*, U.S. Court of Appeals for the Second Circuit, 700 F.2d 70, argued 20 September 1982, decided 28 January 1983.
47. Strauss, "Informant Tells Court," B19.
48. Strauss, "Witness Tells of Bribe," B18.

49. *U.S. v. Mazzei*, 700 F.2d 85 C.A.2 (N.Y.).

50. "Motion to Dismiss Shave Charge against Ex-Player Is Denied," *New York Times*, 4 November 1981, B8.

51. "Shave Trial Nears End," *New York Times*, 19 November 1981, B13.

52. Visser, "Threat by Kuhn Alleged," 1.

53. "F.B.I. Agent Says Player Confessed," *New York Times*, 10 November 1981, B20; John Radosta, "Summations Completed in Point-Shaving Trial," *New York Times*, 20 November 1981, B8.

54. "Conflicts Raised in Fix Trial," *New York Times*, 17 November 1981, C16.

55. Visser, "Coach Saw No Intent," 1; Radosta, "Summations Completed," B8.

56. Kindred, "BC Case," D1; Visser, "Kuhn Receives Landmark 10-Year Sentence," 1.

57. Quoted in Porter, *Fixed*, 205.

58. "Kuhn's Sentence Is Reduced from 10 to Four Years," *Bowling Green (KY) Daily News*, 17 April 1984, 3B.

59. Ibid., 215.

60. "Witness Line Up in Ernie Cobb Point Shaving Trial," *Boston Herald*, 14 March 1984, 72; Visser, "Sweeney Named," 29; Fried, "U.S. Hoping Kuhn Will Aid," B19.

61. Gordon, "Cobb Trial Heads for Jury," 64.

62. Borges, "Cobb Innocent of Point-Shaving," 1, 27.

63. *Sports Wagering Information Packet* (Indianapolis: National Collegiate Athletic Association, 1997), 4–5; Carlson, "Major Ramifications," 10.

Chapter 8

1. Bryant and Underwood, *Bear*, 325–26.

2. Alice Walsh, "Green Wave's Class of 85: The Way Things Used to Be," *New Orleans Times-Picayune*, 11 April 1985, C-1.

3. Keteyian, "Time for Harsh Measures," 67.

4. Goodwin, "Player Says Coach," 15.

5. "4 Charged with Fixing TU Games," *New Orleans Times-Picayune*, 27 March 1985, 1.

6. "Players Got $18,000, Sources Say," *New Orleans Times-Picayune*, 30 March 1985, 1.

7. Philbin, "TU Player, Students Given Probation," A-17.

8. "Jury Declares Williams Innocent in Tulane Bribery Case," *Boston Globe*, 17 June 1986, 70.

9. Malcolm Moran, "Frieder Finds Himself in Role of Wallflower," *New York Times*, 31 March 1989, 63.

10. Stevin Smith and Yaeger, "Confessions of a Point Shaver," 92.

11. Ibid.

12. Keteyian, "NCAA 'Hedake,'" 28.

13. Ibid.

14. Magruder, "Arizona St. Players Plead Guilty," D01.

15. Stevin Smith and Yeager, "Confessions of a Point Shaver," 92; "Outside the Lines: Anatomy of a Fix," espn.com, 31 March 2002, http://espn.go.com/page2/tvlistings/show105transcript.html, accessed 2 June 2012.

16. "Five Men Sentenced in ASU Point Shaving Scandal," CNNSI.com, 22 June 1999, http://sportsillustrated.cnn.com/basketball/college/news/1999/06/21/pointshaving_scandal/, accessed 3 May 2012.

17. "Ex-Arizona State Player Gets 1-Year Term," *Chicago Sun-Times*, 15 November 1999, 76.

18. Figone, "'Student-Bookies.'"

19. Lighty, "Former Northwestern Basketball Player," 87.

20. Quoted in Couch, "Teammate," 116.

21. Lighty, "Former Northwestern Basketball Player," 87.

22. Dizon, "Players Get Prison Time"; "Ex-Northwestern Players Sentenced For Fixing," *Las Vegas Review*, 25 November 1998, 33.

23. Lighty, "Former Northwestern Basketball Player," 87.

24. Figone, "'Student-Bookies.'"

25. Layden, "Bettor Education," 114.

26. Buckley, "Nation Raising," 1.

Chapter 9

1. Slavin, "'Las Vegas Loophole,'" 731.
2. Ibid., 716–19, 720–29.
3. Blinn-Pike, Worthy, and Jonkman, "Disordered Gambling."
4. Coakley, *Sport in Society*, 344–46.
5. Sullivan, "Gambling, Payoffs, and Drugs," 41.
6. "Rhode Island Focus of Inquiry," *New York Times*, 28 February 1992, B13.
7. Nakamura, "Partial Reprieve for Terp," F01.
8. Dedman, "College Football," 56.
9. Houlihan-Skilton, "Ballarini Puts Blame on NU," 45; Couch, "NU," 140.
10. Dedman, "College Football," 56.
11. Telander, "Gambling Scandal Casts Die," 110.
12. Dedman, "College Football," 56.
13. O'Connor and Lighty, "Intentional Fumble," 1; Mark Brown, "Lundy Gets Six Months in Jail," 124.
14. Quoted in O'Connor and Lighty, "Intentional Fumble," 141.
15. Morrissey, "Lundy Tells Other Athletes," 1.
16. Dedman, "College Football," 56.
17. Telander, "Gambling Scandal Casts Die," 110.
18. Dedman, "College Football," 56.
19. O'Connor, "Another Guilty Plea," 1.
20. Ibid., 5.
21. Ibid.
22. Ibid.
23. Mark Brown, "NU Gambling Probe Widens," 138.
24. Sampson and Couch, "Feds Probe '94 Gambling," 1; O'Connor, "FBI Probe at NU," 1.
25. O'Connor, "Another Guilty Plea," 1.
26. Mariotti, "Barnett Must Accept His Role," 238.
27. Boyles and Guido, *USA Today College Football Encyclopedia*, 576.
28. "Grand Jury Hears Testimony Involving Colorado Recruiting Scandal,"

USAToday.com, 21 May 2004, http://www.usatoday.com/sports/college/football/big12/2004–05–21-colorado-grand-jury_x.htm, accessed 3 May 2012.

29. Schaller, "Barnett's Up-and-Down Tenure Is Over," 1.

30. Rhoden, "College-Level Gambling Growing," 3; "Gambling on Campus a Big Deal," *Crystal City (IL) Northwest Herald*, 20 September 1998, 1.

31. Callaghan, "Dark Days at BC," 46.

32. Ibid.

33. Ibid., 47.

34. Strosnider, "Boston College Is Embroiled," A51.

35. Golen, "BC Players Get New Suspensions."

36. Haworth, "Boston College Announces Punishment," A34.

37. Ellen O'Brien, "BC Gambling Probe Ends," 1.

38. Carlson, "Major Ramifications," 10.

39. Ibid.

40. Mooney, "Fall of Adrian McPherson," 1.

41. "College Football; F.S.U. Quarterback Gambled, Friend Says," *New York Times*, 5 June 2003, 45.

42. Murphy, "Uncomfortable with McPherson," 1.

43. "Bookmaker Pleas in McPherson Gambling Charge," *Associated Press*, 22 August 2003.

44. Montreal Alouettes website, http://en.montrealalouettes.com/roster/index/team/9/sort/last, accessed 1 June 2012.

45. Rosica and Ellis, "Cops Probe Betting Reports," 1B.

46. Carlson, "F.S.U. Had Indications," 1.

47. "Eight Charged with Point Shaving at Toledo," *USA Today*, 7 May 2009, 1.

48. Fish and Tanber, "As Summer Ends."

49. Tanber, "Oddsmaker with Suspicions."

50. Zack Silka, "Former UT Player Guilty in Bribery," *Toledo (OH) Blade*, 19 July 2011, 52; "Pleas Expected in Toledo Scandal," *Associated Press*, 8 December 2010, http://sports.espn.go.com/espn/news/story?id=5899329, accessed 3 May 2012; "Not-Guilty Pleas for Michigan Man, Former UT Guard in Point Shaving Scheme, *Associated Press*, 12 May 2009, http://www.toledoblade.com/UT/2009/05/12/Not-guilty-pleas-for-Michigan-man-former-UT-guard-in-point-shaving-scheme.html, accessed 5 June 2012.

51. Brennan, "Betting Scandal Makes USD Coach Sick."

52. Doyle and Albach, "Campus Sports Betting," 64.

Afterword

1. Quoted in Norlander, "According to *ESPN the Magazine*."

2. Bud Withers, "NCAA Gambling Director Saum Reassigned," *Seattle Times*, 22 April 2005, 55.

3. Daniel Seligman, "Taste: At Odds with Odds—Is Wagering on College Sports under Attack? You Bet; But Why?" *Wall Street Journal*, 24 November 2000, W15.

4. Ira Berkow, "Gamblers at Odds with U.N.L.V.," *New York Times*, 31 March 1990, 45.

Bibliography

Abadinski, Howard. *Organized Crime*. Chicago: Nelson-Hall, 1990.

Abrams, Roger I. *The Dark Side of the Diamond: Gambling, Violence, Drugs, and Alcoholism in the National Pastime*. Burlington, MA: Rounder, 2007.

Abramson, Martin. "One Man's Fight for Justice: The Strange Case of Basketball's Nat Holman." Long *Beach (CA) Independent Press-Telegram*, 6 February 1955.

Adler, Patricia A., and Peter Adler. *Backboards and Blackboards: College Athletics and Role Engulfment*. New York: Columbia University Press, 1991.

Adolph Rupp: Myth, Legend, and Fact. DVD. Team Marketing, 2006.

Albom, Mitch. *Fab Five: Basketball, Trash Talk, the American Dream*. New York: Warner, 1993.

Alfieri, Gus. *Joe Lapchick: The Life of a Legendary Player and Coach in the Glory Days of Basketball*. Guilford, CT: Lyons, 2006.

Algeo, Matthew. *Last Team Standing: How the Steelers and the Eagles—the Steagles—Saved Pro Football during World War II*. Cambridge, MA: Da Capo, 2006.

Allen, Frederick Lewis. *Only Yesterday: An Informal History of the 1920s*. New York: Harper, 1931.

———. *Since Yesterday: The 1930s in America: September 3, 1929–September 3, 1939*. New York: Harper and Row, 1939.

Anti-Crime Legislation, 1950–1964 Legislative Chronology. CQ Press Electronic Library, Congress and The Nation Online, catn45-4-3660-184050. Originally published in *Congress and The Nation*, 1945–1964. Washington, DC: CQ Press, 1965.

Ashbury, Herbert. *Sucker's Progress: An Informal History of Gambling in America*. New York: Thunder's Mouth, 1938.

Asinof, Eliot. *Eight Men Out: The Black Sox and the 1919 World Series*. New York: Holt, Rinehart, and Winston, 1963.

Axthelm, Pete. *The City Game: From the Gardens to the Playgrounds*. Lincoln: University of Nebraska Press, 1970.

Barke, Robert, and Philip Santora. "Murphy Will Sift Charge of Gag on '49 Hoop Fix." *New York Daily Mirror*, 23 February 1951.

Bartlett, Donald, L., and James B. Steele. "Throwing The Game." *Time*, 17 September 2000.

Bee, Clair. *Championship Ball*. Nashville, TN: Broadman and Holman, 1998.

———. "Coach's Judgment Not Infallible." *Sporting News*, 14 February 1951.

———. *Freshman Quarterback*. 1952; Nashville, TN: Broadman and Holman, 1998.

———. *A Pass and a Prayer*. Nashville, TN: Broadman and Holman, 1999.

Bee, Clair, as told to Stanley Frank. "I Know Why They Sold Out to the Gamblers." *Saturday Evening Post*, 2 February 1952.

Bee, Clair, as told to Bruce Jacobs. "Cage Coach." *Sport Stars*, November 1951.

Benagh, Jim. *Making It to #1: How College Football and Basketball Teams Get There*. Cornwall, NY: Cornwall, 1976.

Berger, Meyer. "Two Ex-Stars Held in Basketball 'Fix' at $2,000 a Game." *New York Times*, 18 January 1951.

Berger, Phil. *Big Time*. Roanoke, VA: Dryad, 1990.

Bernstein, Mark F. *Football: The Ivy League, Origins of an American Obsession*. Philadelphia: University of Pennsylvania Press, 2001.

Betts, John Rickards. *America's Sporting Heritage, 1850–1950*. Reading, MA: Addison-Wesley, 1974.

Bjarkman, Peter C. *Hoopla: A Century of College Basketball*. Indianapolis: Masters, 1998.

Blackwell, James. *On, Brave Old Army Team: The Cheating Scandal That Rocked the Nation: West Point, 1951*. Novato, CA: Presidio, 1996.

Blakey, G. Robert. "Legal Regulation of Gambling since 1950." *Annals of the American Academy of Political and Social Science* 474 (1984): 12–22.

Blinn-Pike, L., S. L. Worthy, and J. N. Jonkman. "Disordered Gambling among College Students: A Meta-Analytic Synthesis." *Journal of Gambling Studies* 23 (2007):175–83.

Boorstin, Daniel, J. *The Americans: The Democratic Experience*. New York: Random House, 1973.

———. *The Americans: The National Experience*. New York: Random House, 1965.

Borges, Ron. "Cobb Innocent of Point Shaving." *Boston Globe*, 24 March 1984.

Boyle, Robert H. "The Brain That Gave Us the Point Spread." *Sports Illustrated*, 10 March 1986.

Boyles, Bob, and Paul Guido. *50 Years of College Football: A Modern History of America's Most Colorful Sport*. New York: Skyhorse, 2007.

———. *The USA Today College Football Encyclopedia: A Comprehensive Reference to America's Most Colorful Sport, 1953–Present*. New York: Skyhorse, 2008.

Bradley, Bill. *Life on the Run: A Vision of America through the Eyes of One of Its Heroes*. New York: Bantam, 1977.

Brennan, Eamonn. "Betting Scandal Makes USD Coach Sick." ESPN.com, 22 April 2011, http://espn.go.com/blog/collegebasketballnation/post/_/id/30124/betting-scandal-makes-usd-coach-sick. Accessed 3 May 2012.

Breslin, Jimmy. "The Fix Was On." *Saturday Evening Post*, 23 February 1963.

———. "The Untold Facts behind the Basketball Scandal." *Sport*, November 1962.

Brown, Gene, and Robert Lipsyte, eds. *Sports and Society: The Great Contemporary Issues*. New York: Arno, 1980.

Brown, Lou, as told to Dick Herbert. "I Worked with Basketball's No. 1 Briber." *Look*, 27 February 1962.

Brown, Mark. "Lundy Gets Six Months in Jail." *Chicago Sun-Times*, 6 May 1999.

———. "NU Gambling Probe Widens to Include ex-CB." *Chicago Sun-Times*, 23 April 1999.

Bryant, Paul W., and John Underwood. *Bear: The Hard Life and Good Times of Alabama's Coach Bryant*. Boston: Sports Illustrated, 1974.

Buckley, J. Taylor. "Nation Raising 'A Generation of Gamblers.'" *USA Today*, 5 April 1995.

Budin, Steve, with Bob Schaller. *Bets, Drugs, and Rock and Roll*. New York: Skyhorse, 2007.

Burton, Lewis. "Coaches Can Clean It Up." *Sporting News*, 31 January 1951.

Byers, Walter, with Charles Hammer. *Unsportsmanlike Conduct: Exploiting College Athletes*. Ann Arbor: University of Michigan Press, 1995.

Callaghan, Gerry. "Dark Days at BC." *Sports Illustrated*, 18 November 1996.

Carlson, Doug. "F.S.U. Had Indications of QB's Gambling." *Tampa Tribune*, 3 April 2003.

———. "Major Ramifications in McPherson Trial." *Tampa Tribune*, 1 June 2000.

Carroll, John M. *Red Grange and the Rise of Modern Football*. Urbana: University of Illinois Press, 1999.

Cave, Ray. "Portrait of a Fixer." *Sports Illustrated*, 8 May 1961.

Chandler, Joan M. *Television and National Sport: The United States and Britain*. Urbana: University of Illinois Press, 1988.

Christgau, John. *Jump Shot: Eight Men Who Shook the World of Basketball*. Lincoln: University of Nebraska Press, 1999.

Chu, Donald. *The Character of American Education and Intercollegiate Sport*. Albany: State University of New York Press, 1989.

Claerbaut, David. *Recruiting Confidential: A Father, a Son, and Big-Time College Football*. New York: Taylor, 2003.

Clark, Alfred E. "Judge in Fix Condemns Kentucky Teams and Coach." *New York Times*, 30 April 1952.

Coakley, Jay. *Sport in Society: Controversies and Issues*. Boston: McGraw-Hill, 2001.

Cohane, Tim. *Great Football Coaches of the Twenties and Thirties*. New Rochelle, NY: Arlington House, 1973.

———. "Irresponsible Recruiting Is the Chief Reason behind the Basketball Scandal." *Look*, 13 February 1962.

Cohen, Leonard. "College Authorities Warned of Upcoming Basketball Fix." *New York Post*, 10 January 1948.

Cohen, Stanley. "The 1951 Basketball Scandals: The Scars Never Vanish." *New York Times*, 1 January 1978.

———. *The Game They Played*. New York: Farrar, Straus, and Giroux, 1977.

College Basketball on Television in the United States: Big Ten Network, Raycom Media, Sports Broadcasting Contracts in the United States. Memphis, TN: Books, 2010.

The College Football Book. New York: Sports Illustrated Books, 2008.

Constable, Nick. *This Is Gambling*. London: Sanctuary, 2003.
Cook, William A. *The Louisville Scandal of 1877: The Taint of Gambling at the Dawn of the National League*. Jefferson, NC: McFarland, 2005.
Cooney, John. *The Annenbergs*. New York: Simon and Schuster, 1982.
Cope, Myron. *The Game That Was: The Early Days of Pro Football*. New York: World, 1970.
Couch, Greg. "NU: Don't Blame Us." *Chicago Sun-Times*, 3 December 1998.
———. "Teammate: NU Gambling No Secret." *Chicago Sun-Times*, 30 March 1998.
Cox, James A. "Was 'the Gipper' for Real? You Can Bet He Was." *Smithsonian*, 16 December 1985.
Daley, Arthur. "Caesar Was Ambitious." *New York Times*, 20 November 1952.
———. "Court Scandal." *New York Times*, 31 January 1945.
———. "Menace to All Sports—The 'Fix.'" *New York Times Magazine*, 5 January 1947.
Danforth, Harold R., and James Horan. *The D.A.'s Man*. New York: Crown, 1957.
Davies, Richard O., and Richard G. Abram. *Betting the Line: Sports Wagering in American Life*. Columbus: Ohio State University Press, 2001.
Deardorff, Donald L. *Sports: A Reference Guide and Critical Commentary, 1980–1999*. Westport, CT: Greenwood, 2000.
Dedman, Bill. "College Football: 4 Are Indicted in Northwestern Football Scandal." *New York Times*, 4 December 1998.
Deford, Frank. "The Baron of the Bluegrass." *Sports Illustrated*, 7 March 1966.
Devaney, Sean. *The Original Curse: Did the Cubs Throw the 1918 World Series to Babe Ruth's Red Sox and Incite the Black Sox Scandal?* New York: McGraw-Hill, 2010.
Dickey, Glenn. *The Jock Empire: Its Rise and Deserved Fall*. Radnor, PA: Chilton, 1974.
Dizon, Nicole Zeigler. "Players Get Prison Time in Northwestern Betting Scandal." *AP Online*, 24 November 1998. http://www.tmnews.com/stories/1998/11/25/archive.310535.tms. Accessed 3 May 2012.
Donaghy, Tim. *Personal Foul: A First-Person Account of the Scandal That Rocked the NBA*. Largo, FL: VTi, 2009.
Donovan, Herman Lee. *Keeping the University Free and Growing*. Lexington: University of Kentucky Press, 1959.
Don't Bet on It, Put Your Money on a Real Winner: Yourself: A Guide for College Athletes and Everyone Involved in Sports. Denver: National Endowment for Financial Education and the National Collegiate Athletic Association, 1999.
Dowling, William D. *Confessions of a Spoilsport: My Life and Hard Times Fighting Sports Corruption at an Old Eastern University*. University Park: Pennsylvania State University Press, 2007.
Doyle, Pat, and Susan Albach. "Campus Sports Betting Raises Concerns: With Studies Revealing Student Problems with Gambling, Colleges and High Schools Are Facing New Challenges." *Minneapolis Star-Tribune*, 29 January 1999.
Duderstadt, James J. *Intercollegiate Athletics and the American University*. Ann Arbor: University of Michigan Press, 2009.
Dunnivant, Keith. *Coach: The Life of Paul "Bear" Bryant*. New York: Dunne, 2006.
———. *The Fifty-Year Seduction: How Television Manipulated College Football,*

from the Birth of the Modern NCAA to the Creation of the BCS. New York: Dunne, 2004.
Durso, Joseph. *Madison Square Garden: 100 Years of History*. New York: Simon and Schuster, 1979.
Eads, John M. *Gambling Addiction: The Problem, the Pain, and the Path to Recovery*. Ann Arbor, MI: Servant, 2003.
Edwards, Harry. *Sociology of Sport*. Homewood, IL: Dorsey, 1973.
Eitzen, Stanley D. *Fair and Foul: Beyond the Myths and Paradoxes of Sports*. Lanham, MD: Rowman and Littlefield, 2006.
Eskenazi, Gerald. "Kentucky's Baron Still Holding Court." *New York Times*, 14 March 1976.
Feinberg, Alexander. "L.I.U. Star of 2 Years Ago Seized after Night Questioning about 'Fix.'" *New York Times*, 27 February 1951.
Feinstein, John. *The Last Amateurs: Playing for Glory and Honor in Division I College Basketball*. Boston: Little, Brown, 2000.
Figone, Albert J. "The 1978–79 Point-Shaving Scandal at Boston College: College Basketball's Incurable Habit." Paper presented at the North American Society for Sport History Conference, Tempe, Arizona, 29 May 1987.
———. "Gambling and College Basketball: The Scandal of 1951." *Journal of Sport History*, 16 (1989): 44–61.
———. "Jack Molinas and the 1951–61 Gambling Scandals." Paper presented at the North American Society for Sport History Conference, Saskatoon, Saskatchewan, 30 May 1994.
———. "'Student-Bookies': College Basketball's Newest Problem." Paper presented at the North American Society for the Sociology of Sport Conference, Las Vegas, Nevada, 6 November 1998.
Findlay, John M. *People of Chance: Gambling in American Society From Jamestown to Las Vegas*. New York: Oxford University Press, 1986.
Fish, Mike, and George J. Tanber. "As Summer Ends, Heat Is on in Toledo Point-Shaving Case." ESPN.com, 2 September 2009. http://www.espn.go.com/espn/news/story?id=2988714. Accessed 3 May 2012.
Fleisher, Arthur A., Brian L. Goff, and Robert D. Tollison. *The National Collegiate Athletic Association: A Study in Cartel Behavior*. Chicago: University of Chicago Press, 1992.
Francis, Melissa. "Illegal Gambling: CNBC Investigates: Illegal Gambling: Where Fortunes Are on the Line and Lives Hang in the Balance." CNBC.com, 10 December 2009. www.illegalgambling.cnbc.com. Accessed 3 May 2012.
Frank, Stanley. "Basketball's Big Wheel." *Saturday Evening Post*, 15 January 1949.
Frauenheim, Norm. "Flying with Hawk: Suns' Hall of Famer Was Ahead of His Time as Dunker and Showman." *Arizona Republic*, 2 October 1995.
Frey, Darcy. *The Last Shot: City Streets, Basketball Dreams*. Boston: Houghton Mifflin, 2004.
Fried, Joseph. "Ex-Player and 4 Are Indicted." *New York Times*, 30 July 1981.
———. "U.S. Hoping Kuhn Will Aid 'Fix' Case." *New York Times*, 9 February 1982.
Frieder, Bill, with Jeff Mortimer. *Basket Case: The Frenetic Life of Michigan Coach Bill Frieder*. Chicago: Bonus, 1988.
Friedrich, Otto. *The Death Struggle of the Saturday Evening Post: Decline and Fall*. New York: HarperCollins, 1970.

Funk, Gary D. *Major Violation: The Unbalanced Priorities in Athletics and Academics*. Champaign, IL: Leisure, 1991.

Gallico, Paul. *Farewell to Sport*. New York: International Polygonics, 1966.

Getter, Doyle K. "How to Bet on Sports—And Win!" *American Mercury Magazine*, July 1951.

Gildea, Dennis. "Muckraking for a Young Audience: Reader Response to Clair Bee's Sports Fiction in the Wake of the 1951 Basketball Gambling Scandal." Paper presented at "Defining Print Culture for Youth: Children and Reading since 1876," Center for the History of Print Culture in Modern America, Madison, WI, 9–10 May 1997.

Ginsburg, Daniel E. *The Fix Is In: A History of Baseball Gambling and Game Fixing Scandals*. Jefferson, NC: McFarland, 1995.

Gipe, George. *The Great American Sports Book: A Casual but Voluminous Look at American Spectator Sports from the Civil War to the Present Time*. Garden City, NY: Doubleday, 1978.

Gold, Eli, with M. B. Roberts. *Bear's Boys*. Nashville, TN: Nelson, 2007.

Golen, Jimmy. "BC Players Get New Suspensions." *Associated Press*, 25 July 1997.

Golenbock, Peter. *Personal Fouls: The Broken Promises and Shattered Dreams of Big Money Basketball at Jim Valvano's North Carolina State*. New York: Carroll and Graf, 1989.

Goodman, Robert. *The Luck Business: The Devastating Consequences and Broken Promises of America's Gambling Expansion*. New York: Kessler, 1995.

Goodwin, Michael. "Player Says Coach, Now at Fairleigh, Paid Him at Tulane." *New York Times*, 6 April 1985.

Gordon, Joe. "Cobb Trial Heads for Jury." *Boston Herald*, 22 March 1984.

Gorn, Elliott J., and Warren Goldstein. *A Brief History of American Sports*. New York: Farrar, Straus, and Giroux, 1993.

Goudsouzian, Adam. *King of the Court: Bill Russell and the Basketball Revolution*. Berkeley: University of California Press, 2010.

Graebner, William, and Leonard Richards, eds. *The American Record: Images of the Nation's Past*. New York: Knopf, 1982.

Graffis, Herbert, ed. *Esquire's First Sports Reader*. New York: Barnes, 1945.

Graham, Frank, Jr. *A Farewell to Heroes*. New York: Viking, 1981.

———. "The Story of a College Football Fix: A Shocking Report of How Wally Butts and 'Bear' Bryant Rigged a Game." *Saturday Evening Post*, 23 March 1963.

Greaves, William, and Robert Williams. "3 LIU Stars Confess Bribes: Game May Die in Garden." *New York Post*, 20 February 1951.

Gross, Milton. "Speaking Out." *New York Post*, 20 February 1951.

Grundy, Pamela. *Learning to Win: Sports, Education, and Social Change in Twentieth-Century North Carolina*. Chapel Hill: University of North Carolina Press, 2001.

Grutzner, Charles. "Basketball Fixer Aids Race Inquiry." *New York Times*, 9 September 1966.

———. "Gross' Borrowing from Police Cited." *New York Times*, 9 November 1951.

———. "Gross' Tale of Graft Quoted as 30 Policeman Go on Trial." *New York Times*, 6 November 19511.

———. "The Impact of Athletics on Education." *New York Times*, 18–23 March 1951.

Guttmann, Allen. *A Whole New Ball Game: An Interpretation of American Sports*. Chapel Hill: University of North Carolina Press, 1988.

Haller, Mark H. "The Changing Structure of American Gambling in the Twentieth Century." *Journal of Social Issues* 35 (1979): 87–114.

Harp, Richard L., and Joseph B. McCullough. "The Myth of the College Basketball Coach." *Journal of American Culture* 4 (2004): 49–57.

Harris, David. *The League: The Rise and Decline of the NFL*. New York: Bantam, 1986.

Haworth, Karla. "Boston College Announces Punishment for 21 Students Linked to Gambling Scandal." *Chronicle of Higher Education*, 24 January 1997.

Hill, Henry, and Douglas S. Looney. "How I Put the Fix In." *Sports Illustrated*, 16 February 1981.

Hobson, Howard. "How to Stop Those Basketball Scandals." *Collier's*, 29 December 1951.

Horn, Calvin. *The University in Turmoil and Transition: Crisis Decades at the University of New Mexico, 1981*. Albuquerque: Rocky Mountain, 1981.

Houlihan-Skilton, Mary. "Ballarini Puts Blame on NU." *Chicago Sun-Times*, 1 October 1998.

Iba, Henry P. "1947 Forecast." *Collier's*, 21 December 1946.

Ignatin, George. "Sports Betting." *Annals of the American Academy of Political and Social Science*, 474 (1984): 168–77.

Isaacs, Neil D. *All the Moves: A History of College Basketball*. New York: Lippincott, 1975.

———. *The Great Molinas*. Bethesda, MD: Wid, 1992.

———. *You Bet Your Life: The Burdens of Gambling*. Lexington: University Press of Kentucky, 2001.

Isaacs, Stan. "The College Scandals, and Questions to Ask." *Washington Post*, 22 February 1981.

Jackson, Kenneth T., ed. *The Encyclopedia of New York*. New Haven: Yale University Press, 1995.

Jackson, V. A. *Beyond the Baron*. Kuttawa, KY: McClanahan, 1998.

Jacobson, Bob. *Sports in America: Business, Education, and Controversy*. Detroit: Gale, 2008.

Jay, Kathryn. *More Than Just a Game: Sports in American Life since 1945*. New York: Columbia University Press, 2004.

Jeffries, James, as told to Charles Oliver. *The Book on Bookies: An Inside Look at a Successful Sports Gambling Operation*. Boulder, CO: Paladin, 2000.

Jenkins, Dan. *You Call It Sports, but I Say It's a Jungle Out There*. New York: Simon and Schuster, 1989.

Johnson, James W. *Dandy Dons: Bill Russell, K. C. Jones, Phil Woolpert, and One of College Basketball's Greatest and Most Innovative Teams*. Lincoln: University of Nebraska Press, 2009.

Jones, Kenneth M. "Cagers Named as 'Fixing' Probe Spreads." *Peoria (IL) Journal*, 25 July 1951.

Kalb, Elliott. *The 25 Greatest Sports Conspiracy Theories of All Time: Ranking Sports' Most Notorious Fixes, Cover-Ups, and Scandals*. New York: Skyhorse, 2007.

Kanfer, Stewart. *A Summer World: The Attempt to Build a Jewish Eden in the*

Catskills, from the Days of the Ghetto to the Rise and Decline of the Borscht Belt. New York: Farrar, Straus, and Giroux, 1989.

Kase, Max. "How Many Scandals Are Needed before Hungry Colleges Act?" *Time*, 18 January 1951.

Katz, Stephen. *Gambling Facts and Fictions: The Anti-Gambling Handbook to Get Yourself to Stop Gambling, Quit Gambling, or Never Start Gambling*. Bloomington, IN: AuthorHouse, 2004.

Keegan, William. "Basketball Star of Late '40s Hunted as Agent for Big Gamblers in 'Fix.'" *New York Post*, 28 February 1951.

Keidan, Bruce. "The Fixer: Out of Prison, Jack Molinas Reveals Taking Bribes as Collegian." *Philadelphia Inquirer*, 6 January 1964.

Kemper, Kurt Edward. *College Football and American Culture in the Cold War*. Urbana: University of Illinois Press, 2009.

Kefauver, Estes. "I Meet the King of the Underworld." *Saturday Evening Post*, 28 April 1951.

Keteyian, Armen. "An NCAA 'Hedake': The Only Fix to the Growing Number of Point-Shaving Scandals Is to Make the Guilty Pay." *Sport*, May 1998.

———. "A Time for Harsh Measures." *Sports Illustrated*, 4 April 1985.

Kindred, Dave. "BC Case: A Sentence Is Punctuated by a Moral Question: Kuhn Sentencing Delayed." *Washington Post*, 8 January 1982.

King, Peter. *Sports Illustrated Football: A History of the Professional Game*. New York: Bishop, 1997.

Kirby, James. *Fumble: Bear Bryant, Wally Butts, and the Great Football Scandal*. New York: Dell, 1986.

Knox, Harvey. "Why Ronnie Knox Quit California." *Sports Illustrated*, 6 September 1954.

Kohout, Martin Donell. *Hal Chase: The Defiant Life and Turbulent Times of Baseball Biggest Crook*. Jefferson, NC: McFarland, 2001.

Koppett, Leonard. *24 Seconds to Shoot: An Informal History of the American Basketball Association*. New York: Macmillan, 1968.

———. *Sport Illusion, Sport Reality: A Reporter's View of Sports, Journalism, and Society*. Boston: Houghton Mifflin, 1981.

Layden, Tim. "Bettor Education: Gambling Is the Dirty Little Secret on College Campuses." *Sports Illustrated*, 3 April 1995.

———. "Special Report: Book Smart: The Bookies Catering to Most College Gamblers Are Fellow Students Such As 'J. P. Browman,' Who Says He Earned $42,000 while Serving More Than 100 Clients a Year at the University of Florida." *Sports Illustrated*, 10 April 1995.

Lears, Jackson. *Something for Nothing*. New York: Penguin, 2003.

Lederman, Douglas. "North Carolina State U. Professors Debate Faculty Role in Basketball Scandal, Vow More Vigilant Oversight." *Chronicle of Higher Education*, 13 September 1989.

Lee, Jason W., and Jeffrey C. Lee, eds. *Sport and Criminal Behavior*. Durham, NC: Carolina Academic, 2009.

Lesieur, Henry R. "Black and White Students Equally Bitten by the Gambling Bug." *Journal of Blacks in Higher Education*, June 30, 1995.

Lester, Robin. *Stagg's University: The Rise, Decline, and Fall of Big-Time Football at Chicago*. Urbana: University of Illinois Press, 1995.

Leveton, Dave. "The Coolest Guy. . . and the Sad Truth about How He Got His Car (My Brush with History)." *American Heritage*, May 2003.

Levin, Melvin. *Life in the Trash Lane: Cash, Cars, and Corruption: A Sports Agent's True Story*. Plantation, FL: Distinctive, 1993.

Lewin, Leonard. "Has Basketball Really Cleaned House?" *Sports Stars*, January 1953.

———. "Hogan Blasts Garden as College Hoop Site." *New York Daily Mirror*, 19 February 1951.

Lieberman, Richard. *Personal Foul: Coach Joe Moore vs. the University of Notre Dame*. Chicago: Academy Chicago, 2001.

Light, Glenn, Karl Rutledge, and Quinton Singleton. "Betting on the U.S. Market: A Discussion of the Legality of the Sports Gaming Businesses." November 2011. http://gaming.unlv.edu/papers/cgr_op12_light_rutledge_singleton.pdf. Accessed 31 May 2012.

Lighty, Todd. "Former Northwestern Basketball Player Lee Talks about Gambling for First Time." *Chicago Tribune*, 24 December 1998.

Longstreet, Stephen. *Win or Lose: A Social History of Gambling in America*. Indianapolis: Bobbs-Merrill, 1977.

Lucas, John A., and Ronald A. Smith. *Saga of American Sport*. Philadelphia: Lea and Febiger, 1978.

Lunquist, Carl. "Grand Jury to Report on Bribe Investigation." *Port Arthur (TX), News*, 31 January 1945.

Lupica, Mike, ed. *The Best American Sports Writers*. Boston: Houghton-Mifflin, 2005.

MacCambridge, Michael. *America's Game: The Epic Story of How Pro Football Captured a Nation*. New York: Random House, 2004.

Magruder, Jack. "Arizona St. Players Plead Guilty; Smith and Burton Agreed to Fix Games." *Washington Post*, 6 December 1997.

Maitland, Leslie. "Fix Suspect Indicted on New Drug Charge." *New York Times*, 21 January 1981.

———. "Basketball Inquiry Is Widened." *New York Times*, 20 January 1981.

Mandel, Stewart. *Bowls, Polls, and Tattered Souls: Tacking the Chaos and Controversy That Reign over College Football*. Hoboken, NJ: Wiley, 2007.

Mandelbaum, Michael. *The Meaning of Sports: Why Americans Watch Baseball, Football, and Basketball and What They See When They Do*. Cambridge, MA: Perseus, 2004.

Mariotti, Jay. "Barnett Must Accept His Role in Scandal." *Chicago Sun-Times*, 4 December 1998.

Markoe, Arnold, and Kenneth T. Jackson, eds. *The Scribner Encyclopedia of American Lives*. Vol. 1, *Sports Figures*. New York: Scribner's, 2002.

Mays, Benjamin. "Students May Have to Show Us the Way to Reducing the Athletic Proselytizing." *Pittsburgh Courier*, 11 February 1950.

McCarthy, Michael. "Point-Shaving Remains a Concern in College Athletics." *USA Today*, 9 May 2007.

McClelland, George S., Thomas W. Hardy, and Jim Caswell. *Gambling on Campus*. San Francisco: Jossey-Bass, 2006.

McCloskey, John, and Julian Bailes. *When Winning Costs Too Much: Steroids, Supplements, and Scandal in Today's Sports*. New York: Taylor, 2005.

McDonough, Will, Peter King, Paul Zimmerman, Vic Carucci, Greg Gergen, Harold Rosenthal, C. W. Nevius, Ed Bouchette, Ted Brock, Tom Barnidge, and Phil Barber. *75 Seasons: A Complete Story of the National Football League, 1920–1995*. Atlanta: Turner, 1994.

McFadden, Robert. "The Lonely Death of a Man Who Made a Scandal." *New York Times*, 5 April 1986.

McMullen, Paul. *Maryland Basketball: Tales from Cole Field House*. Baltimore: Johns Hopkins University Press, 2002.

Meier, Ted. "Garden Games Given Clean Bill." *Lowell (MA) Sun*, 21 February 1945.

Melchiorre, Gene, as told to Tim Cohane. "How I Fell for the Basketball Bribers." *Look*, 13 January 1953.

Merchant, Larry. *The National Football Lottery*. New York: Holt, Rinehart, and Winston, 1973.

Michener, James A. *Sports in America*. New York: Random House, 1976.

Miller, Richard I. *The Truth about Big-Time Football*. New York: Sloane, 1953.

Moldea, Dan E. *Interference: How Organized Crime Influences Professional Football*. New York: Morrow, 1989.

Molinas v. National Basketball Association. 190 F. Supp. 241; 1961 U.S. Dist. LEXIS 5846; 1961, Trade Cas. (CCH) P69, 903, 11 January 1961.

Mooney, Roger. "The Fall of Adrian McPherson." *Bradenton (FL) Herald*, 2 May 2003.

Moore, William Howard. *The Kefauver Committee and the Politics of Crime, 1950–1952*. Columbia: University of Missouri Press, 1974.

Morris, Ron. "Scandal That Rocked ACC." *Charlotte Observer*, 27 March 2010.

Morris, Willie. *The Courting of Marcus Dupree*. Garden City, NY: Doubleday, 1983.

Morrissey, Mark. "Lundy Tells Other Athletes Not to Repeat His Mistakes." *Chicago Tribune*, 26 February 1999.

Munson, Lester. "Special Report: Mob Scene." *Sports Illustrated* 10 April 1995.

Murphy, Brett. "Uncomfortable with McPherson, USF Says No." *Tampa Tribune*, 8 August 2003.

Murray, Jim. "Athletics' Victim." *Oakland Tribune*, 2 November 1961.

Naismith, James. *Basketball: Its Origin And Development*. 1941; Lincoln: University of Nebraska Press, 1996.

Nakamura, Dave. "Partial Reprieve for Terp; NCAA Cuts Milanovich Suspension to Four Games." *Washington Post*, 25 August 1995.

Nathan, Daniel A. *Saying It's So: A Cultural History of the Black Sox Scandal*. Urbana: University of Illinois Press, 2003.

Nelli, Humbert S. "Adolph Rupp, the Kentucky Wildcats, and the Basketball Scandal of 1951." *Register of the Kentucky Historical Society* 84 (1986): 51–56.

Norlander, Matt. "According to *ESPN the Magazine*, 1 in 4 Players Would Throw a Game for Cash." CollegeHoopsJournal.com, 8 November 2010. http://www.collegehoopsjournal.com/2010/11/08/according-to-espn-the-magazine-1-in-4-players-would-throw-a-game-for-cash/. Accessed 3 May 2012.

O'Brien, Ellen. "BC Gambling Probe Ends with Convictions of 6." *Boston Globe*, 8 February 1998.

O'Brien, Timothy L. *Bad Bet: The Inside Story of the Glamour, Glitz, and Danger of America's Gambling Industry*. New York: Random House, 1998.

O'Connor, Matt. "Another Guilty Plea in NU Betting Probe." *Chicago Tribune*, 28 August 1998.

———. "FBI Probe at NU." *Chicago Tribune*, 22 August 1998.

O'Connor, Matt, and Todd Lighty. "Intentional Fumble at NU." *Chicago Tribune*, 3 January 1999.

Offit, Sidney. *Memoir of the Bookie's Son*. New York: St. Martin's, 1995.

Olbermann, Keith, and Dan Patrick. *The Big Show: Inside ESPN's SportsCenter*. New York: Pocket, 1997.

Omalu, Bennet. *Play Hard, Die Young: Football Dementia, Depression, and Death*. Lodi, CA: Neo-Forenxis, 2008.

Oriard, Michael. *Bowled Over: Big-Time College Football from the Sixties to the BCS Era*. Chapel Hill: University of North Carolina Press, 2009.

———. *The End of Autumn: Reflections on My Life in Football*. Garden City, NY: Doubleday, 1982.

Pallette, Philip. *Game Changer: How Hank Luisetti Revolutionized America's Great Indoor Game*. Bloomington, IN: AuthorHouse, 2005.

Parker, Dan. "Inside Story of Basketball Scandal." *Sport Magazine*, February 1947.

———. "Judge Targets Coaches and Madison Square Garden in Sentencing of Players." *New York Daily Mirror*. 21 November 1951.

Parrish, Bernie. *They Call It a Game: Shoulders the NFL Stands On*. New York: Dial, 1971.

Parrott, Harold. "School Fires Players in Bribe Case." *Sporting News*, 8 February 1945.

Patton, Phil. *Razzle Dazzle: The Curious Marriage of Television and Football*. Garden City, NY: Dial, 1984.

People of the State of New York v. Jacob Molinas. Supreme Court of New York, Appellate Division, First Department, 21 A.D. 2d 384; 250, N.Y.S. 2d 684; 1964 N.Y. App. Div. Lexis 3504, 16 June 1964.

Perkins, Brett. *Frantic Francis: How One Coach's Madness Changed Football*. Lincoln: University of Nebraska Press, 2009.

Philbin, Walt. "TU Player, Students Given Probation, Fines." *New Orleans Times-Picayune*, 26 November 1985.

Plasket, Bruce. *Buffaloed: How Race, Gender, and Media Bias Fueled a Season of Scandal*. N.p., 2005.

Pont, Sally. *Fields of Honor: The Golden Age of Football and the Men Who Created It*. New York: Harcourt, 2001.

Pope, S. W. *The New American Sport History: Recent Approaches and Perspectives*. Urbana: University of Illinois Press, 1997.

Porter, David. *Fixed: How Goodfellas Bought Boston College Basketball*. Dallas: Taylor, 2000.

Porto, Brian L. *A New Season: Using Title Nine to Reform College Sports*. Westport, CT: Praeger, 2003.

Powers, Ron. *Super Tube: The Rise of Television Sports*. New York: Coward-McCann, 1984.

Pritchard, Henry S. "A Substitute for Football." *Atlantic Monthly*, October 1932.

Rader, Benjamin J. *American Sports: From the Age of Folk Games to the Age of Televised Sports*. Upper Saddle River, NJ: Prentice-Hall, 2004.

———. *In Its Own Image: How Television Has Transformed Sports*. New York: Free Press, 1984.

Raglund, Shannon. *The Thin Thirty: The Untold Story of Brutality, Scandal, and Redemption for Charlie Bradshaw's 1962 Kentucky Football Team*. Louisville, KY: Set Shot, 2007.

Reynolds, Bill. *Fall River Dreams: A Team's Quest for Glory—A Town's Search for Its Soul*. New York: St. Martin's Griffin, 1994.

Reynolds, Quentin. "Court Marshall." *Collier's*, 14 January 1949.

Rhoden, William C. "College-Level Gambling Growing All across the Country: The New Major?" *Houston Chronicle*, 10 May 1992.

Rice, Grantland. *The Tumult and the Shouting*. New York: Barnes, 1963.

Rice, Robert. *The Business of Crime*. Westport, CT: Greenwood, 1974.

Rice, Russell. *Adolph Rupp: Kentucky's Basketball Baron*. Champaign, IL: Sagamore, 1994.

Riess, Steven A. *The American Sporting Experience: A Historical Anthology of Sport in America*. Champaign, IL: Leisure, 1984.

———. *City Games: The Evolution of American Urban Society and the Rise of Sports*. Urbana: University of Illinois Press, 1989.

Riffenburgh, Biff, and Jack Clary. *The Official History of Pro Football*. London: Hamlyn, 1990.

Roberts, Randy, and James S. Olson. *Winning Is the Only Thing: Sports in America since 1945*. Baltimore: Johns Hopkins University Press, 1989.

Roche, George. *The Fall of the Ivory Tower: Government Funding, Corruption, and the Bankrupting of American Higher Education*. Washington, DC: Regnery, 1994.

Rogers, Rex M. *Seducing America: Is Gambling a Good Bet?* Grand Rapids, MI: Baker, 1997.

Rose, Pete, with Rick Hill. *Pete Rose: My Prison without Bars*. New York: St. Martin's, 2004.

Rosen, Charley. *Barney Polan's Game: A Novel of the 1951 College Basketball Scandals*. New York: Seven Stories, 1998.

———. *The First Tip-off: The Incredible Story of the Birth of the NBA*. New York: McGraw-Hill, 2009.

———. *Scandals of '51: How the Gamblers Almost Killed College Basketball*. 1978; New York: Seven Stories, 1999.

———. *The Wizard of Odds: How Jack Molinas Almost Destroyed the Game of Basketball*. New York: Seven Stories, 2001.

Rosica, James L., and Steve Ellis. "Cops Probe Betting Reports." *Tallahassee (FL) Democrat*, 13 December 2002.

Rudolph, Frederick. *The American College and University: A History*. New York: Vantage, 1962.

Runyon, Damon. *The Best of Damon Runyon*. New York: Pocket Books, 1940.

Russell, Bill, with David Faulkner. *Russell Rules: 11 Lessons on Leadership from the Twentieth Century's Greatest Winner*. New York: Penguin Putnam, 2001.

Russell, John. *Honey Russell: Between Games, between Halves*. San Francisco: Dyad, 1986.

Sack, Allen. *Counterfeit Amateurs: An Athlete's Journey through the Sixties to the Age of Academic Capitalism*. University Park: Pennsylvania State University Press, 2008.

Sampson, Cam, and Greg Couch. "Feds Probe '94 Gambling on NU Football." *Chicago Sun-Times*, 28 August 1998.

Sarandis, Ted. *Boston College Eagles Men's Basketball: Boston College Point Shaving Scandals of 1978–79*. Memphis, TN: Books, 2010.

Schaller, Jake. "Barnett's Up-and-Down Tenure Is Over." *Colorado Springs Gazette*, 8 December 2005.

Schlichter, Art, with Jeff Snook. *Busted: The Rise and Fall of Art Schlichter*. Wilmington, OH: Orange Frazier, 2009.

Schmidt, Raymond. *Shaping College Football: The Transformation of an American Sport, 1919–1930*. Syracuse: Syracuse University Press, 2007.

Schwartz, David G. *Roll the Bones: The History of Gambling*. New York: Penguin, 2006.

Seibel, Max. "Bradley Officials Stunned by Bribe Charge." *Peoria (IL) Star*, 25 July 1951.

Seidel, Larry R. *College Investing in Basketball*. Bloomington, IN: AuthorHouse, 2004.

Sharnik, Morton, and Robert Creamer. "A Rough Day for the Bear." *Sports Illustrated*, 26 November 1962.

Sharpe, Wilton. *Wildcat Madness: Great Eras in Kentucky Basketball*. Nashville, TN: Cumberland House, 2005.

Shulman, James L., and William G. Bowen. *The Game of Life: College Sports and Educational Values*. Princeton: Princeton University Press, 2001.

Shumsky, Neil Larry, ed. *Encyclopedia of Urban America: The Cities and Suburbs*. 2 vols. Santa Barbara, CA: ABC-CLIO, Inc., 1998.

Sifakis, Carl. *Encyclopedia of Gambling*. New York: Facts on File, 1990.

Simmons, Bill. "Strapped Jocks: College Athletic Programs Rake in Big Bucks, but the Athletes Never Get to See a Penny of It. It's Time They Got Paid." 14 November 1996. http://www.bostonphoenix.com/alt1/archive/news/96/11/14/BOSTON_COLLEGE.html. Accessed 1 June 2012.

Slavin, Aaron J. "The 'Las Vegas Loophole' and the Current Push in Congress towards a Blanket Prohibition on Collegiate Sports Gambling." *University of Miami Business Law Review* 10 (2002): 715–42.

Small, Collie. "The Crafty Wizard of Lexington." *Saturday Evening Post*, 15 February 1947.

Smith, Ronald A., ed. *Big-Time Football at Harvard 1905: The Diary of Coach Bill Reid*. Urbana: University of Illinois Press, 1994.

———. *Play-by-Play: Radio, Television, and Big-Time College Sport*. Baltimore: Johns Hopkins University Press, 2001.

———. *Sports and Freedom: The Rise of Big-Time College Athletics*. New York: Oxford University Press, 1988.

Smith, Stevin, and Don Yaeger. "Confessions of a Point Shaver." *Sports Illustrated*, 9 November 1998.

Soderstrom, Robert M. *The Big House: Fielding Yost and the Building of Michigan Stadium*. Ann Arbor, MI: Huron River, 2005.

Sperber, Murray. *College Sports, Inc.: The Athletic Department vs. the University*. New York: Holt, 1990.

———. *Onward to Victory: The Crises That Shaped College Sports*. New York: Holt, 1998.

Starr, Kevin. *Material Dreams: Southern California through the 1920s*. New York: Oxford University Press, 1990.

Steptoe, Sonja. "Anatomy of a Scandal: Florida State Won the 1994 National Football Championship, but Because of Unsavory Agents, Rule-Breaking Players, and Its Own Lack of Vigilance, It Ended Up a Loser." *Sports Illustrated*, 16 May 1995.

Strauss, Michael. "Informant Tells Court of Point Shaving." *New York Times*, 29 October 1981.

———. "Witness Tells of Bribe." *New York Times*, 3 November 1981.

Strosnider, Kim. "Boston College Is Embroiled in Scandal over Gambling." *Chronicle of Higher Education*, 15 November 1996.

Stuhldreher, Harry A. *Knute Rockne: Man Builder*. New York: Grosset and Dunlap, 1931.

Sullivan, Robert. "Gambling, Payoffs, and Drugs." *Sports Illustrated*, 30 October 1989.

Tanber, George J. "Oddsmaker with Suspicions Filed Report on Toledo." ESPN.com, 6 April 2007. http://sports.espn.go.com/ncf/news/story?id=2823507. Accessed 3 May 2012.

Tarkanian, Jerry, with Dan Wetzel. *Runnin' Rebel: Shark Tales of "Extra Benefits," Frank Sinatra, and Winning It All*. Champaign, IL: Sports Publishing, 2005.

Telander, Rick. "Gambling Scandal Casts Die for Many." *Chicago Sun-Times*, 23 December 1998.

———. *Hundred Yard Lie: The Corruption of College Football and What We Can Do to Stop It*. New York: Simon and Schuster, 1989.

Teitelbaum, Stanley H. *Sports Heroes, Fallen Idols*. Lincoln: University of Nebraska Press, 2005.

Thelin, John R. *Games Colleges Play: Scandal and Reform in Intercollegiate Athletics*. Baltimore: Johns Hopkins University Press, 1996.

"Trouble at West Point." *Time*, 13 August 1951.

Underwood, John. *The Death of an American Game: The Crisis in Football*. Boston: Little, Brown, 1979.

Underwood, John, Robert H. Boyle, Douglas S. Looney, Armen Keteyian, Greg Kelly, Austin Murphy, Martin Dardis, and Jack Tobin. "The Biggest Game In Town." *Sports Illustrated* 10 March 1986. 30.

U.S. v. James Burke, Anthony Perla, Rocco Perla, and Richard Perry. 700 F. 2d; 70; 1983 U.S. App. Lexis 30957; 9 Media L. Rep. 1211.

Van Leuven, Hendrik. *Touchdown UCLA: The Complete Account of Bruin Football*. N.p., 1982.

Veysey, Laurence, R. *The Emergence of the American University*. Chicago: University of Chicago Press, 1965.

Vincent, Ted. *Mudville's Revenge: The Rise and Fall of American Sport*. Lincoln: University of Nebraska Press, 1981.

Visser, Lesley. "Coach Saw No Intent." *Boston Globe*, 18 November 1981.

———. "Kuhn Receives Landmark 10-Year Sentence." *Boston Globe*, 6 February 1982.

———. "Sweeney Named in Cobb Trial." *Boston Globe*, 14 March 1984.

———. "Threat by Kuhn Alleged." *Boston Globe*, 5 November 1981.

Vogel, Jennifer, ed. *Crapped Out: How Gambling Ruins the Economy and Destroys Lives*. Monroe, ME: Common Courage, 1997.

Viuker, Steve. "When Gambling Nearly Destroyed College Hoops." 3 April 2000. http:///www.apnews.com/media/celebnews/2000/04/03/hoops_main0403_01.html.1.

Walker, Michael B. *The Psychology of Gambling*. New York: Pergamon, 1992.

Watterson, John Sayle. *College Football: History—Spectacle—Controversy*. Baltimore: Johns Hopkins University Press, 2000.

Weiler, Paul. *Leveling the Playing Field: How the Law Can Make Sports Better for Fans*. Cambridge: Harvard University Press, 2000.

Wells, Joseph T., and Richard B. Carozza. "Corruption in College Sports." *Internal Auditor*, April 2000.

Weltech, Bob. *Crooked Zebra*. Bloomington, IN: AuthorHouse, 2004.

Wenner, Lawrence W., ed. *Media Sport*. London: Routledge, 1998.

Wetzel, Dan, Josh Peter, and Jeff Passan. *Death to the BCS: The Definitive Case against the Bowl Championship Series*. New York: Gotham, 2010.

Wetzel, Dan, and Don Yaeger. *Sole Influence: Basketball, Corporate Greed, and the Corruption of America's Youth*. New York: Warner, 2000.

Weyand, Alexander M. *The Cavalcade of Basketball*. New York: Macmillan, 1960.

White, Sherman. "The Basketball Fix Wrecked My Life." *Sport*, July 1951.

Whittingham, Richard. *Rites of Autumn: The Story of College Football*. New York: Free Press, 2001.

Williams, Joe. "Bank President Explains Bookie Tie-In." *New York World-Telegram and Sun*, 6 March 1954.

Wilson, Harry B. "They Took the Back Door to the Big Time." *Saturday Evening Post*, 25 February 1950.

Wiggins, David K., ed. *African-Americans in Sports*. Vol. 2. Armonk, NY: Sharpe, 2004.

———. *Sport in America: From Wicked Amusement to National Obsession*. Champaign, IL: Human Kinetics, 1995.

Wolf, David. *Foul! Connie Hawkins*. New York: Warner, 1972.

Wolff, Alexander. "As Point-Shaving Charges Rocked N.C. State's Basketball Program, Coach Jim Valvano Prepared to Step Aside." *Sports Illustrated*, 12 March 1990.

Woodward, Stanley. "Basketball Betting: An Open Scandal." *Sport*, January 1951.

Wright, John D., Jr. *Lexington: Heart of the Bluegrass*. Lexington, KY: Lexington–Fayette County Historic Commission, 1982.

Yaeger, Don. *Undue Process: The NCAA's Injustice for All*. Champaign, IL: Sagamore, 1991.

Yost, Mark. *Varsity Green: A Behind the Scenes Look at Culture and Corruption in College Athletics*. Stanford, CA: Stanford University Press, 2010.

Young, Dick. "Bee Stung by Whispers, Challenges Met Teams." *Seawanhaka*, 11 January 1950.

Ziegler, Valarie H. "C6-Ho: The Centre-Harvard Game of 1921." N.d. http://www.centre.edu/web/library/sc/special/C6ho/ziegler.html. Accessed 3 May 2012.

Zimbalist, Andrew. *Unpaid Professionals: Commercialism and Conflict in Big-Time College Sports*. Princeton: Princeton University Press, 1999.

Zimmiuch, Fran. *Crooked: A History of Cheating in Sports*. New York: Taylor, 2009.

Index

Page numbers in *italics* refer to illustrations.

ALBERT J. FIGONE has seen sports from all sides. He is a professor emeritus of kinesiology and a former head baseball and assistant football coach at Humboldt State University, and he previously coached football, baseball, and track at California high schools. He lives in Folsom, California.

Sport and Society

A Sporting Time: New York City and the Rise of Modern Athletics, 1820–70 *Melvin L. Adelman*

Sandlot Seasons: Sport in Black Pittsburgh *Rob Ruck*

West Ham United: The Making of a Football Club *Charles Korr*

Beyond the Ring: The Role of Boxing in American Society *Jeffrey T. Sammons*

John L. Sullivan and His America *Michael T. Isenberg*

Television and National Sport: The United States and Britain *Joan M. Chandler*

The Creation of American Team Sports: Baseball and Cricket, 1838–72 *George B. Kirsch*

City Games: The Evolution of American Urban Society and the Rise of Sports *Steven A. Riess*

The Brawn Drain: Foreign Student-Athletes in American Universities *John Bale*

The Business of Professional Sports *Edited by Paul D. Staudohar and James A. Mangan*

Fritz Pollard: Pioneer in Racial Advancement *John M. Carroll*

A View from the Bench: The Story of an Ordinary Player on a Big-Time Football Team (*formerly* Go Big Red! The Story of a Nebraska Football Player) *George Mills*

Sport and Exercise Science: Essays in the History of Sports Medicine *Edited by Jack W. Berryman and Roberta J. Park*

Minor League Baseball and Local Economic Development *Arthur T. Johnson*

Harry Hooper: An American Baseball Life *Paul J. Zingg*

Cowgirls of the Rodeo: Pioneer Professional Athletes *Mary Lou LeCompte*

Sandow the Magnificent: Eugen Sandow and the Beginnings of Bodybuilding *David Chapman*

Big-Time Football at Harvard, 1905: The Diary of Coach Bill Reid *Edited by Ronald A. Smith*

Leftist Theories of Sport: A Critique and Reconstruction *William J. Morgan*

Babe: The Life and Legend of Babe Didrikson Zaharias *Susan E. Cayleff*

Stagg's University: The Rise, Decline, and Fall of Big-Time Football at Chicago *Robin Lester*

Muhammad Ali, the People's Champ *Edited by Elliott J. Gorn*

People of Prowess: Sport, Leisure, and Labor in Early Anglo-America *Nancy L. Struna*

The New American Sport History: Recent Approaches and Perspectives *Edited by S. W. Pope*

Making the Team: The Cultural Work of Baseball Fiction *Timothy Morris*

Making the American Team: Sport, Culture, and the Olympic Experience *Mark Dyreson*

Viva Baseball! Latin Major Leaguers and Their Special Hunger *Samuel O. Regalado*
Touching Base: Professional Baseball and American Culture in the Progressive Era (rev. ed.) *Steven A. Riess*
Red Grange and the Rise of Modern Football *John M. Carroll*
Golf and the American Country Club *Richard J. Moss*
Extra Innings: Writing on Baseball *Richard Peterson*
Global Games *Maarten Van Bottenburg*
The Sporting World of the Modern South *Edited by Patrick B. Miller*
The End of Baseball As We Knew It: The Players Union, 1960–81 *Charles P. Korr*
Rocky Marciano: The Rock of His Times *Russell Sullivan*
Saying It's So: A Cultural History of the Black Sox Scandal *Daniel A. Nathan*
The Nazi Olympics: Sport, Politics, and Appeasement in the 1930s *Edited by Arnd Krüger and William Murray*
The Unlevel Playing Field: A Documentary History of the African American Experience in Sport *David K. Wiggins and Patrick B. Miller*
Sports in Zion: Mormon Recreation, 1890–1940 *Richard Ian Kimball*
Sweet William: The Life of Billy Conn *Andrew O'Toole*
Sports in Chicago *Edited by Elliot J. Gorn*
The Chicago Sports Reader *Edited by Steven A. Riess and Gerald R. Gems*
College Football and American Culture in the Cold War Era *Kurt Edward Kemper*
The End of Amateurism in American Track and Field *Joseph M. Turrini*
Benching Jim Crow: The Rise and Fall of the Color Line in Southern College Sports, 1890–1980 *Charles H. Martin*
Pay for Play: A History of Big-Time College Athletic Reform *Ronald A. Smith*
Globetrotting: African American Athletes and Cold War Politics *Damion L. Thomas*
Cheating the Spread: Gamblers, Point Shavers, and Game Fixers in College Football and Basketball *Albert J. Figone*

Reprint Editions

The Nazi Olympics *Richard D. Mandell*
Sports in the Western World (2d ed.) *William J. Baker*
Jesse Owens: An American Life *William J. Baker*

The University of Illinois Press
is a founding member of the
Association of American University Presses.

Designed by Kelly Gray
Composed in 9.5/14 Trump Mediaeval
with Univers display
by Jim Proefrock
at the University of Illinois Press
Manufactured by Sheridan Books, Inc.

University of Illinois Press
1325 South Oak Street
Champaign, IL 61820-6903
www.press.uillinois.edu